RENAISSANCE DRAMA

New Series XIII ❧ 1982

Renaissance Drama

New Series XIII

Drama and Society

Edited by Leonard Barkan

Northwestern University Press

EVANSTON 1982

PN
1785
.R4
1982
Vol.13

37,714

The front and back cover illustrations are "The distinction between . . .
patrician, and plebeian": A Lord Mayor of London's lady and the daughter
of an ordinary citizen, from Wenceslaus Hollar's *Theatrum Mulierum*
(London, 1643), pp. 10, 12, reproduced by permission of the Syndics of
Cambridge University Library.

Publication of this volume was made possible by a grant from the College
of Arts and Sciences, Northwestern University.

Editorial Note

RENAISSANCE DRAMA, an annual publication, provides a forum for scholars in various parts of the globe: wherever the drama of the Renaissance is studied. Coverage, so far as subject matter is concerned, is not restricted to any single national theater. The chronological limits of the Renaissance are interpreted liberally, and space is available for essays on precursors, as well as on the use of Renaissance themes by later writers. Editorial policy favors articles of some scope. Essays that are exploratory in nature, that are concerned with critical or scholarly methodology, that raise new questions or embody fresh approaches to perennial problems are particularly appropriate for a publication that originated from the proceedings of the Modern Language Association Conference on Research Opportunities in Renaissance Drama.

The Editor gratefully acknowledges his debt to the members of the Editorial Committee, and similar warm thanks are due to the editorial assistant, Mary Ann Creadon, and to our administrative assistant, Marjorie Weiner. The efficient and expert help of the assistant editor, Janice Feldstein, has been absolutely indispensable.

Volume XIV of *Renaissance Drama* will be concerned with Relations and Influences, Literary and Dramatic. Correspondence, submissions, and enquiries regarding future volumes should be addressed to Professor Leonard Barkan, Editor, *Renaissance Drama*, English Department, Northwestern University, Evanston, Illinois 60201.

Contents

THOMAS PETTITT *English Folk Drama and the Early German*
Fastnachtspiele   1

CATHERINE MINSHULL *Marlowe's* "Sound Machevill"   35

PETER BEREK Tamburlaine's *Weak Sons: Imitation as Interpretation*
Before 1593   55

CATHERINE BELSEY *Alice Arden's Crime*   83

DON E. WAYNE Drama and Society in the Age of Jonson:
An Alternative View   103

WILLIAM SHULLENBERGER *"This For the Most Wrong'd*
of Women": A Reappraisal of The Maid's Tragedy   131

MARTIN BUTLER *Massinger's* The City Madam
and the Caroline Audience   157

KATHARINE EISAMAN MAUS *Arcadia Lost: Politics and Revision in*
the Restoration Tempest   189

Notes on Contributors   211

RENAISSANCE DRAMA

New Series XIII ❧ 1982

English Folk Drama and the Early German Fastnachtspiele

THOMAS PETTITT

I N ANY STUDY of early folk-drama traditions the absence of texts is a
serious obstacle. In England, the earliest surviving text of the mummers' plays familiar in recent tradition is from 1780.[1] The earliest chapbook text is from the middle decades of the eighteenth century,[2] while the
earliest account of a performance resembling the mummers' plays takes us
back only as far as 1737.[3] From echoes and parallels in mystery plays,
moralities, interludes, and Elizabethan and Jacobean stage plays we have
good reason to suspect the tradition goes back to the sixteenth or fifteenth

---

1. From Islip, Oxfordshire. See Michael J. Preston, "The Oldest British Folk Play,"
Folklore Forum, VI (1973), 168–174. The controversial *Sword Play* from Revesby, Lincolnshire, dated 1779, is discussed later in this study.

2. See M. J. Preston, M. G. Smith, and P. S. Smith, *Chapbooks and Traditional
Drama*, pt. I, *Alexander and the King of Egypt Chapbooks* (Sheffield, 1977), p. 1.

3. Andrew Brice, *The Mobiad, or Battle of the Voice* (London, 1770), p. 90, written in
1737, and referring to events in Exeter. There is an account of a traditional performance
said to have occurred in Cork in 1685 in a MS in the Library of Trinity College, Dublin.
The MS itself, however, is much later. See W. Smith Clark, *The Early Irish Stage* (Oxford,
1955), pp. 4–5.

1

centuries,[4] but as far as texts are concerned we have only three dramatizations of Robin Hood ballads, belonging to a different folk-drama tradition.[5] The situation on the Continent is very similar. For example the only type of folk drama which was widespread in Scandinavia, the Epiphany play of the Star and the Three Kings, is amply documented in Norway, Sweden, and Denmark, as well as the German-speaking areas of central Europe, in the nineteenth and twentieth centuries. While there are enough external references to show that the tradition goes back at least to the sixteenth century, there are no early texts of the play.[6] As in England, historical and pictorial evidence, and echoes in other kinds of plays suggesting the existence of vigorous traditions of folk drama on the Continent in the Middle Ages and the Renaissance, are matched by a chronic paucity of texts.[7]

I

This situation is radically altered if it is appreciated that the 150 or so early German *Fastnachtspiele* from the fifteenth and early sixteenth centuries provide startlingly rich evidence of a particular phase of folk-drama tradition in a specific social and cultural context.

The identification of the early *Fastnachtspiele* as folk drama offered here is not based on factors such as definition or origins. It is possible simply to define folk drama to include the *Fastnachtspiele*, and indeed there is a tendency among German folklorists to define the *Volksschauspiel* in fairly

4. For the kind of evidence involved, see, e.g., Richard Axton, "Folk Play in Tudor Interludes," in *English Drama: Forms and Development: Essays in Honour of Muriel Clara Bradbrook*, ed. Marie Axton and Raymond Williams (Cambridge; Eng., 1977), pp. 1–23; W. K. Smart, "Mankind and the Mumming Plays," *MLN*, XXXII (1917), 21–25; Thomas Pettitt, "The Folk Play in Marlowe's *Doctor Faustus*," *Folklore*, XCI (1980), 72–77; Martin W. Walsh, "Thomas Randolph's *Aristippus* and the English Mummers' Play," *Folklore*, LXXXIV (1973), 157–159.

5. "Robin Hood and the Sheriff" (ca. 1475, from the Paston Papers); "Robin Hood and the Friar" and "Robin Hood and the Potter" (both printed by Wm. Copland, ca. 1560). For all three texts see *Rymes of Robyn Hood*, ed. R. B. Dobson and T. Taylor (London, 1976), Nos. 19, 20, and 21.

6. Hilding Celander, *Stjärngossarna, deras visor och julspel* (Stockholm, 1950), p. 23.

7. See, for example, Richard Axton's discussion of folk-drama elements in Adam de la Halle's *Jeu de la Feuillée* (thirteenth cent.), in *European Drama of the Early Middle Ages* (London, 1974), pp. 144–158.

broad terms, to include, for example, the medieval mystery plays.[8] Within such limits there is plenty of room for the *Fastnachtspiele*,[9] but the
concrete nature of the identity between *Fastnachtspiel* and folk drama
remains to be demonstrated. Similarly, it might be argued that since both
the folk drama and the *Fastnachtspiele* derive ultimately from primitive
ritual, they must be intimately related. Certainly there is much in the
German plays that the ritualist student of folk drama would recognize.
These and other parallels of motif will be noted in due course, but the
assertion of common ritual origins for folk drama and *Fastnachtspiele* is a
thoroughly unsatisfactory basis for arguing their identity. The assertion is,
in both instances, controversial. It is also irrelevant: whatever their origins
it is clear that in the fifteenth and sixteenth centuries neither form had
ritual status or function, and their identity must be sought on other
grounds. Indeed, the ritual connection has had a singularly damaging
impact on research into traditions of popular drama. In England the
post-Frazerian obsession of folk-drama scholarship with ritual origins has
diverted attention from the plays themselves—their occasion, performance, milieu, and function—to quite extraneous matters, and at a time
when the traditions could be studied in a good deal more vigorous state
than they are now a lot of significant questions were simply not asked.[10] In
Germany the possible relationship of the *Fastnachtspiele* to primitive ritual
attracted the attention and enthusiasm of adherents of National Socialism,
the ritual origins sought in this instance being the initiation rites of the

8. For example, Leopold Schmidt's anthology of European folk drama, *Le Théatre
Populaire Européen* (Paris, 1965), contains not only folk plays such as the English Pace Egg
Play and a Swedish Star and Three Kings Play, but an early German Passion Play and the
Newcastle Mystery Play of Noah.

9. Leopold Schmidt's standard *Das Deutsche Volksschauspiel: Ein Handbuch* (Berlin,
1962) regularly includes *Fastnachtspiele* in its regional surveys.

10. This imbalance is now being belatedly corrected with such studies as Henry Glassie,
All Silver and No Brass (Bloomington, Ind., and London, 1975); Susan Pattison, "The
Antrobus Soulcaking Play: An Alternative Approach to the Mummers' Play," *Folklife*, XV
(1977), 5–11; Barry James Ward, "A Functional Approach to English Folk Drama,"
Ph.D. diss., Ohio State University, 1972. Much of this work has been inspired by the
pioneering studies of traditional custom published in *Christmas Mumming in Newfoundland:
Essays in Anthropology, Folklore and History*, ed. Herbert Halpert and G. M. Story (Toronto,
1969).

warrior brotherhoods—the *kultischen Männerbünde*—of the ancient Teuton tribes.[11] Not unnaturally, postwar German scholarship has fought shy of this aspect, preferring rather to see the plays simply as a distinct dramatic genre, amenable to appreciation with the usual tools of literary criticism.[12] Ironically, this has led to neglect of the evident parallels between *Fastnachtspiele* and folk drama (some pointed out by the ritualists), which are valid quite independently of the relationship of either form to any kind of primitive ritual.

The following remarks will demonstrate the identity of the two traditions on an empirical basis, by drawing parallels between two corpuses of material representing the folk drama and the *Fastnachtspiele*, respectively. By folk drama I refer to the "mummers' plays," which have been observed and collected in England from the later eighteenth century to the present. They fall fairly neatly into the three categories which have been current in English scholarship for a number of years, and which are usually designated as the Hero Combat Play (found over most of England), the Sword Dance Play (Northeastern England), and the Wooing Play (confined to Lincolnshire and parts of adjoining counties). Their characteristic features will become apparent in the course of the following discussion.[13] It would

11. An early attempt by M. J. Rudwin to link the *Fastnachtspiele* on Frazerian lines to fertility cult, "The Origin of the German Carnival Comedy," *JEGP*, XVIII (1920), 402–454, was soon overshadowed by the work of the German ritualists, particularly Robert Stumpfl's "Der Ursprung des Fastnachtspiels und die kultischen Männerbünde der Germanen," *Zeitschrift für Deutschkunde*, XLVIII (1934), 286–297, and *Kultspiele der Germanen als Ursprung des Mittelalterlichen Dramas* (Berlin, 1936). As the title of the latter indicates, Stumpfl seeks to demonstrate a ritual origin for medieval drama as a whole, the *Fastnachtspiele* being discussed in pt. I, chap. 1. To be fair it should be noted that Stumpfl's book itself is only sporadically marked by considerations of race, and his scholarship, compared to which many English ritualist studies look decidedly amateurish, deserves to be assessed on its own merits.

12. The major exponent of this newer trend is Eckehard Catholy, whose *Das Fastnachtspiel des Spätmittelalters: Gestalt und Funktion* (Tübingen, 1961) is the standard exposition of this approach.

13. The standard presentation of these categories, with a comprehensive geographical and bibliographical index of the materials to which they apply, is E. C. Cawte, Alex Helm, and N. Peacock, *English Ritual Drama* (London, 1967). Alan Brody's *The English Mummers and Their Plays* (London, 1969), which is primarily concerned with ritual origins, is nonetheless a lively and illuminating presentation of the characteristic features of the three types of play.

defeat the purposes of the task in hand to offer here any original or controversial remarks on the plays themselves, and my comparisons will be based on aspects of the plays which are familiar and generally agreed on. [14] Similar results could be achieved by the more obvious choice of recent German traditions of folk drama as a basis of comparison with the *Fastnachtspiele*. But the impact of the parallels will be greater, and their implications less confused, in comparing traditions which are geographically widely separated. My aim is to demonstrate the essential identity of folk drama and *Fastnachtspiel*, as belonging to the same species of drama, not the derivation of the one from the other, and no one would argue that English folk drama is derived from the German *Fastnachtspiele*, or vice versa. Furthermore, my ultimate hope is that the *Fastnachtspiele* may eventually tell us something about medieval and sixteenth-century traditions of *English* folk drama.

By *Fastnachtspiel* I refer to the approximately 150 German plays surviving from the fifteenth and early sixteenth centuries, the majority of them associated with Nuremberg, which were traditionally performed at Shrovetide, the period of carnival immediately preceding the beginning of Lent on Ash Wednesday, characterized by a wide range of seasonal customs. These early plays do not belong to the more familiar phases of the *Fastnachtspiel* tradition. Students of English drama have been more interested in the plays of the early seventeenth century, such as those of Jakob Ayrer, which were influenced by the jigs and shows of the professional English companies touring the Continent at that time. [15] In terms of literary and dramatic achievement the tradition is dominated by the Nuremberg shoemaker Hans Sachs, who in the course of a long and astonishingly productive literary career in the first half of the sixteenth century wrote about 85 *Fastnachtspiele*, as well as many comedies and tragedies, not to mention several thousand songs and occasional poems. [16] In their most developed form his *Fastnachtspiele* were fully fledged dramatic productions, involving plot, dialogue, action, and interaction among the

14. As presented for example in E. K. Chambers, *The English Folk-Play* (1937; rpt. Oxford, 1969), and Cawte et al., *English Ritual Drama*.

15. Charles Read Baskervill, *The Elizabethan Jig* (1929; rpt. New York, 1965), pp. 302 ff.

16. For a concise review of Sachs's life and works see Barbara Könneker, *Hans Sachs* (Stuttgart, 1971).

characters, and performed on some kind of formal stage. The *Fastnachtspiele* of the earlier phase of tradition (and perhaps some of Sachs's early pieces) involved a much simpler and altogether less theatrical context and performance.[17] Again, it is not my purpose to say anything particularly original or controversial about the plays themselves: I shall take some of the generally agreed-upon features of these early *Fastnachtspiele* as a special kind of performance, and point out their identity with the corresponding characteristics of recent English folk drama.[18]

II

The most immediately visible parallels between folk drama and the *Fastnachtspiele* are the features of plot, character, and action which they have in common. A student of English folk drama would greet with a nod of recognition those *Fastnachtspiele* which are built up of a series of short speeches in which a succession of male characters woo a lady, each urging his claims to her favor (e.g., Keller Nos. 12, 15, 70, and, in more complex fashion, Zingerle No. XI). This parallels exactly the action of the English Wooing Plays, particularly in those instances (Keller Nos. 15 & 70) where the lady replies with a short speech rejecting each suitor in turn. Equally familiar is the sequence of action in a number of German plays where an altercation between two or more characters leads to a combat in which one or several participants are wounded. A Doctor is sent for, and after a discussion which may touch on his abilities, his fee, and the powers of his medicine, he administers a cure (e.g., Keller Nos. 21, 57, 66; Zingerle No. XXVI). This is the sequence of action in the English Hero

17. For recent reviews of Sachs's controversial relationship to tradition, see Eckehard Catholy, *Fastnachtspiel* (Stuttgart, 1966), pp. 50 ff.; Könneker, *Hans Sachs*; Joel Lefebvre, "Vie et Mort du Jeu de Carneval à Nuremberg: *Neidhart et la Violette*, de Hans Sachs," in *Les Fêtes de la Renaissance*, Vol. III, ed. Jean Jacquot and Elie Konigson (Paris, 1975), pp. 557–568.

18. In my approach to the *Fastnachtspiele* as traditional performances I have relied particularly on Catholy's *Fastnachtspiel* (which is a clearer and more readable account than his otherwise more substantial treatment in *Das Fastnachtspiel des Spätmittelalters*), and Joel Lefebvre, "Le Jeu du Carnaval de Nuremberg au xve siècle et au xvie," in *Le Lieu Théatral à la Renaissance*, ed. Jean Jacquot and Elie Konigson (Paris, 1964), pp. 183–190. In citing *Fastnachtspiele* my references will be to Adalbert Keller's edition of fifteenth-century texts, *Fastnachtspiele aus dem 15. Jahrhundert*, 4 vols. (1853–1858; rpt. Darmstadt, 1965), and to the sixteenth-century plays from the Austro-Italian Tyrol, *Sterzinger Spiele: Nach Aufzeichnungen des Vigil Raber*, ed. O. Zingerle, 2 vols. (Vienna, 1886).

Combat Plays, and in some of the German examples the Doctor is accompanied by a humorous servant (Keller No. 57, Zingerle No. XXI), analogous to the entertaining Jack Finney of that important subtradition of English Hero Combat Plays with an extended cure scene.[19] Individual elements of this sequence of action also occur separately in a considerable number of German *Fastnachtspiele*. Many consist of an altercation leading to a fight (e.g., Keller Nos. 2, 3, 4, 7, 8, 37, 53, 56), although in most cases the dispute is resolved before leading to serious injury. In one instance, however (Keller No. 62), a combat between two knights concludes with the victor beheading his defeated opponent. In another (Keller No. 54), the slaying takes the form of an execution (a beheading) following a trial, echoing the (rudimentary) trial and execution of the Fool in some English Sword Dance Plays.

Alternatively, we encounter the Doctor and his cure scene independent of any combat. In such examples the play usually starts by introducing the Doctor (e.g., Keller Nos. 6, 48, 82, 120; Zingerle Nos. IV, VI), who is then provided with a patient (say a constipated peasant), and proceeds to diagnosis and a cure, which is not always successful. In other *Fastnachtspiele* the Doctor's role may be restricted to a comic diagnosis (e.g., Keller No. 85) or a harangue to the audience on the variety and virtues of his medicines (e.g., Keller Nos. 98 and 101); these features both characterize the performance of the Doctor in the English folk plays. Other, miscellaneous, parallels include a series of boasts by young men of their abilities and adventures in love (Keller No. 13; cf. the boasts of the dancers in the calling-on sequence of the Sword Dance Plays), and a series of belligerent boasts exchanged between Christian knights and Turkish warriors (Keller No. 39; cf. the taunts exchanged between St. George and the Turkish Knight in the Hero Combat Plays). Even on the verbal level the topsy-turvy world sometimes evoked by the folk plays ("I went on a bit further, I came to King Charles up a cast iron pear tree"[20]), is matched by the *Fastnachtspiele*:

19. Cf. Chambers, *English Folk-Play*, p. 58.

20. Quoted, by Chambers, *English Folk-Play*, p. 47, from the Weston-sub-Edge (Gloucestershire) play, and see Chamber's discussion, pp. 48–50. Keller's text No. 9 consists entirely of a series of speeches by eight peasants competing to tell the strangest marvel they have seen, all very much on a par with the extraordianry adventures narrated by Beelzebub in the Weston-sub-Edge play.

Ich kam gen Trebetzen gezogen,
Ein ku was auf ein baum geflogen.
(Keller No. 9, p. 93, 11. 3–4)

Such parallels are striking and suggestive, but are not in themselves decisive. The early *Fastnachtspiele* also contain features reminiscent of courtly poetry (*Minnesang*), and dramatize episodes from romance, popular tales, and classical legend, and even borrow figures and scenes from the religious drama (e.g., Keller No. 68, the Coming of Antichrist). Indeed the frequent appearance of the Doctor and his medicines has been taken by the evolutionist school of German drama scholarship to demonstrate the derivation of the *Fastnachtspiel* from the Easter liturgical plays, in which the herbalist (*Salbenkrämer*) from whom the three Marys purchase their ointments on their way to the tomb, has many features (including a comic servant) in common with the Doctor.[21] As Richard Axton has pointed out in discussing a similar problem in early medieval drama, both verbal parallels and analogous narrative elements are of only secondary importance in establishing the relationship between two traditions. A tradition is characterized essentially by its mode of performance, comprising dialogue, gesture, action, movement, interaction between performers and between performers and audience, all related to a particular physical environment, and evolved in a particular social and cultural context. It is the mode of performance which both distinguishes dramatic traditions and facilitates study of relationships between them,[22] and it is on the same basis that I seek to establish the essential identity of folk drama and *Fastnachtspiel*.

The *Fastnachtspiel* is a seasonal performance, associated with one of the major festival seasons of the year, carnival, just as the English folk drama now usually has its seasonal context in the Christmas festivities. Both are performed exclusively by men, including the female roles (which occur in

---

21. E.g., Viktor Michels, *Studien über die Ältesten deutschen Fastnachtspiele* (Strasbourg, 1896), pp. 48–49. The opposite view—that the liturgical drama stems from Germanic ritual, of which both the folk plays and the *Fastnachtspiele* are derivatives—is urged at length by Stumpfl, *Kultspiele der Germanen*, pp. 222 ff.

22. Richard Axton, "Popular Modes in the Earliest Plays," in *Medieval Drama*, ed. Neville Denny, Stratford-upon-Avon Studies, XVI (London, 1973), p. 15.

many *Fastnachtspiele*). The performers are amateurs, with full-time occupations and a work-a-day role and status which are in no way affected by their strictly seasonal function as dramatic performers. Most significantly, performance of the early *Fastnachtspiele*, in an exact parallel to the folk plays, occurs in the context of a house-to-house visit. On Shrove Tuesday night the *Fastnachtsrotten* obtain leave to enter a house in which people are already assembled and enjoying the seasonal festivities. The visitors perform their show, take their leave, and go on to another house where the same sequence is observed, and so on. It seems that the houses thus visited were mostly taverns. Such establishments are among the favorite ports of call of the English mummers, although this is usually reckoned a fairly recent development. The early *Fastnachtspiele*, like the folk plays, may also have been taken to private houses: some of the texts refer to the presence of women and children in the audience, which may imply domestic auspices rather than a hostelry.

As in the case of the folk plays, the event may also be considered a "Good Luck Visit," in the sense that the performers bring seasons greetings and good wishes to the assembled company.[23] In the context of seasonal custom such house-to-house visits are often associated with formalized begging, or at least the demand for largesse or refreshment, and accordingly labeled *quête* (the usual English term) or *Heischegang*. Most English folk plays conclude with an explicit demand for money, food, or drink. This aspect of the auspices of the *Fastnachtspiele* has been neglected, but there are hints in the texts, some quite broad, that the performers expected to be rewarded with some kind of refreshment:

> Herr wirt, wolt ir der gest abkomen,
>   so gebt ain mal zu trineken herume
> Vnd last uns vrlab von euch nemenn
>   wir wollen pald herwider khemenn.

to which this text, exceptionally, adds the explicit direction: *Da soll man trinkhn* (Zingerle No. X; cf. Keller Nos. 21, 34, 44, etc.).

The German plays are short, lasting at most half an hour, usually a good

---

23. On this aspect of the folk plays see M. J. Preston, "The British Folk Play: An Elaborated Luck-Visit?" *Western Folklore*, XXX (1971), 45–48.

deal less, and performed by smallish companies of five to fifteen men. The performers are disguised, and to judge by the attempts of the authorities to suppress the practice, may often have worn masks. The plays often involve several characters in identical type-roles—fools, peasants, knights—and we may imagine them costumed uniformly. The whole performance may therefore have given a visual impression similar to that of the traditional English mummers.[24] This is reinforced by a more significant feature, the absence of any stage separating performers and audience. As in the case of the folk plays, the early German *Fastnachtspiele* are performed at floor level, with no physical arrangements necessary to facilitate the action, beyond the clearing of a space in the room in which people are already assembled. There is no scenery, and no properties are used beyond simple portable items (e.g., swords).

The performance opens with a presenter who is usually designated *Vorläufer* or *Einschreier*, the terms reflecting two of his functions which correspond precisely to the opening of the folk plays: he is the one who "comes before" to prepare the audience for the performance, and who "calls on" the other players. Eckehard Catholy's list of the tasks of the *Vorläufer* fits equally well the corresponding figure of the folk plays: greeting to those present, request for room in which to perform, request for attention, presentation of the players, and perhaps introduction of the plot.[25] Such introductions comprise a series of verbal commonplaces of which the following provides a representative sample:

> Got gruss euch, herren uberal
> Und alle, die do sitzen in disem sal.
> Hie kumen zu euch, ab got wil, frum leut, als ir secht;
> Sie hoffen, sie werden von euch nicht versmeht,
> Und in nicht fur ubel haben,
> Dann es sein werlich gut knaben,
> In sunderlicher freuntschaft kumen sie her
> Und verkunden euch neue mer
> Von einem arzt, der ist hochgelert,
> Als ir in seinem werken sehen wert;

---

24. On modes of costuming in English folk plays see Brody, *The English Mummers*, pp. 21–26.

25. Catholy, *Fastnachtspiel*, p. 21.

Darumb biten wir den herren und die frauen,
Das sie diesem werk wollen zuschauen,
Und sich des nit Verdrissen lasser,
Dan es is kurz auss der massen.
Nu schweigt und habt ru!
Knecht Quenzepelzsch, trit herzu . . .

(Keller No. 6, p. 58, 11. 4–19. For the request for
room, not explicit here, see e.g., No. 1, p. 1, 1. 5:
"Weicht ab, tret umbe und raumet auf")

Compare the opening speech of the English Hero Combat Plays, here in Chamber's "normalized text," which assembles the more common formulas from a large number of versions:

I open the door, I enter in;
I hope your favour we shall win.
Stir up the fire and strike a light,
And see my merry boys act to-night.
Whether we stand or whether we fall,
We'll do our best to please you all.
Room, room, brave gallants all,
Pray give us room to rhyme;
We've come to show activity,
    This merry Christmas time;
Activity of youth,
    Activity of age,
The like was never seen
    Upon a common stage.
And if you don't believe what I say,
    Step in St George . . . [26]

With the calling on of the first character the action of the performance in both forms gets under way.

The *Fastnachtspiele* likewise conclude with an address by the Presenter to the audience. He usually recalls the festive occasion of the performance, apologizes for any offense it may have given, promises he and his colleagues will come again next year, and takes leave of the assembled company on behalf of the performers. He may also, as we have seen, suggest that some refreshment would be in order, and in many plays calls on the

26. Chambers, *English Folk-Play*, p. 6, 11. 1–16.

musician to "Pfeiff auf" to accompany a concluding dance.[27] While there is not much uniformity in the conclusions of the English folk plays, they can provide parallels to most of these functions. The reference to the festive season and the concern for the audience's response usually come at the start of the play (see quotation above). In the Hero Combat Plays the concluding speech is dominated by the *quête*, but the Lincolnshire Wooing Plays generally end with a formal leave-taking:

> You see our song is ended,
> You see our fool is gone;
> We're making it our business,
> To follow him along.
> We thank you for civility, and what you gave us here;
> We wish you all good-night and another Happy New Year.[28]

As just noted, the *Fastnachtspiele* often conclude with a dance. It is usually the Presenter who, in the course of his concluding speech, calls on the minstrel to play, and the dance intervenes before he speaks the formal farewell.[29] A dance likewise concludes many English folk plays. This is of course the case with the Sword Dance Plays, where the play is sometimes little more than a device for calling on the dancers. Closer to the *Fastnachtspiele* are those Hero Combat Plays in which one of the speakers in the final parade of characters introduces himself as a dancer, often with the formula:

> In come I, as ain't been yet,
> With my big head and little wit,

27. Catholy, *Fastnachtspiel*, p. 23; Lefebvre, "Le Jeu du Carneval de Nuremberg," p. 187.

28. Carleton-le-Moorland, Lincolnshire, published by E. H. Rudwin in *Folklore*, L (1939), 88–92.

29. In most cases this is to be inferred from the speeches themselves, but in one of the Doctor plays, characterized by unusually explicit directions, the pause for the dance is made quite clear:

> AUSZSCHREYER
> Pawcher, pfeyff auff, lass uns verdrehen,
> So wil ich meyster stuck lan sehen.
> *Man tantzt, dan spricht wider der Ausschreyer*
> (then comes the Farewell proper)
>
> (Keller No. 120, p. 13, 11. 22 ff.)

(then comes the Farewell proper)

> My head so big, my wit so small,
> I will dance a jig to please you all.[30]

Or he may be a musician and offer to play a tune "to please you all," presumably to accompany a dance by the other performers.[31] This is confirmed occasionally when directions have been recorded along with the text: " . . . they all dance round while Tom Pinny sings to his fiddle" (Kempsford, Gloucestershire);[32] "Father Christmas, Dr. Lamb, Policeman and Old Woman plays the music and the other four begin dancing" (Burghclere, Hampshire).[33] As in the *Fastnachtspiele*, the dance can be inserted before the final speech (usually the *quête*).[34]

While in any one English village or town the same play will be performed year after year, in the German cities in the late fifteenth and sixteenth centuries new *Fastnachtspiele* were composed and performed each year. Further consideration will be given to this problem in due course, but it may be noted now that the contrast is not as great as might appear. The early German *Fastnachtspiele* operate with a fairly limited number of type characters—the knight, the peasant, the fool, the man-woman, the doctor, and the comic servant—all familiar in English folk drama, and the plots, such as they are, tend to manifest themselves in a small range of simple patterns, such as contests, altercation, trial, combat, and cure. But more important than either of these in demonstrating the equivalence of folk drama and *Fastnachtspiel* are their presentational character and the recurrent patterns of movement and action which mark their characteristic common dramaturgy.

The folk plays and the *Fastnachtspiele* are presentational in the sense that they are performed throughout predominantly as a conscious and often explicit offering to an audience, in which only fitfully, if at all, is there any attempt to *represent* an autonomous dramatic world distinct from the social

---

30. Chambers's normalized text, *English Folk-Play*, p. 9, ll. 91–94.

31. *Ibid.*, p. 64.

32. R.J.E. Tiddy, *The Mummers' Play* (Oxford, 1923), p. 253.

33. *Ibid.*, p. 188.

34. *Ibid.*, p. 168: a stage direction in the text places a "three-handed reel" before Father Christmas's concluding *quête*-speech, "If this old frying pan had but a tongue, / He'd say chuck in your money and think it no wrong."

reality in which the performance occurs.[35] Such a dramaturgical mode is inherent in the performance context, where there is no stage to distinguish the world of the play from that of the audience, and no scenery or complex properties to establish dramatic illusion. The direct relationship between performance and audience is marked by the opening and closing addresses of the Presenter, which frame the action. It is sustained throughout by the performers' habit of addressing the audience directly, and by the opening formulas with which new characters explicitly introduce themselves: "Ich bin ein ritter aus Meilant"; "Here comes I, St George."

The two traditions share above all characteristic patterns of action and movement, whatever the motivation of those patterns on the level of plot. The early *Fastnachtspiele* are often constructed, in whole or in part, as a *Reihespiel* (or *Revue*): "a simple sequence of separate comic speeches."[36] At its most elementary, the *Reihespiel* consists of a series of quite unrelated speeches, usually of equal length, by a number of characters who step forward one after another and address the audience directly, without reference to or interaction with each other. Each speech is usually little more than a self-characterization of the speaker.[37] Students of English folk drama will recognize this as the pattern of the *Quête* section of the Hero Combat Plays, a simple parade of several new characters (Beelzebub, Big Head, Little Johny Jack, etc.), who present themselves in turn to the audience, without getting involved with each other or with the characters already in the acting area. As in the *Reihespiele*, these *Quête*-figures often describe their own appearance ("with my big head"; "In my hand I carries my club").[38]

The next stage of dramaturgical complexity is represented by those *Reihespiele* in which the speakers in the sequence refer to or interact with

35. The distinction between "presentational" and "representational" modes is fairly standard in the study of dramaturgical technique, but my appreciation of their significance and usefulness has benefited greatly from reading Barbara A. Mowat, *The Dramaturgy of Shakespeare's Romances* (Athens, Ga., 1976).

36. "Eine einfache Aneinanderreihung komischer Einzelvorträge," Catholy, *Fastnachtspiel*, p. 26.

37. *Ibid.*, p. 27.

38. Cf. Catholy, *Fastnachtspiel*, p. 33: "Die einfachste Form der Reden in Rsp. bildet jener Typus, in dem der jeweilige Sprecher eine Eigentümlichkeit seines Körperbaus oder seines Kostüms beschreibt . . ."

each other.[39] English Sword Dance Plays provide an example of this pattern in the denial-of-responsibility sequence following the execution of the Fool:

> KING
>
> Bold Hector he is dead, and on the ground is laid
> You'll have to suffer for him, young man I'm sore afraid.
>
> MR. SPARKS
>
> I'm sure its none of I, I'm clear of the fact;
> It's he that follows I, that did this dirty act.
>
> MR. STOUT
>
> Nay I'm sure it's none of I, I'm clear of the crime;
> It's 'e that follows I, that drew his sword so fine.
>
> SQUIRE'S SON
>
> Don't lay the blame on me . . .[40]

In the most complex type of *Reihespiel* we find a more concentrated organization with a tendency for the speakers to focus on a central character, with whom they have a relationship grounded in the fiction of the play. A typical situation, notes Catholy, is the contest, in which the central figure is the judge who is to award the prize.[41] A series of fools, say, narrate their follies, and the prize goes to the greatest fool among them. Although the motivation is different, the dramaturgical pattern is clearly identical in the English Wooing Plays, where the prize the Lady has to award is herself, and she is treated to a series of speeches by a variety of wooers, each competing to present himself in the most favorable light: "I am my father's eldest son, / And heir to all his land . . ." As noted earlier, there are some early *Fastnachtspiele* in which a Lady is wooed by a series of suitors, but this parallel in motif is less important than the identical mode in which the English and German wooings are performed.[42]

39. *Ibid.*, p. 29: "Die verschiedenen Sprecher werden untereinander in Beziehung gesetzt, z.B. wenn der folgende auf die Rede des vorhengehenden eingeht oder wenn der gegenwärtige Sprecher bereits auf den folgenden hinweist."

40. N. Peacock, "The Greatham Sword Dance," *Journal of the English Folk Dance and Song Society*, VIII (1956), 29–39; hereafter cited as *JEFDSS*.

41. Catholy, *Fastnachtspiel*, p. 30. See also Lefebvre, "Le Jeu du Carneval de Nuremberg," pp. 187–188.

42. Also similar to the "concentrated" *Reihespiel* is the calling-on sequence of the Sword Dance plays, in which the dancers enter and present themselves in turn, each in response to the instruction of the leader.

There remain the considerable number of *Fastnachtspiele* which present action of sufficient complexity to be characterized as plot, the so-called *Handlungsspiele*. But the complexity is not very great: there are relatively few early *Fastnachtspiele* that actually dramatize a pre-existing narrative, and in most cases the plot, although it provides the action with a degree of motivation going beyond the *Reihespiele*, can be resolved into a few very simple dramaturgical movements. One of the simplest and more common of such movements is the confrontation. Two characters confront each other and participate in an altercation based on some slightly motivated disagreement, exchanging speeches of insult, accusation, and defiance. The same simple confrontation occurs in the Hero Combat Plays, with the exchange of boasts and defiance between St. George and his antagonist. The parallel is complete in those *Fastnachtspiele* where the confrontation reaches a climax in a fight (see discussion of combat motif, above). Alternatively, the dispute is brought before a court, and judges or jurors give their verdict in a series of speeches, the action reverting to the *Reihespiel* form (e.g., Keller Nos. 8, 10, 18, etc.).

III

Altogether, there is a striking equivalence between the early German *Fastnachtspiele* and the English folk plays, in such fundamental generic features as performance context and dramaturgy, in addition to the common motifs noted earlier, and we may legitimately ask what perspectives this may offer for the understanding and appreciation of the two traditions concerned.

It may not show too much temerity for an outsider to suggest that study of the *Fastnachtspiele* may be considerably facilitated by the equivalence offered here, which obliges one to designate them as a species of folk drama belonging to a specifically urban and guild context. The thesis may at least provoke useful contextual and dramaturgical studies to complement the current interest in the literary qualities of the *Fastnachtspiele*, and may also go some way to resolve the long-running and rather arid debate on their origins.[43] One view has assigned the early *Fastnachtspiele* to the

---

43. Catholy, *Fastnachtspiel*, pp. 3–5, provides a convenient review and commentary on the theories that have been offered.

wandering scholars of the Middle Ages, the *vagantes*, who may have inherited something of the dramatic traditions of the antique *mimus*. But
indebtedness to the *mimus*, direct or indirect, seems extremely unlikely for
a genre which, as the parallels to folk drama suggest, is so singularly
lacking in *mimesis*,[44] and it is hard to imagine the *vagantes*, by definition
wanderers, contributing significantly to a dramatic activity which functions so intimately within the social interrelationships of a particular
community. At most a wandering scholar, like any other individual
author, could provide the script for a play: but the generic framework
within which this might be done was largely determined in advance by the
performance context out of which the form emerged.[45] The *Fastnachtspiel*
is likewise revealed as a species of performance generically distinct from
the liturgical drama with which it has frequently been linked, as an
antecedent or derivative. Specific plots, motifs, or characters (the Coming
of Antichrist, Lucifer and his devils, the Doctor) might be exchanged
between them, but they remain quite different dramaturgical systems.[46]
Eckehard Catholy, while reluctant to pursue the question of origins, nonetheless tends to see the *Fastnachtspiele* emerging from the humorous
speeches, the "turns" (*Einzelvorträge*) with which participants in carnival
revelry might entertain each other. A string of such party-pieces gives us
at once the simplest form of *Fastnachtspiel*, the *Reihespiel*.[47] But there is a
fundamental difference between such a situation and the mimetic context
of the *Fastnachtspiele*, which, like the folk plays, are specifically characterized by the house-to-house visit, involving the intrusion from outside of a
group of performers whose function in the custom is measurably distinct
from that of the revelers they visit.

44. On the characteristic mimetic talents of the Roman *mimus* and his medieval successors, see Axton, *European Drama of the Early Middle Ages*, chap. 1.

45. This is the major weakness of Catholy's own preference (*Fastnachtspiel*, p. 5) to
concentrate on the literary character of the plays, independently of their context in seasonal
custom, and as the creation of individual authors.

46. On the characteristic dramaturgy of the liturgical plays, see Axton, "Popular Modes
in the Earliest Plays," pp. 19 ff.

47. Catholy, *Fastnachtspiel*, p. 16. As this implies, Catholy tends to assume that the
simplest form of *Fastnachtspiel* is also the earliest. This may be unwarranted: there is a
chronological problem in the sequence of the early forms of the *Fastnachtspiel* reminiscent of
the evolutionary problem in liturgical drama.

The time may soon be ripe for something of a rehabilitation of a cluster of earlier theories which all connected the *Fastnachtspiele* with seasonal custom (and hence with folk drama), but which are currently out of favor, largely, and justly, on account of their unnecessary introduction of extraneous factors. Some have suggested the derivation of the *Fastnachtspiele* from an earlier tradition of secular drama, which in turn emerged from seasonal customs. The interpolated intermediate stage here makes for easy refutation—there are simply not enough earlier secular plays on which to build a case [48]—and it is quite unnecessary: the *Fastnachtspiele* are patently directly related to the seasonal customs of Shrovetide. Adherents of the latter view, meanwhile, have made their task unnecessarily difficult by appeal to carnival customs quite distinct from the *Fastnachtspiele*, such as the processional *Schembartlauf*.[49] Finally the theory of ritual origins (in addition to its unfortunate ideological affiliations) introduced a factor essentially irrelevant to the medieval status and function of the plays, although since seasonal customs of various kinds, including folk drama, were also believed to derive from primitive ritual their juxtaposition with the *Fastnachtspiele* was a useful by-product. The parallels explored above suggest not so much that the early *Fastnachtspiele* derive from seasonal custom as that they *are* a—dramatic—seasonal custom: they are folk drama. There may have been earlier, simpler forms, say the house-to-house visits of disguised Shrovetide mummers,[50] the kind of thing regulated in the records of the Nuremberg authorities,[51] and probably common to many rural and urban communities. The early German *Fastnachtspiele* can be said to derive from (i.e., to be more than) such customs only to the extent that they may have achieved a degree of elaboration through their cultivation in a particular urban and guild milieu.

IV

It may be anticipated that the equivalence between *Fastnachtspiele* and the folk plays argued above will be of particular value in supplementing the very fragmentary and sporadic evidence available on English folk drama in the medieval and early modern periods. The parallels noted

48. *Ibid.*, p. 4.

49. On the distinction between *Fastnachtspiel* and *Schembartlauf*, see Lefebvre, "Le Jeu du Carneval de Nuremberg," pp. 183–184.

50. Derek van Abbé, *Drama in Renaissance Germany and Switzerland* (Melbourne, 1961), pp. 27–28.

51. Stumpfl, *Kultspiele der Germanen*, pp. 19–20.

between the two forms are so strong, and, I would argue, so fundamental, that any residual features by which the *Fastnachtspiele* differ from English folk plays as recorded in the last two centuries, rather than giving pause, may be turned to account in charting the earlier phases of English tradition.

A case in point is the evident institutional context of the *Fastnachtspiele* provided by the urban guilds (for example, the craft guilds of Nuremberg), from whose younger members the performers seem to have been recruited.[52] This does not mean that early English folk drama must have had the same context, but does suggest that it may be worth looking for one. Indeed an awareness of the German situation is salutary, prompting the disconcerting realization that we still lack systematic analysis of the institutional framework of English folk drama. The available surveys do not tell us about the social, professional, or economic status of the performers, or their personal or social relationship to each other or to their audiences; such information, indeed, is only sporadically recorded in even the firsthand accounts of English folk drama. It is consequently hard to generalize, but I imagine there would be some agreement that at least for the very recent phases of tradition there is no regular institutional context for the English folk plays, which are generally performed by an ad hoc group, whose play-performing activity is not a function of their common membership of a particular social or institutional grouping. In any one company the men are likely to have different occupations, to be of different generations, or even to come from different communities.[53] The one social institution that can occasionally be glimpsed in the accounts is the family, with brothers, fathers, and sons, or uncles and nephews prominent in a particular company, or with one family dominant in a local tradition for a number of generations.[54]

52. For example in Lübeck the guild responsible for the *Fastnachtspiele* decided formally in 1499 that the twelve most junior members should be responsible for performing the play (Catholy, p. 69).

53. These remarks are of necessity based on impressions gained from sporadic references. But see, for example, the accounts of a number of companies in Barry J. Ward's dissertation, "A Functional Approach to English Folk Drama," based on fieldwork undertaken in the early 1970s.

54. For examples see Ward, *ibid.*, pp. 72–73, 115; Ian Russell, "A Survey of Traditional Drama in North East Derbyshire 1970–8," *Folk Music Journal*, III, no. 5 (1979), 403, 410, 414, etc.; N. Peacock, "The Greatham Sword Dance," *JEFDSS*, VIII (1956), 29.

We cannot be certain, however, that these contextual features can be extrapolated back to the earlier phases of tradition prior to the social upheavals occasioned by the Agrarian and Industrial Revolutions, or even that similar conditions obtained prior to the cataclysm of World War I, which literally killed off the folk-play tradition of many towns and villages. For the social function and context of early English folk drama there is very little evidence indeed, but the example of the *Fastnachtspiele* and other Continental traditions may provide guidance and encouragement in the task.[55] The connection of the German plays with guilds is paralleled for example by the late-medieval tradition (now lost) of folk plays re-enacting the combat of St. George and the Dragon (a legend which also achieved dramatization as a *Fastnachtspiel*—Keller No. 126). In the fifteenth and sixteenth centuries these St. George "ridings," performed on the saint's day, April 23, were "in the hands of a guild, founded not as a trade guild, but as a half social, half religious fraternity, for the worship of the saint, and the mutual aid and good fellowship of its members."[56] On the other hand the context of the Robin Hood plays, often associated with the May games, seems to have been an administrative unit, the parish or borough, with the churchwardens or municipal officials collecting money to support the plays, and supervising expenditure on them.[57]

<hr />

55. The most revealing evidence for the social perspectives of early folk-play traditions, both English and Continental, is often provided in connection with social disorder and rebellion, these being among the few occasions on which the lower classes figure at all prominently in the historical records, and the way in which seasonal folk traditions are exploited as a vehicle for social protest and insurrection is attracting increasing interest among scholars. See, for example, Yves-Marie Bercé, *Fête et Révolte: Des Mentalités Populaires du xvie au xviie siècle* (Paris, 1976); Emmanuel Le Roy Ladurie, *Carnival in Romans: A People's Uprising at Romans 1579–80* (London, 1981); Norman Simms, "Ned Ludd's Mummers Play," *Folklore*, LXXXIX (1978), 166–178, and "Nero and Jack Straw in Chaucer's *Nun's Priest's Tale*," *Parergon*, VIII (1974), 2–12. Much of the English evidence is assembled and discussed in my study, "'Here Comes I, Jack Straw': English Folk Drama and Social Revolt," forthcoming in *Folklore*, XCV.

56. E. K. Chambers, *The Medieval Stage* (1903; rpt. London, 1967), I, 222. See also John Wasson, "The *St George* and *Robin Hood Plays* in Devon," *Medieval English Theatre*, II (1980), 66–69. For the guilds and their purposes see H. F. Westlake, *The Parish Guilds of Medieval England* (London, 1919).

57. Chambers, *Medieval Stage*, I, 176.

Other traditions could function in less formal, but nonetheless tangible, social contexts. Early Continental sources assign the primary role in much seasonal custom to the young men of the community, the bachelors who have attained physical maturity but not yet taken on the responsibilities of family life or acquired an established position in the community through occupation or proprietorship.[58] In France, such groups went by the name of *bachelleries* or *abbayes*, in Germany *Burschenschaften* or *Jungmannschaften*,[59] and there are occasional glimpses of similar youth-groupings in the early English records. A celebrated Norwich record, to be discussed more fully later, associates a traditional Shrovetide festival performed in 1443 with the "Bachery guild,"[60] evidently the English equivalent of the *bachelleries* of rural France. It must also be the gathering of such a group which is described so vividly in Philip Stubbes's diatribe against the "Lords of Misrule" in Elizabethan England:

all the wilde-heds of the Parish, conuenting togither, chuse them a Graund-Captain . . . whome they innoble with the title of my Lord of Misrule. . . . This king anointed, chuseth forth twentie, fortie, threescore or a hundred lustie Guttes like himself to waighte vppon his lordly Maiestie . . .

this as a prelude to a rowdy summer game reaching its climax with the whole company invading the church.[61] Such an informal arrangement for seasonal revelry is by no means incompatible with the guild context documented for the German *Fastnachtspiele*. In a village or small town, all the eligible young men would presumably belong to the community's one "Bachery." In a more decidedly urban setting, however, as Natalie Davis has shown, diversification occurs, and the functions of the rural youth-groups are taken over by other institutions; by neighborhood groupings (sixteenth-century Lyons, for example, had about twenty youth-abbeys), or, more significantly for present purposes, by occupational groupings,

---

58. See, e.g., Natalie Zemon Davis, *Society and Culture in Early Modern France* (Stanford, Calif., 1975), pp. 104–109; Bercé, *Fête et Révolte*, chap. I.

59. Davis, *Society and Culture in Early Modern France*; Schmidt, *Das Deutsche Volksschauspiel*, p. 32.

60. William Tydeman, *The Theatre in the Middle Ages* (Cambridge, Eng., 1978), p. 19.

61. Philip Stubbes, *The Anatomie of Abuses* (1583; facs. rpt., New York and London, 1973), sig. M.2ᵃ.

such as the craft guilds.[62] It is therefore possible to assert that the parallels already discussed are supplemented by a contextual equivalence between the *Fastnachtspiele* and certain types of early English folk drama.

At the same time it is evident that while the example of the *Fastnachtspiele* has prompted a significant question concerning English traditions, it has not provided the full answer. Indeed the most salutary effect of the German example may be the realization that in charting early traditions of folk drama it is necessary to be aware of the correlation between different traditions and their specific social contexts. The discussion above, for example, has not touched on the three types of folk drama which have been prominent in the last couple of centuries. It is striking that despite their recent visibility the Hero Combat, Sword Dance, and Wooing Plays are entirely absent from the historical records of the late medieval and early modern periods: no arrangements are made for them by parochial, municipal, or ecclesiastical authorities, and neither medieval bishops nor Puritan moralists include them in their many fulminations against popular seasonal revelry. At the same time the frequent echoes and parallels in the other dramatic traditions of the period leave little room for doubt that such folk plays existed then.[63] This suggests that their function was such that it neither needed to figure in administrative documents nor provoked the ire of contemporary guardians of morality: perhaps a private social function, rather than institutional; interpersonal rather than public.

Considerations of space do not permit a full exploration here, nor is the ground so certain as to warrant one at this stage, but I suggest a likely context may be offered by personal and group relationships within the manorial system. Even among the more recent records the dominant pattern of folk-drama activity seems to be performance by fairly humble members of the community, visiting their social superiors—squire, clergyman, schoolmaster, doctor, etc.—at the "big houses" of the village, and there are hints in the early records that the subservient relationship of the mummers to their audience may have been of contextual significance. The earliest surviving folk play related to the modern traditions, the *Revesby Sword Play*, was performed in 1779 by tenants of the Revesby

62. Davis, *Society and Culture*, pp. 110–111.
63. See above, n. 4.

estate at Revesby Abbey, the seat of their landlord, Sir Joseph Banks.[64] One of the few late medieval records suggesting a performance at all similar to the modern folk plays is the Scottish "Pleugh Song," from ca. 1500, which as interpreted by Helena Shire and Kenneth Elliott emerges as a seasonal performance by a group of men before their lord, involving processional movements, the harnessing of the performers to the plough, the execution of the lead "ox," and his replacement by a younger one.[65] The parallels to later Plough Monday customs are clear enough, but more interesting for the moment is the evident function of the performance as an offering to the lord before whom it takes place. In the words of Richard Axton:

the ceremony is a "ritual of social relationships," in which the ploughlads act out their allegiance and are literally bound together in the service of their lord, the ox and plough representing an undying obligation to work. The mutual social advantages are affirmed.[66]

It may therefore be worth exploring if the medieval progenitors of the modern English folk plays were similar "rituals of social relationships," expressing and confirming the mutual obligations of the manorial lord and his villeins, tenants, or laborers. Manorial relationships were very much a matter of custom, not all of it recorded, and a seasonal custom with such a function need not have been looked upon by contemporary churchmen as immoral, or as a devilish alternative to the established religion; hence the otherwise baffling silence of the historical sources. It may also be anticipated that exploration of their function in relation to the differing complexes of relationships within the manorial system will ultimately explain the striking correlation, often noted, between the geographical incidence

---

64. Paul and Georgina Smith, "The *Plouboys or Modes Dancers* at Revesby," *EDS*, XLIII, no. 1 (1980), 7–9. On the relationship of the Revesby text to folk-play traditions, see my "English Folk Drama in the Eighteenth Century: A Defense of the *Revesby Sword Play*," *CompD*, XV (1981), 3–29.

65. Helena M. Shire and Kenneth Elliott, "Pleugh Song and Plough Play," *Saltire Review*, II, no. 6 (1955), 39–44.

66. *European Drama of the Early Middle Ages*, p. 42.

of the modern folk plays and the regions of England dominated by champion husbandry before the Enclosures. [67]

A further contrast to the *Fastnachtspiele* may prompt consideration of other aspects of English folk-play tradition. We have become accustomed to contemplating a fairly high degree of uniformity in the traditions recorded since ca. 1800. There are few genres of folk play (three main types plus a few minor forms like the "Old Tup" ceremony), and there is relative stability in the tradition of any one community: the mummers in a particular village will be content to go on performing the same play year after year, even generation after generation, and their play will not differ so very much from the one performed in the next village. This sometimes leads to the suspicion that idiosyncratic plays, like those from Revesby or Ampleforth, must be nontraditional, or affected by literary intervention. [68] The German *Fastnachtspiele* therefore present us with the provocative spectacle of a species of drama, evidently traditional, but comprised of "one off performances": a new play composed as each *Fastnacht* came round. This suggests that folk drama may likewise be properly termed "traditional" not so much because the separate plays bear substantial textual similarities to each other, as because it is marked by a traditional dramaturgy, a characteristic mode of performance, which can provide the vehicle for any number of quite different texts. The example of the *Fastnachtspiele* may therefore warn us to be more tolerant of the exceptional plays within the surviving English folk-play corpus. It is not merely that there may have been more kinds of folk drama in the past: the specific traditions may have shown a much greater textual and structural flexibility from year to year and from place to place.

It is relevant to recall in this connection that texts of English folk drama start to be collected in reasonable quantities from about the 1830s, coinciding significantly with the period that saw the final impoverishment of

67. The correlation is discussed briefly in Cawte et al., *English Ritual Drama*, p. 33. For medieval champion husbandry and the characteristic social and economic relationships associated with it, see Caspar Homans, *English Villagers of the Thirteenth Century* (New York, 1970).

68. Cf. Michael Preston, "The Revesby Sword Play," *JAF*, LXXXV (1972), 51–57, and "Solutions to Classic Problems in the Study of Oral Literature," in *Computing in the Humanities*, ed. S. Lusignan and J. S. North (Waterloo, Can., 1978), pp. 117–132.

the English rural laborers and the failure of the last serious movement of violent social protest in the countryside, the "Swing" riots of 1830–1831. The relative uniformity of modern English folk drama may reflect the social, economic, and cultural demoralization of the English peasantry, and before the Agrarian Revolution folk-drama traditions may have evinced more vigorous flexibility and originality. We need not go so far as to suggest that early English mummers matched the German *Fastnachtsrotten* in putting on a completely new play (within the traditional framework) each year; the latter are clearly advantaged by their prosperous urban milieu—the availability of poets who could provide new texts, and the financial resources to commission them. But even in the eighteenth century in England there is evidence of a greater variety of folk-drama traditions,[69] and flexibility within traditions is suggested, ironically, by the many chapbook-texts (which we may presume ultimately contributed to the later inflexibility). The commercial publication of the chapbooks must have been based on the assumption that the mummers were willing to replace whatever play they performed before by purchasing a new one.[70] The commercial printing of the two Robin Hood plays by William Copland, ca. 1560, offered to buyers as "verye proper to be played in Maye Games,"[71] has similar implications.

We may turn, finally, to the most concrete question prompted by the results offered and discussed above: were there *Fastnachtspiele* in England? The question can be answered affirmatively in two complementary ways: in the surviving dramatic corpus from the later Middle Ages and the sixteenth century there are plays (without specific seasonal affiliations) which provide sometimes striking parallels to the German *Fastnachtspiele*; there is also evidence of a species of traditional drama directly associated with the festivities of Shrovetide. The parallels in nonseasonal plays are the

69. Cf. the evidence offered in my "English Folk Drama in the Eighteenth Century."

70. On the extent of chapbook printing of folk-drama texts see Alex Helm, *The Chapbook Mummers' Plays* (Ibstock, Eng., 1969), and M. J. Preston, M. G. Smith, and P. S. Smith, "The Lost Chapbooks," *Folklore*, LXXXVIII (1977), 160–174. The studies of Michael Preston and Paul and Georgina Smith promise further insights into the significance of the chapbook texts: a series of editions and studies is currently being published by the Centre for English Cultural Tradition and Language, University of Sheffield.

71. *Rymes of Robyn Hood*, ed. Dobson and Taylor, pp. 208–209.

least significant of the two phenomena, but are nonetheless intriguing, and may be illustrated by an early and a late example from English popular drama.

The Croxton *Play of the Sacrament*, from the late fifteenth century, is not a *Fastnachtspiel*: as a miracle of the Host its seasonal affiliations, if any, are more likely to be with the feast of Corpus Christi.[72] Nor is it a folk play: its auspices are uncertain—they may be professional, ecclesiastical, or parochial—but it is a piece of regular drama, and may have been written specifically to counter the attack on the Real Presence by the Lollards, who were particularly strong in East Anglia.[73] Nonetheless it is generally recognized that an episode in the play, which may be an interpolation, is an importation from seasonal folk drama.[74] In the course of his attempts to injure a host, which he has obtained surreptitiously, one of the wicked Jews, Sir Jonathan, has his hand wrenched off.[75] The Jews withdraw and there enters Colle, "þe lechys man" (l. 524 S.D.) who greets the audience (significantly the first direct address since the play's opening prayer), and regales them with a jaundiced account of the qualities and activities of his employer, "Mayster Brendyche of Braban, . . . þe most famous phesycyan / þat euer sawe vryne" (ll. 533–536). The Doctor duly appears, and there follows a comic dialogue in which the Doctor's self-praise is deflated by Colle's disrespectful asides. At his master's instruction, Colle makes a public proclamation of the Doctor's arrival and invites patients to visit him, listing the many diseases for which he has a sovereign (by implication, mortal) remedy. Colle tells the Doctor of the injury suffered by Sir Jonathan, and together they hail him and offer their services. He angrily refuses and with the other Jews drives the Doctor and his man from the stage.

72. Axton, *European Drama in the Early Middle Ages*, p. 199.

73. Celia Cutts, "The Croxton Play—An Anti-Lollard Piece," *MLQ*, V (1944), 45–60. On the play's affiliation with East Anglia, see Axton, *European Drama in the Early Middle Ages*.

74. E.g., Anna J. Mill, "The Miracle Plays and Mysteries," in *A Manual of the Writings in Middle English*, vol. V, ed. A. E. Hartung (Hamden, Conn., 1975), pp. 4–5; Hardin Craig, *English Religious Drama of the Middle Ages* (1955; corr. rpt., Oxford, 1964), pp. 326–327.

75. In what follows, references to the play will be to the text in *Non-Cycle Plays and Fragments*, ed. Norman Davis, EETS, ss. 1 (London, 1970), pp. 58–89; the Doctor episode is on pp. 74–78.

There is much here reminiscent of the Cure Scene common to all three types of recent English folk play: the Doctor and his medicines, boasts of earlier cures, lists of diseases, etc. The relationship between Master Brendyche and his servant parallels very closely the interplay of the Doctor and his servant Jack Finney in that important regional subtradition of Hero Combat plays with an extended Cure Scene. But, extraordinarily, the specific parallels with the *Fastnachtspiele* are even stronger. In several instances the action of the *Fastnachtspiele* (unlike the English folk plays) opens with a speech by the servant giving the same kind of dissillusioned characterization of the Doctor and his activities as Colle provided in the Croxton *Sacrament* (e.g., Keller No. 6; Zingerle Nos. VI, XXI). At the Doctor's behest, the servant makes a declaration of the powers of his medicines, and advertises for custom. A patient duly appears, and the play moves into a cure scene. The sequence of action here duplicates closely that of the Doctor episode in the Croxton *Sacrament*, and the ironic accounts of the physicians by their servants are very similar:

> Von einem maister wil ich euch sagen neue mer,
> Der ist kumen auss fremden landen her
> . . . .
> Mit seiner erznei hat er ertot munch und pfaffen,
> . . . .
> Wer do ist gesunt, den macht er sich.
> Maister Viviam ist er genant.
> (Keller No. 6, p. 58, 11. 25 ff.)

> Mayster Brendyche of Braban,
> I tell yow he ys þat same man,
> . . . .
> He had a lady late in cure;
> I wot be þis she ys full sure;
> There shall neuer Cristen creature
> > Here hyr tell no tale.
> (ll. 533 ff.)

The blunt warning of the German servant, "Wer do ist gesunt, den macht er sich," is matched by Colle's later declaration, "Thowh a man were ryght heyle, he cowd soone make hym sek" (l. 619).

A hundred years later in English popular tradition we encounter a similar phenomenon in Marlowe's *Tragical History of the Life and Death of*

Doctor Faustus. Here, too, there are evident parallels to the modern English folk plays, particularly in the scene where Faustus is attacked and beheaded by a group of swordsmen at the court of the German Emperor. They discuss dismembering his corpse, only to be dismayed by the Doctor's revival (scene xiii).[76] As in the case of the Croxton *Sacrament*, these borrowings from folk-play tradition are supplemented by equally specific parallels to the *Fastnachtspiele*. Among the pageants, processions, and other shows that characterize this play's variegated dramaturgy is a passage which in all respects reproduces the structural pattern of an early *Fastnachtspiel*. Following Faustus's recovery from one of his frequent bouts of remorse, the devils entertain him with what Lucifer terms a "show" (vi. 110). It is introduced by Beelzebub who functions as Presenter/*Vorläufer*:

Faustus, we are come from hell in person to show thee some pastime. Sit down, and thou shalt behold the Seven Deadly Sins appear to thee in their own proper shapes and likeness.

> (vi. 104–107)

The context is very much that of the *Fastnachtspiele*, with the performers intruding on Faustus at home (he is "in his study," as the scene opens), and in proper fashion Beelzebub announces their arrival ("we are come"; cf. the *Vorläufer*'s formula *Wier khumen herein*), declares their purpose ("to show thee some pastime"; cf. *Wir wollen haben ain fasnachtspill*), asks the audience to settle down ("Sit down"; cf. *siczet nider*), and announces the nature of the show ("thou shalt behold . . . "; cf. *Ier werdet sehen . . .*). The Seven Deadly Sins parade onto the stage, evidently costumed (and perhaps masked) to suit their qualities. Each in turn, in response to a question from Faustus (who here usurps the function of the *Vorläufer*) delivers a short speech of self-characterization: "I am Pride . . . ," "I am Covetousness . . . ," etc. The structure and content of the action here correspond precisely to the *Reihespiele* examined by Catholy (see above). The sequence completed, the performers leave accompanied by a piper.

One of the first comic scenes in the play shows us Wagner, Faustus's

---

76. *Doctor Faustus*, ed. John D. Jump, Revels Plays (Manchester, 1978). All further references will be to this edition. See my note, "The Folk-Play in Marlowe's *Doctor Faustus*," *Folklore*, XCI (1980), 72–77.

servant, recruiting the Clown, Robin, into the Doctor's service (scene iv). The scene is important within the play for its parody of Faustus's conjuration and his own contractual relationship to the devil, but more interesting for present purposes because of distinct parallels with some *Fastnachtspiele* (e.g., Keller No. 4). The motif of the Doctor and his comic servants is common to both, as is the recruitment action. The Doctor of the *Fastnachtspiele* (like his counterpart in the related scene of the German Easter Plays)[77] is sometimes shown hiring a servant, and specific parallels include the discussion of conditions of service and the name of the servant (*Rubein / Rubin* in the German plays, Robin in *Faustus*).

It would be absurd to suggest that both the anonymous author of the Croxton *Play of the Sacrament* and the collaborator who furnished Marlowe's play with its comic scenes were directly influenced by the German *Fastnachtspiele*. This evidence, rather, suggests that the German plays preserve for us features of those early traditions of folk drama which are now lost in England, and which only sporadically left their traces in the drama of the popular theater. In this way, at least, we can say that England once had performances like the *Fastnachtspiele*.

But this assertion may also be made in a more concrete and positive manner: England also once had a traditional drama affiliated to the Shrovetide season. Recent conditions are naturally of little value as a guide, since the Reformation, supplemented by the efforts of the Puritans, has left little remaining of the medieval English carnival tradition.[78] Nor does it seem that the urban craft guilds provided the context for the medieval English Lent-eve-plays: the larger English provincial cities had a rich tradition of seasonal custom,[79] but it may be that their dramatic resources were devoted rather to the Corpus Christi cycles and other forms of religious drama. But even if this should be the case, the discussion

---

77. Viktor Michels, *Studien über die Ältesten Fastnachtspiele*, pp. 52–59.

78. Modern English folklore has recorded a rather sad little Shrove-Tuesday *quête*, in which groups of poor children went from house to house and chanted a rhyme begging for food, often the seasonal pancake. A. R. Wright, *British Calendar Customs*, vol. I, *Movable Festivals* (London, 1936), pp. 16 ff.

79. See Charles Pythian-Adams, "Ceremony and the Citizen: The Communal Year at Coventry 1450–1650," in *Crisis and Order in English Towns 1500–1700: Essays in Urban History*, ed. Peter Clark and Paul Slack (London, 1972), pp. 57–85.

above implies that there could be English folk-drama equivalents to the *Fastnachtspiele* in other social or institutional contexts.

C. R. Baskervill, in his review of the dramatic features of medieval seasonal customs, observes pessimistically that the evidence for England is strikingly poor compared to that for Germany, but he does cite a record of a Shrovetide performance at Norwich in 1443 which is interesting both in itself and for its assertion that the performance was a seasonal tradition both there and elsewhere. A certain John Gladman,

of disporte as is and ever hath ben accustomed in ony Cite or Burgh thrugh al this realme on fastyngong tuesday made a disporte w^t his neighburghs having his hors trapped with tyneseyle and otherwyse dysgysyn things crowned as King of Kristmesse in token that all merthe shuld end with ye twelve mothes of ye yer, afore hym eche moneth disgysed after ye seson yerof, and Lenten cladde in white with redde herrings skinnes and his hors trapped with oyster shelles after him in token y^t sadnesse and abstinence of merthe shulde followe and an holy tyme; and so rode in diverse stretes of ye Cite w^t other peple w^t hym disgysed making merthe and disporte and pleyes.[80]

As we meet them in this account, John Gladman and his neighbors are not performing a *Fastnachtspiel*; this part of the custom is evidently processional, but the reference to "making . . . pleyes" in various parts of the city is certainly suggestive. Perhaps the Norwich record describes them parading between house visits. The sequence of figures representing the twelve months of the year would make a perfect *Reihespiel*,[81] and the personification of Lent is also known in the *Fastnachtspiele* (e.g., Keller No. 73). Be that as it may, the description is enough as it stands to suggest that European carnival customs, familiar from written accounts and pictorial sources such as Bruegel's *Fight between Carnival and Lent*, had analogues in England, encouraging the search for English equivalents of the early German *Fastnachtspiele*.

Such a quest will not be undertaken here, but I might offer, by way of conclusion and challenge, some hints of the directions it might usefully

80. Charles Read Baskervill, "Dramatic Aspects of Medieval Folk Festivals in England," *SP*, XVII (1920), 39–40.

81. Cf. the Italian folk play of "The Months" (*I Mesi*), in which twelve performers representing the months deliver a series of self-descriptive speeches, with appropriate gestures and properties. *Le Théatre Populaire Européen*, ed. Schmidt, no. 3.

follow. Particularly interesting, not least because much information about them survives, are the English court masques, and the simpler traditions of mumming and disguising that preceded them. The masque, it is generally acknowledged, has a relationship to the folk drama analogous to that postulated here for the *Fastnachtspiele*.[82] Court masques belong to the festive season generally, but some were specifically intended for a Shrovetide performance, and their seasonal affiliations may repay further study along the lines recently sketched by R. C. Hassel.[83] These Shrovetide masques may be seen as a specifically courtly elaboration of the folk-drama traditions of the season, parallel to the urban / guild elaboration which produced the *Fastnachtspiele*. There is a curious parallel between some *Fastnachtspiele* and the court masque in the "taking out" of members of the audience by the performers for the concluding dance, the "revels."[84] And contrary to what might be expected, even the elaborate Jacobean court masque could, like both folk drama and the *Fastnachtspiel*, be performed in a sequence of house visits, although the visits, not unnaturally, were spread over a number of nights. The contemporary term for the phenomenon was the "running masque," and in a letter describing the country sports of the court in February 1620, John Chamberlain connects the performance of a running masque with Shrovetide festivities, designated by what must be the traditional expression for house-to-house visits at this season, "to go ashroving":

they passe the time merrilie at Newmarket and the running maske raunges over all the countrie, where there be fit subjects to entertain yt, as lately they have ben at Sir John Crofts neere Berrie, and in requitall those Ladies have invited them to

82. Usually referred to in this connection is Margaret Dean-Smith's "The Folk-Play Origins of the English Masque," *Folklore*, LXV (1954), 74–86. Its general treatment should be supplemented by the concrete documentation in Charles Read Baskervill, "The Sources of Jonson's *Masque of Christmas* and *Love's Welcome at Welbeck*," *MP*, VI (1908–1909), 257–269.

83. R. Chris Hassel, Jr., *Renaissance Drama and the English Church Year* (Lincoln, Nebr., and London, 1979), chap. 6, "The Shrovetide Masques and Plays."

84. This aspect of the German plays is discussed by Catholy, *Fastnachtspiel*, p. 25. There are signs in some texts that the number of female dancers required exceeded the available "female" characters in the cast (e.g., Keller No. 5, p. 57, 11. 27 ff.; No. 51, p. 390, 11. 2 ff.).

a maske of theyr owne invention, . . . so that on Thursday next the King, Prince and all the court go thither ashroving.[85]

Turning to a more humble milieu, a case could surely be made for a reassessment of the fifteenth-century morality, *Mankind*, in relation to an English tradition of Shrovetide folk plays analogous to the *Fastnachtspiele*. The play's appropriateness to Shrovetide performance has long been accepted: its references to late winter activities (threshing, sowing), to February, to football (a common Shrove Tuesday sport), to winter weather, and to Saint David (whose day is March 1). The play even quotes from the Ash Wednesday liturgy.[86] Even the singing of a "Crystemes songe" (l. 332),[87] which has caused some doubt about the seasonal affiliation, is compatible with this association, since Shrovetide marks the end of that long season of revels which starts at Christmas (cf. the presence of the "King of Kristmesse" in the Norwich Shrovetide procession discussed above). At the same time the play is significantly indebted to folk-drama traditions. Mankind lashes out with his spade at the three subsidiary vices, Neu Gyse, Nowadays, and Nought (ll. 380 ff.), causing grievous injuries which necessitate their treatment by Mischief in a sequence (ll. 433 ff.) which is strongly reminiscent of the Cure Scene in the English folk plays.[88] In an earlier scene (ll. 45 ff.), whose exact status has not yet been fully appreciated, the vices intrude on Mercy in a disrespectful perversion of the good-luck visit of the mummers, and offer a performance which might in itself preserve something of the traditional drama of Shrovetide. After Mischief as Presenter / *Vorläufer* has announced to the perturbed Mercy, "I am cumme hedyr to make yow game" (l. 69)—and following an unfortunate gap in the text—the three minor vices come on,

85. Quoted in Paul R. Sellin, "The Performance of Ben Jonson's *News from the New World Discover'd in the Moon*," *ES*, LXI (1980), 495.

86. W. K. Smart, "Some Notes on *Mankind*," *MP*, XIV (1916), particularly pp. 45–58.

87. *The Macro Plays*, ed. Mark Eccles, EETS, o.s 262 (London, 1969).

88. For a perceptive interpretation of the action in this rather obscure scene, see Axton, *European Drama of the Early Middle Ages*, pp. 200–201. For this and other echoes of folk drama in the play see W. K. Smart, "*Mankind* and the Mumming Plays," *MLN*, XXXII (1917), 21–25; Neville Denny, "Aspects of the Staging of *Mankind*," *Medium Ævum*, XLIII (1974), 252–263.

with Nought apparently being goaded into an athletic dance by the other two (ll. 72 ff.).

Glynne Wickham has offered the intriguing suggestion that this action is a deliberate parody of a bearward and his dancing bear, with Nought "dressed up in a pantomime bearskin with a detachable head."[89] Wickham may be right about the bear, but if so the scene may more closely correspond to the English seasonal custom of the "Straw Bear," belonging to a date a few weeks earlier than Shrovetide, the Tuesday following Plough Monday. The following account of the custom, as observed at Whittlesey, Cambridgeshire, in the late nineteenth century, is strikingly close to the situation in *Mankind*: "the straw bear was a man completely swathed in straw, led by means of a string and made to dance before people's houses, in return for which money was expected."[90] In several Continental countries, similar customs involving men dressed as bears belong to the season of Shrovetide.[91]

As a Shrovetide play, with strong links to folk drama, Mankind invites appreciation in the light of the *Fastnachtspiele*. This might, for example, give more body to the idea, which some have already hinted at, that behind the struggle of Mischief and Mercy for the allegiance of Mankind we may glimpse something of the traditional contest between Carnival and Lent. And much that remains problematic about the play—its auspices, staging, its built-in *quête*, its odd combination of occasional Latinity with pervasive vulgarity—might be resolved by such an approach.[92]

This concluding discussion of the earlier phases of English traditional drama has been necessarily brief, and somewhat speculative; the matter

89. Glynne Wickham, ed., *English Moral Interludes* (London, 1976), p. 5.

90. A. R. Wright, *British Calendar Customs*, vol. II, *Fixed Festivals, January-May* (London, 1938), p. 104.

91. Richard Bernheimer, *Wild Men in the Middle Ages* (Cambridge, Mass., 1952), pp. 54–55; Schmidt, *Das Deutsche Volksschauspiel*, pp. 47, 264, 338 ff., etc. (*Bärenjagen*).

92. For conflicting views on the topic mentioned, see David M. Bevington, *From Mankind to Marlowe: Growth and Structure in the Popular Drama of Tudor England* (Cambridge, Mass., 1962), pp. 15–18, and "Popular and Courtly Traditions on the Early Tudor Stage," in *Medieval Drama*, ed. N. Denny, Stratford-upon-Avon Studies, XVI (London, 1973), pp. 97–99; Neville Denny, "Aspects of the Staging of *Mankind*"; Axton, *European Drama of the Early Middle Ages*, pp. 199–203; Lawrence M. Clopper, "*Mankind* and Its Audience," *CompD*, VIII (1974), 347–355.

deserves fully fledged analysis and documentation in its own right. But it is along such lines, I suggest, that the "discovery" of 150 or so early German folk plays announced in the preceding pages may provide some supplementary avenues of exploration into those early traditions of popular drama in England for which our sources are otherwise so frustratingly limited.

Marlowe's "Sound Machevill"

CATHERINE MINSHULL

P ROBLEMS OF DRAMATIC unity and purpose are posed by *The Jew of Malta* to such a degree that most critics are in accord that it is a difficult play to interpret. Efforts to fit the play into a conventional moral framework tend not to be satisfactory. The determination to view the play in terms of an orthodox tradition of morality drama leads one critic to describe it improbably as "a patriotic play . . . a Christian play . . . the story of Malta's heroic resistance."[1] Another writer finds the play flawed because accepted notions of plot design fail to explain it: "The structure of the play demands a relationship between cause and effect in Barabas's career. The difficulty is that in rationalizing Barabas's original plight Marlowe has created villains out of those very persons who must later become agents of retribution."[2] Interpretation of the play as a conventional moral homily is precluded by the unscrupulous methods the Christians ruling Malta employ to maintain their power and emerge triumphant at the end of the play. Despite his assiduous claims to piety, Ferneze's successful resumption of power at the end of the play can in no way be termed a moral triumph. If his closing words

1. Bernard Spivack, *Shakespeare and the Allegory of Evil* (New York, 1958), p. 346.
2. D. M. Bevington, *From Mankind to Marlowe* (Cambridge, Eng., 1962), p. 232.

35

> So, march away, and let due praise be given
> Neither to fate nor fortune, but to heaven[3]
>
> (V.v. 122–123)

are to be taken literally then heaven must be credited with a catalog of mass murder, treachery, and duplicity, for which it is characteristic of Ferneze to hold heaven, not himself, responsible. Just as the portrayal of Ferneze does not conform to expectations if he is intended to be seen as the virtuous restorer of order at the end of the play, so, similarly, the characterization of Barabas contains anomalous elements not wholly in keeping with his role of comic villain destined for a bad end. In the first part of the play, his passionate denunciation of Christian hypocrisy gives him potential tragic stature which is lost in the comic machinations of his later career and ludicrous indignity of his death. It is hard to reconcile the Barabas who witheringly exposes Christian "piety,"

> What! Bring you scripture to confirm your wrongs?
> Preach me not out of my possessions
>
> (I.ii. 111–112)

with the later clownish villain who boasts

> As for myself, I walk abroad o'nights,
> And kill sick people groaning under walls;
> Sometimes I go about and poison wells
>
> (II.iii. 176–178)

Not least among the difficulties posed by the characterization of Barabas is his presentation as a disciple of Machiavelli. "Machevil" introduces him as such in the Prologue:

> I come not, I,
> To read a lecture here in Britany,
> But to present the tragedy of a Jew,
> Who smiles to see how full his bags are crammed,
> Which money was not got without my means
>
> (ll. 28–32)

3. Quotations from *The Jew of Malta* are taken from the Revels edition, edited by N. W. Bawcutt (Manchester, Eng., 1978).

Although "Machevil" claims that it is adherence to his code which has made Barabas rich, as Edward Meyer points out, "Machiavelli nowhere instructs how to obtain wealth."[4] The problem is, why should Marlowe make the appetite for wealth such a prominent feature of his supposedly Machiavellian villain when Machiavelli's works have so little to say about financial matters? Was Marlowe ignorant that Machiavelli's works give no sanction for the portrayal of a Machiavellian as one primarily motivated by desire for wealth? This was the view of Edward Meyer, who maintained that in *The Jew of Malta* "there is not a single line taken directly from Machiavelli."[5] He asserted that the distortions of Machiavelli's doctrine found in *The Jew of Malta* derived from Gentillet's *Discours . . . Contre Nicholas Machiavel*, which he saw as the source of Marlowe's knowledge of Machiavelli.[6]

But the debate about Marlowe's knowledge of Machiavelli has led critics, as Irving Ribner remarks, into a "welter of contradictions."[7] More recent scholarship has questioned the assumption that Marlowe would not have read Machiavelli in the original. Drawing attention to the illegal Italian editions of *The Prince* and *The Discourses* printed in England in the 1580s, and to the English translations of these works circulating in manuscript, Felix Raab dismisses as "the myth of Gentillet"[8] the theory that the Elizabethans' main access to Machiavelli was through Gentillet's attack. Irving Ribner argues that, if *The Jew of Malta* contains ideas that cannot be traced to Machiavelli, this does not necessarily imply ignorance of Machiavelli's works on Marlowe's part. Unlike *Tamburlaine the Great*, which he interprets as a dramatization of Machiavelli's actual creed, Ribner sees *The Jew of Malta* as an exploitation for comic and dramatic purposes of the popular misconception of Machiavelli's thought. In his view the play contains "absolutely no reflection of Machiavelli's own ideas" and was without "any political purposes whatsoever."[9]

4. *Machiavelli and the Elizabethan Drama* (Weimar, 1897), p. 63.

5. *Ibid.*, p. 41.

6. Quotations from this work are taken from the English translation by Simon Patericke, *A Discourse . . . Against Nicholas Machiavell* (London, 1602), from now on referred to as *Discourse*.

7. "Marlowe and Machiavelli," *CL*, VI (1954), 348.

8. *The English Face of Machiavelli* (London and Toronto, 1964), p. 56.

9. "Marlowe and Machiavelli," p. 353.

The idea that Marlowe made a neat distinction between real Machiavellianism and "Elizabethan" Machiavellianism, exploiting the latter in *The
Jew of Malta*, has in its turn come in for criticism. According to Antonio
de Andrea, even if Marlowe had read Machiavelli's works in the original,
there are no grounds for supposing that "he would have arrived at an
interpretation of them different from that of his contemporaries." [10]
N. W. Bawcutt finds it impossible in *The Jew of Malta* to distinguish
between those elements, if any, which are directly derived from
Machiavelli's writings, and those which derive from secondhand notions
about them. He says, "it . . . becomes impossible to define just how
much of Machiavelli Marlowe knew at first hand, and this is partly due to
the varied and sometimes muddled and even contradictory nature of the
total Elizabethan response to Machiavelli." [11]

Part of the reason for the lack of consensus about the relationship of *The
Jew of Malta* to Machiavelli's works seems to be that the play contains
elements which could have been derived directly from Machiavelli's works,
together with elements which could not have been so derived. But this
situation does not necessarily support Bawcutt's view that Marlowe made
no clear distinction between what Machiavelli said and what he was
popularly believed to have said. The fact that most Elizabethans may not
have distinguished between the two does not mean that Marlowe shared
their confusion. If Francis Bacon could perceive the true impact of Machiavelli's philosophy and praise it for describing "what men do and not what
they ought to do" [12] it is likely that the keen intellect of Marlowe was also
capable of forming a clear idea of Machiavelli's actual code. Marlowe's
Prologue to *The Jew of Malta* bears witness to the fact that he had considerable insight into Machiavelli's philosophy, that is until its puzzling introduction of Barabas as an arch-Machiavellian. The image of Machiavellianism
which emerges from the main body of the Prologue is one of power politics
in which conventional religious and moral scruples play little part. Although presented in a deliberately outrageous and provocative way, this
image is compatible with what Machiavelli actually wrote. Power is seen in

10. "Studies in Machiavelli and His Reputation in the Sixteenth Century," *Mediaeval
and Renaissance Studies*, V (1961), 238.

11. Introduction to *The Jew of Malta*, p. 15.

12. *The Advancement of Learning*, in *Works*, ed. J. Spedding (New York, 1951), III, 430.

Marlowe's Prologue, as in Machiavelli's works, as something to be seized, rather than conferred by divine right. The Duke of Guise and the Pope are cited in the Prologue as modern examples of political climbers, and Caesar as an ancient one. The line

> What right had Caesar to the empery?
>
> (l. 19)

recalls a passage from Machiavelli's *Discourses* in which Caesar's right to rule is questioned and his bid for power distinguished from Catiline's only by its success.

Nor should anyone be deceived by Caesar's renown, when he finds writers extolling him before others, for those who praise him have either been corrupted by his fortune, or overawed by the long continuance of the empire which, since it was ruled under that name, did not permit writers to speak freely of him. If, however, anyone desires to know what writers would have said, had they been free, he has but to look what they say of Catiline. [13]

It is interesting to note that the tyrant Phalaris is referred to twice by Machiavelli in the paragraph preceding this passage in the *Discourses*. This fact, in conjunction with the fact that Caesar and Phalaris are also mentioned in close proximity by Marlowe in his Prologue, perhaps suggest that Marlowe had this section of the *Discourses* in mind when composing his Prologue.

The view of religion which emerges from Marlowe's Prologue is also close to the one found in Machiavelli's works. "Machevil's" claim to "count religion but a childish toy" is in keeping with the treatment of religion in Machiavelli's works as a political tool to be conformed with outwardly, but disregarded in essence. [14] It has been objected that Marlowe's Prologue cannot be based closely upon Machiavelli's writings because "Machevil's" remark that Phalaris made a mistake in not putting his trust in "a strong-built citadel" is incompatible with the attitude toward fortresses found in Machiavelli's works. [15] It is true that Machiavelli advises rulers not to put their trust in fortresses, for the love of their

---

13. *Discourses*, I. 10 [4]; quotations are taken from the translation by Leslie J. Walker, 2 vols. (Boston, 1950).

14. E.g., *Discourses*, I. 11–14.

15. Irving Ribner, "Marlowe and Machiavelli," p. 352.

subjects was the best protection rulers could have, [16] but by the same argument fortresses were indispensable to tyrants like Phalaris who had forfeited their subjects' love, and Machiavelli admits that fortresses are "useful in time of peace because they give you more courage in ill-treating your subjects." [17] In his Prologue, Marlowe mischievously suggests that a tyrant as hated as Phalaris would have been better employed in building a fortress to protect himself from his subjects than in composing his famous letters.

In view of the fact that "Machevil" offers a frank, if inflammatory, exposition of Machiavelli's political code in the prologue to *The Jew of Malta*, it is particularly strange that he concludes his prologue with the introduction of Barabas to the audience as one of his favored disciples. Barabas's behavior diverges widely from the image of Machiavellianism found in the rest of the Prologue as an art devoted to gaining and maintaining political power. In the opening scene of the play, Barabas, the supposed arch-Machiavellian, disclaims all interest in ruling, saying of his race:

> I must confess we come not to be kings.
> That's not our fault: alas, our number's few,
> And crowns come either by succession,
> Or urg'd by force; and nothing violent,
> Oft have I heard tell, can be permanent.
> Give us a peaceful rule, make Christians kings,
> That thirst so much for principality
>
> (I.i. 128–134)

Machiavelli's works teem with observations on military routes to power, yet in *The Jew of Malta* Barabas's lack of interest in military matters is abundantly evident. Ferneze remarks to him, "Tut, Jew, we know thou art no soldier" (I.ii. 52), and Barabas makes it plain that he is indifferent to the Turkish threat to Malta, except insofar as it affects him personally, scoffing,

---

16. *The Prince*, chap. 20, p. 119; quotations are taken from the translation by George Bull, Penguin Classics Series (Harmondsworth, Eng., 1961).

17. *Discourses*, II.24 [2].

> Nay, let 'em combat, conquer, and kill all,
> So they spare me, my daughter, and my wealth.
>
> (I.i. 151–152)

So small is Barabas's interest in ruling that, when given the opportunity to be governor of Malta, he merely exchanges the position with Ferneze in return for yet more wealth. His attitude makes an ironic contrast with that of Machiavelli's ideal hero, who, according to Machiavelli "should never let his thoughts stray from military exercises." [18]

The suspicion presents itself that perhaps Marlowe was being intentionally ironic in presenting Barabas to the audience as an arch-Machiavellian. "Machevil's" introduction of Barabas

> . . . let him not be entertained the worse
> Because he favours me
>
> (ll. 34–35)

is ironic on the obvious level that a personal recommendation from Machiavelli could hardly be anything but damning in the eyes of an Elizabethan audience. It may also be ironic on a deeper level in being an item of disinformation of the type to be expected from a politician renowned for cunning and dissimulating arts. If anyone in the play conforms to the Machiavellian code set out in the Prologue to the play, it is not Barabas, but Ferneze, who in true Machiavellian fashion is primarily interested in power politics and military matters. Ferneze resembles Machiavelli's ideal prince in that he seldom allows his mind to stray from military affairs, and he admits that the tribute money owed to the Turks is overdue "by reason of the wars, that robbed our store" (I.ii. 48). During the play, instead of handing over the newly raised tribute money to the Turks as agreed, he follows the advice of his First Knight, and wages war with it instead. [19] At the end of the play, his power safely regained, Ferneze states his continuing ambition to hold on to his power against all comers:

> As sooner shall they drink the ocean dry,
> Than conquer Malta, or endanger us
>
> (V.v. 120–121)

18. *The Prince*, chap. 14, p. 88.
19. II.ii. 26–27.

His attitude could hardly be in more marked contrast with that of Barabas, who takes the earliest opportunity to relinquish the power he has unexpectedly gained.

Was Marlowe playing a joke on his audience, not only by introducing a character to them as a "Machiavellian" who turns out to be profoundly uninterested in Machiavellian political and military theory, but also by presenting them unsuspectedly with a real Machiavellian in the character of Ferneze? This suggestion is in keeping with the insight revealed in the Prologue that real Machiavellians do not advertise where their true allegiance lies. "Machevil's" claims that "such as love me guard me from their tongues" (1. 6) and "admired I am of those that hate me most" (1. 9) are borne out by the behavior of Ferneze, who unobtrusively puts into practice Machiavelli's major political precepts, chief among which is the axiom that rulers should appear to be models of Christian and moral behavior. Barabas's colorful but inaccurate impersonation of a "Machiavellian" acts as a red herring, distracting attention from the real embodiment of Machiavelli's creed represented by Ferneze. Once it is recognized that Barabas's dramatic function is to act as a foil to the true Machiavellians in the play, the inconsistencies in his characterization become easier to understand.

In the first part of the play his dealings with the Christians serve to expose their pose of piety and virtue, with which, true to Machiavelli's teaching, they seek to validate all their actions, however expedient these may be. In the second half of the play, Barabas's comically villainous exploits throw into relief by contrast their cool power politics, which, unlike Barabas's disastrous adventures, are in authentic Machiavellian style. Although Barabas gets all the odium directed in the Elizabethan age against Machiavellians, it is Ferneze who actually implements Machiavelli's code. Ferneze escapes the blame of being a Machiavellian in a manner analogous to his evasion of responsibility for the events of the last scene of the play, which he claims illustrate "the unhallowed deeds of Jews" (V.v. 91). Marlowe's audience must have watched with tremendous glee as Barabas, the hated and feared Machiavellian monster boiled in the cauldron at the end of the play, and Marlowe must have been equally amused that while Barabas, the seeming Machiavellian boiled, Machiavellianism itself presided over his destruction, unrecognized in the figure of the Governor of Malta.

The concept of Barabas as a comic caricature has of course been well known since Eliot advanced it as part of his analysis of the play as a savage farce. [20] The idea that Marlowe in *The Jew of Malta* was satirically contrasting Barabas's burlesque of Machiavellianism with the thing itself is less familiar. J. L. Smith in his essay *"The Jew of Malta* in the Theatre" [21] describes how a production of the play at Reading University in 1954 was designed to bring out this satiric contrast. The evidence of the text supports the theory that Marlowe was contrasting Machiavelli's actual theories with the distorted version of them popularly current. Ferneze's character conforms closely to Machiavelli's actual code as set out in his own works. Barabas's character conforms rather to the picture of Machiavellianism disseminated by Gentillet.

It would have been possible for Marlowe to construct the character of Barabas almost entirely from hints found in one chapter of Gentillet's *Discourse*. [22] In this chapter, the first in the section of the book entitled "Of Religion," Gentillet presents, as elsewhere in his book, a selective and distorted image of Machiavelli's code. In this chapter Gentillet follows his usual practice of presenting Machiavelli's ideas in the form of extracts from his works. These extracts are emotively selected and paraphrased in order to show Machiavelli's views in the worst possible light. In the Preface to his work, Gentillet claims that in doing this, he is not distorting Machiavelli's ideas, but presenting them in their true colors, omitting only material which Machiavelli had taken from other authors in order to camouflage his real message. Gentillet argues that in his method of dealing with Machiavelli's works he has "extracted and gathered that which is properly his owne," excluding "some good places drawne out of *Titus Livius*, or some other authors," in order to isolate the major doctrines of Machiavelli, deliberately obscured by the author in his works by the cunning technique of "enterlacing and mixing some good things amongst them, doing therin as poysoners doe, which never cast lumpes of poyson upon an heape, least it bee perceived, but doe most subtillie incorporate it as they can, with some other delicate and daintie morsels." [23]

20. "Christopher Marlowe" (1919), in *Selected Essays*, 3d ed. (New York, 1951), p. 123.

21. *Christopher Marlowe*, Mermaid Critical Commentaries, ed. Brian Morris (London, 1968), pp. 13–14.

22. Bk. II, maxim 1, pp. 92 ff.

23. *Discourse*, Preface, sig. A iii.

Gentillet asserts that his analysis of Machiavelli separates out the kernel of Machiavellian doctrine from the extraneous material which obscures it in Machiavelli's works. But although he claims to be paring down Machiavelli's works to reveal their true significance, what he actually does in the chapter at issue is interpolate material which bears no relation to anything that Machiavelli wrote. The chapter portrays Machiavellians in an unprecedented way as experts in unscrupulous financial malpractices. The novelty of this allegation against Machiavellians leads Bawcutt to suggest that Marlowe may have been indebted to Gentillet for his portrayal of Barabas. [24] Gentillet attacks the sharp practices of some of his fellow Frenchmen who were ruining the country and enriching themselves by methods he claims they had learned from Machiavelli. There is an obvious similarity between Gentillet's "Machiavellians" who gather "great heapes of money" [25] and collect "riches and heapes of the treasure of the Realme, whilest it is in trouble and confusion," [26] and Barabas who is indifferent to the Turkish threat to Malta except insofar as it affects him personally, and who says,

> Howe'er the world go, I'll make sure for one,
> And seek in time to intercept the worst,
> Warily guarding that which I ha' got.

> (I.i. 185–187)

In other respects, too, Barabas conforms to the image of Machiavellians set out by Gentillet in the same chapter. Barabas's ingenious villainy, over which he gloats,

> Now tell me, wordlings, underneath the sun
> If greater falsehood ever has been done

> (V.v. 49–50)

resembles that ascribed by Gentillet to Machiavelli's disciples, of whom he says, "There is no wickednesse in the world so strange and detestable, but they wil enterprise, invent, and put it in execution, if they can." [27]

24. "Machiavelli and Marlowe's *The Jew of Malta*," *RenD*, N.S. III (1970), 49; notes to the Revels edition, Prologue l. 32 and IV.i.54.

25. *Discourse*, p. 93.

26. *Discourse*, p. 94.

27. *Discourse*, p. 94.

During the course of the play, Barabas manages to poison a nunnery and blow up a monastery, in addition to engineering the death of two friars. His anti-religious sentiments accord with Gentillet's portrayal of Machiavellians as enemies of "good Catholickes and Cleargie men." [28] Perhaps Barabas's most shocking exploit in the play is the poisoning of his daughter Abigail, which he follows up with the attempted poisoning of his accomplice Ithamore. Gentillet portrays such exploits as the kind to be expected of Machiavellians who "make not scruple" at "betraying or impoysoning." [29] Barabas is unrepentant of the murder of Abigail, remarking, "I grieve because she lived so long" (IV.i.18). He is similarly indifferent to the death of the nuns:

> How sweet the bells ring, now the nuns are dead,
> That sound at other times like tinkers' pans
>
> (IV.1.2–3)

His attitude is in keeping with Gentillet's observation that Machiavellians contemplate their victims' sufferings "without having any commiseration or compassion upon them, no more than upon brute beasts," [30] an outlook which is also illustrated by Barabas's and Ithamore's mocking of the dead friar, whom they stand up against a wall, joking, "he stands as if he were begging of bacon" (IV.1.154–155). The guiding sentiment of Barabas's life is summed up in his words "so I live, perish may all the world" (V.iv.10), which is in perfect accord with Gentillet's judgment that Machiavellians "have neither love to their neighbour, nor to their countrey." [31] This is in no way a reflection of the actual ideas of Machiavelli, whose political works were motivated by the patriotic desire to free Italy from foreign domination, and who stressed that "it cannot be called prowess to kill fellow citizens, to betray friends, to be treacherous, pitiless, irreligious." [32]

Marlowe cannot have been unaware of the gulf between Machiavelli's creed personified by Barabas, and Machiavelli's actual teaching, because he

28. *Discourse*, p. 93.
29. *Discourse*, p. 93.
30. *Discourse*, p. 93.
31. *Discourse*, p. 93.
32. *The Prince*, chap. 8, p. 63.

makes Ferneze and the Christians ruling Malta astutely put into practice Machiavelli's major political axioms. Ferneze personifies the cornerstone of Machiavelli's creed, which is that it is essential for politicians to maintain an appearance of virtue, however far they diverge from it in actuality. Machiavelli says:

A prince . . . need not necessarily have all . . . good qualities . . . but he should certainly appear to have them. I would even go so far as to say that if he has these qualities and always behaves accordingly he will find them ruinous; if he only appears to have them they will render him service. He should appear to be compassionate, faithful to his word, guileless, and devout. And indeed he should be so. But his disposition should be such that, if he needs to be the opposite, he knows how. [33]

Throughout the play Ferneze assiduously presents to the world a mask of virtue, which never slips. Although he is quick to take advantage of the strategems laid by Barabas in the last scene of the play, he is also quick to condemn them once they have served his turn. He blames the death of Calymath's soldiers upon "a Jew's courtesy" (V.v.107) regardless of the fact that he himself gave the order for their deaths. In contrast with Ferneze, Calymath's career illustrates Machiavelli's maxim that it is disastrous to actually behave honorably instead of just pretending to do so. His courteous response to Barabas's invitation to dine,

> Yet would I gladly visit Barabas,
> For well has Barabas deserved of us
>
> (V.iii.24–25)

is rewarded by his own men being blown up, and himself narrowly escaping being boiled alive.

Machiavelli attached primary importance to the need for a ruler to appear to be a religious man, saying, "there is nothing so important as to seem to have this . . . quality," [34] and Ferneze accordingly takes care to justify all his actions on moral and religious grounds. Pretending to believe that Malta's troubles were a punishment for the sin of harboring infidels, Ferneze claims that the Jews' goods must be confiscated in atonement,

> For through our sufferance of your hateful lives,
> Who stand accursed in the sight of heaven,
> These taxes and afflictions are befallen
>
> (I.ii.63–65)

Ferneze's combination of observance of the letter of religion with disregard for it in spirit is in accord with Machiavelli's observations on the use of religion as a political tool, demonstrated by the Roman generals' pragmatic manipulation of the auguries to justify whatever course of action they found expedient. [35] His flexible attitude toward keeping his promises is also in copybook Machiavellian style. Machiavelli wrote:

A prudent ruler cannot, and should not, honour his word when it places him at a disadvantage and when the reasons for which he made his promise no longer exist. [36]

Ferneze observes this advice by breaking faith first with Calymath, then with Barabas. In each case his glib dexterity in justifying his actions illustrates Machiavelli's maxim that "a prince will never lack good excuses to colour his bad faith." [37] The breach of faith with Calymath is dressed up in warlike rhetoric,

> Proud-daring Calymath, instead of gold,
> We'll send thee bullets wrapped in smoke and fire.
>
> (II.iii.53–54)

And his trickery of Barabas is disguised as a desire to see justice done and "treachery repaid" (V.v.73).

Ferneze triumphs at the end of the play because unlike Barabas, he does not make the mistake, warned against by Machiavelli, of trusting former enemies. Machiavelli wrote, "whoever believes that with great men new services wipe out old injuries deceives himself," [38] and Barabas commits a

35. *Discourses*, I.14 [1–3].
36. *The Prince*, chap. 18, pp. 99–100.
37. *The Prince*, chap. 18, p. 100.
38. *The Prince*, chap. 7, p. 61.

major error in Machiavellian policy by believing he could make an ally of the governor whose son he had, after all, murdered. In contrast Ferneze's behavior in double-crossing Barabas at the end of the play is in accord with Machiavelli's observation that "old injuries are never cancelled by new benefits." [39] In financial matters, by evading the payment of the ten-years' overdue tribute money for as long as possible, and, when the necessity for payment seemed imminent, by raising the required sum from the Jews' rather than his own coffers, Ferneze follows Machiavelli's advice that a ruler should not be afraid of a reputation for miserliness, since "miserliness is one of those vices which sustain his rule." [40] His seizure of Barabas's property might be mistaken for an error in Machiavelli's warning that "a prince should abstain from the property of others; because men sooner forget the death of their father than the loss of their patrimony." [41] But this view would fail to take into account that Barabas was not regarded as a citizen of Malta, but as an outsider tolerated on sufferance. In robbing him, Ferneze is following the course recommended by Machiavelli when he said, "the prince gives away what is his own or his subjects', or else what belongs to others. In the first he should be frugal; in the second, he should indulge his generosity to the full." [42]

Finally, throughout the play, Ferneze demonstrates the ability to adapt rapidly to different circumstances, and in this he shows the "flexible disposition, varying as fortune and circumstances dictate," [43] which Machiavelli recommends as a recipe for success. Barabas, in contrast, behaves inflexibly and is unwilling to adapt to a new religious faith or to the unexpected opportunity to rule Malta which comes his way. Ferneze's success illustrates the political wisdom of Machiavelli's maxims, whereas, ironically, Barabas's failure is in large part due to elementary errors in Machiavellian policy. Although it is difficult to show conclusively that Marlowe had firsthand knowledge of Machiavelli's works, the accuracy with which the character of Ferneze reflects Machiavellian policy makes it probable that Marlowe was acquainted with these ideas in the original and

39. *Discourses*, III.4 [2].
40. *The Prince*, chap. 16, pp. 93–94.
41. *The Prince*, chap. 17, p. 97.
42. *The Prince*, chap. 16, p. 94.
43. *The Prince*, chap. 18, p. 101.

was not reliant upon the garbled form in which they were presented by Gentillet. [44] *The Jew of Malta* shows an assimilation of Machiavelli's thought at a fundamental level, an impression supported by the fact that the theme of boundless ambition, which is a recurrent feature of Marlowe's plays, is in deep accord with observations found in Machiavelli, but not in Gentillet, that

Nature has so constituted man that, though all things are objects of desire, not all things are attainable; so that the desire always exceeds the power of attainment. [45]

Human appetites are insatiable, for by nature we are so constituted that there is nothing we cannot long for, but by fortune we are such that of these things we can attain but few. [46]

Although Marlowe may have had a clear enough conception of Machiavellian theory to be able to satirize the misconceptions about Machiavelli current in Elizabethan England, is it credible that he would have employed an ironic technique so subtle that his meaning was lost to those not so well versed in Machiavelli as himself? The fact that the play has proved so much of a puzzle to critics perhaps lends support to the otherwise improbable theory that there may be a level of meaning in the play which has not been fully explained. Also, Marlowe's other plays abound in ironic devices which suggest that irony was a habitual mode of communication for him. In *Tamburlaine the Great* Marlowe plays upon the ironic gap between the audience's conventional expectations of plot and the events actually taking place on stage. He mischievously thwarts his audience's expectations that divine retribution will catch up with those who deserve it, and constructs the end of the play in such a way as to suggest that if Tamburlaine's death is in any way due to divine retribution, then Mohammed is the agent of it in punishing Tamburlaine for burning the Koran. In this way Marlowe covertly mocks the Christian belief that God was active in their concerns, but in such a manner that his meaning need only be taken by those who appreciate his irony.

Marlowe's technique of allowing some conclusions to be drawn by the audience without him fully spelling them out can also be seen at work in

44. E.g., *Discourses*, Bk. II, maxim 1; Bk, III, maxims 6, 18, 21, 26, 27.
45. *Discourse*, I.37 [1].
46. *Discourses*, II, Preface [7].

Edward II. The Queen succeeds against all the odds in persuading
Mortimer to allow Gaveston to return to the country after the barons have
only recently banished him. Their conversation takes place in sight of the
audience, but its content is not revealed. The Queen's method of persuasion has to be surmised from the course of action that Mortimer proceeds
to take, which is that Gaveston should be allowed to return, but only in
order to be murdered. Challenged as to why he did not make this proposal
earlier, Mortimer explains that he could not, "because, my lords, it was
not thought upon." [47] The conclusion to be drawn by the audience is that
the plan had not been thought of before because the Queen had only just
suggested it. This means that Isabel does not in fact undergo the sudden
implausible transformation from loving wife to scheming murderess which
has often been held to mar the play. Her plotting starts while she is still
posing as a devoted wife. By leaving her early treachery so near-perfectly
concealed, even from the audience, Marlowe shows its insidious nature,
doubly dangerous because going almost undetected.

Marlowe's ironic technique is pervasive in *Dr. Faustus*, which, seconded
by *The Jew of Malta*, G. K. Hunter terms "the greatest ironic structure in
Marlowe's work." [48] The irony of the play lies in the gap between the
salvation promised by Christ and the damnation which overtakes Faustus.
The legend which Marlowe dramatizes shows the trend of the new Protestant thought on the Continent, in which, contrary to Christ's promises,
salvation is not available to everyone. If one argues that in *Dr. Faustus*
Marlowe employs ironic devices to protest against the injustice of the
religion which condemns Faustus, the play takes on an anti-religious cast
in keeping with the subversive elements in his other works and his contemporary reputation for unorthodoxy and atheism. But in writing such a
play Marlowe shows himself to be true to Bacon's definition of an atheist as
one cauterized by holy things. [49]

The evidence of large-scale structural ironies in Marlowe's other works
supports the suggestion that his presentation of Barabas in *The Jew of
Malta* as a Machiavellian is another example of irony of this type. Close
reading of the text reveals smaller ironies on a verbal level which are

47. I.iv.273; *The Plays of Christopher Marlowe*, ed. Roma Gill (London, 1971).
48. "The Theology of Marlowe's *The Jew of Malta*," *JWCI*, xxvii (1964), 213.
49. "Of Atheism," *Essays*, 16, in *Works*, ed. Spedding, vi, 414.

further evidence that Marlowe was writing a secret play between the lines of his official play. G. K. Hunter perceives an irony in Marlowe's choice of the name Barabas for his anti-hero. He points out that the name also figures in Baines's testimony against Marlowe, where Marlowe is alleged to have claimed that "Christ deserved better to die than Barabas." [50] Viewed in the context of Baines's testimony, Marlowe's choice of the name Barabas supports the contention that his ironic purpose in the play is to suggest that it is the Christians, not Barabas, who are the real Machiavellians. The view that Marlowe adopted a subtle and indirect mode of communication in *The Jew of Malta* also finds support from Bawcutt's exposition of another irony concerning the allusion to the Knights of Rhodes (II.ii.47–51). Although the Christians defending Malta professed themselves to be ready to emulate the bravery of the Knights of Rhodes and fight to the death, their claim would have been recognized as empty bluster by an audience who knew that Rhodes had been surrendered to the Turks without resistance. [51] By means of this irony Marlowe exposes the propaganda employed by the ruling classes to shore up their image and power.

The implications of *The Jew of Malta* as a comment on the English political scene are subversive. "Machevil" in the Prologue to the play claims, "Admired I am of those that hate me most" (l. 9), and Marlowe's satiric target in his play could be seen as the English politicians who banned Machiavelli's works when in practice their own statecraft more closely resembled the Machiavellian model than it did theocentric Tudor political theory. One of the reasons for the ban on Machiavelli's works in England was that they were considered dangerous because they presented too accurate a picture of the world. An Elizabethan manuscript translation of *The Prince* has verses on the title leaf in which the book is described as teaching "what kings doe in states." [52] The acceptance of *The Prince* by the translator as an accurate depiction of statecraft shows political awareness of the type discouraged by the Tudor authorities. The danger posed to political stability by Machiavelli's works is illustrated by the fact that the

---

50. "The Theology of Marlowe's *The Jew of Malta*," p. 239.

51. Introduction to *The Jew of Malta*, p. 5.

52. Napoleone Orsini, "Elizabethan Manuscript Translations of Machiavelli's *Prince*," *Journal of the Warburg Institute*, I (1939), 167.

dissident political tract *Leycesters Commonwealth* (1584) describes Henry VII's elimination of Stanley in terms of Machiavelli's advice about not trusting former enemies. [53] Too great a familiarity with Machiavelli's works might lead to the recognition that the Tudor government had established itself and maintained itself by methods of the kind outlined by Machiavelli.

Marlowe would have been familiar with the less savory aspects of government if he had been employed in the secret service, and would have been undeceived by the claim made in the letter prefixed to Gentillet's *Discourse* that Machiavelli's arts were unknown to Elizabeth's government:

Shee by maintaining wholesome unitie amongst all degrees, hath hitherto preserved the State of her realme, not onely safe but florishing: not by Machiavelian artes, as Guile, Perfidie, and other villainies practising: but by true vertues, as Clemencie, Iustice, Faith. [54]

Gentillet ends his work with a plea that people should exert themselves to "drive away and banish . . . Machiavell and all his writings, and all such as maintaine and follow his doctrine." [55] On the face of it, the fate of Barabas in *The Jew of Malta* shows Gentillet's wishes being carried out on the artistic plane. But Marlowe's subtle ironic message in *The Jew of Malta* is that in the real world such an enterprise would be no easy task because it is the politicians in power who are the true inheritors of Machiavelli's policies. It was to the authorities' advantage that a popular misconception of Machiavelli should flourish to obscure the import of Machiavelli's works as an analysis of statecraft. The general lack of precise knowledge about Machiavelli's ideas meant that the term "Machiavellian" could be used to describe any type of treachery, villainy, and irreligion. It could be used as an indiscriminate slogan to incite hatred of unpopular sections of society. Gentillet uses the term to attack wealthy speculators whom he would be glad to see go on "another S. Bartholomew journey." [56]

In *The Jew of Malta* it is Barabas's race, as well as his envied wealth, which makes him a convenient candidate for the role of scapegoat

53. Meyer, *Machiavelli and the Elizabethan Drama*, p. 29.
54. *The Epistle Dedicatorie.*
55. *Discourse*, p. 374.
56. *Discourse*, p. 94.

Machiavellian. The popular prejudice against Jews meant that the indiscriminate label "Machiavellian" was likely to stick to them, however inappropriate in an exact sense such a term was for a class without political power. Barabas is described as "a sound Machiavell" by Heywood in his prologue to the 1633 revival of the play at court, because Barabas fits the stereotype of the underhanded, scheming anti-Christian villain which had become popularly synonymous with Machiavellianism. Ironically, Marlowe's play did much to establish this stereotype, although his secret purpose in *The Jew of Malta* was to satirize and undercut it. Ignorant of Machiavelli's writings, Marlowe's audience mistook his caricature of a Machiavellian villain for the real thing. The sixteenth-century ban on Machiavelli's works in England had been successful. Misconceptions about Machiavelli's works had become so strongly rooted that when presented with a real "sound Machiavell" in the person of Ferneze the public failed to recognize him.

Tamburlaine's *Weak Sons:*
Imitation as Interpretation
Before 1593

PETER BEREK

T HE PROLOGUE to Part One of Marlowe's *Tamburlaine* ends, "View but
his picture in this tragicke glasse, / And then applaud his fortunes as
you please." [1] Modern critics seem to have taken this liberating injunction
to heart: some applaud Marlowe's hero for his martial prowess, rhetorical
brilliance, and aspiring mind, while others condemn his cruelty, bombast,
and arrogant neglect of mortal limitations. [2] Recently, Judith Weil has

1. *1 Tamburlaine*, Prologue, in *The Complete Works of Christopher Marlowe*, ed. Fredson
Bowers (Cambridge, Eng., 1973). Subsequent quotations of Marlowe come from this
edition and will be cited in my text.
2. Among those who urge sympathetic admiration for Tamburlaine are: Paul Kocher,
Christopher Marlowe: A Study of His Thought, Learning and Character (Chapel Hill, N.C.,
1946); Harry Levin, *The Overreacher* (London, 1952); F. P. Wilson, *Marlowe and the Early
Shakespeare* (Oxford, 1953), pp. 18–19; Irving Ribner, *The English History Play in the Age of
Shakespeare*, rev. ed. (London, 1965), p. 60; J. B. Steane, *Marlowe: A Critical Study*
(Cambridge, Eng., 1964); Eugene M. Waith, *The Herculean Hero* (London, 1962), chap. 3,
and *Ideas of Greatness: Heroic Drama in England* (London, 1971), chap. 2; J.M.R. Margeson,
The Origin of English Tragedy (Oxford, 1967), p. 133. Among those who condemn
Tamburlaine: Roy Battenhouse, *Marlowe's Tamburlaine: A Study in Renaissance Moral Philos-*

proposed an Erasmian Marlowe who "mocks his heroes in a remarkably subtle fashion."[3] Tamburlaine's "repeated efforts to give his magnificent conceits literal existence in a foolish world bring home to an audience the tragic consequences of his great imagination."[4] At nearly the same time, Joel Altman chastises those who argue that plays like *Tamburlaine* should be read didactically (as presumably even Weil is doing) and asserts that the play arose from a rhetorical tradition of education which emphasized arguing multiple sides of any issue. Thus, it dramatizes a question, not a lesson; the writer moves his audience "toward some fuller apprehension of truth that could be discerned only through the total action of the drama."[5] While denying that he opens the door to critical anarchy, Altman says of Tamburlaine that we are left "ultimately to decide the meaning of his fate for ourselves."[6] Though Altman and Weil see very different *Tamburlaine*s, both writers have the virtue of acknowledging the problematic nature of a play which invites its audience to "applaud his fortunes as you please."

It may be beyond hope to find firm evidence of how Marlowe himself meant us to respond to *Tamburlaine*; my private belief, which I will not try to argue in this essay, is that Marlowe was irretrievably ambivalent about his hero's defiant self-creation: the play is flawed by its brilliant author's own confusions. But we can, I think, discover how Marlowe's society took this enormously popular work. The surviving body of Elizabethan critical comment on *Tamburlaine* is too limited and too cryptic to make safe generalizations possible.[7] But because of its enormous popular success, *Tamburlaine* spawned a brood of offspring—including, presumably, *2 Tamburlaine*—which attempted to attract the same audience avid for Alleyn's strutting as a conqueror. These plays may tell us nothing at all

---

ophy (Nashville, Tenn., 1941); Douglas Cole, *Suffering and Evil in the Plays of Christopher Marlowe* (Princeton, N.J., 1962); Charles G. Masinton, *Christopher Marlowe's Tragic Vision: A Study in Damnation* (Athens, Ohio, 1972); W. L. Godshalk, *The Marlovian World Picture* (The Hague, 1974).

　　3. Judith Weil, *Christopher Marlowe: Merlin's Prophet* (Cambridge, Eng., 1977), p. 2.
　　4. *Ibid.*, p. 109.
　　5. Joel B. Altman, *The Tudor Play of Mind: Rhetorical Inquiry and the Development of Elizabethan Drama* (Berkeley, Calif., 1978), p. 6.
　　6. *Ibid.*, p. 7.
　　7. See Tucker Brooke, "The Reputation of Christopher Marlowe," *Transactions of the Connecticut Academy of Arts and Sciences*, XXV (1922), 347–408.

about Marlowe's ideas or intentions, but they reveal a great deal about what his contemporaries found appealing in *Tamburlaine*. For I assume— and this is the key assumption of this essay—that any writer trying to capitalize on the commercial success of another writer's work is likely to try to imitate those features of the work that in his judgment created its wide appeal. Playwrights and actors in the late 1580s and early 1590s may have no shrewder insights into the ideas of Christopher Marlowe than do modern critics, but their livelihoods depended on their knowledge of what attracted audiences to his plays and their own.

Thus, if *Tamburlaine's* first audience relished seeing human aspiration to match or conquer Jove himself celebrated and affirmed by dramatic action, it is unlikely that the play's imitators would fail to shape their heroes and plots to the same purpose. I am assuming, in other words, that theatrical history can tell us a good deal about the way a society perceived a play, even though it may not tell as much about how an author meant it to be taken. Imitation of a play is a form of criticism. The criticism may not help us to see the object—the play imitated—as it really is, but it can help us assess the tastes and ideals of a society by showing what the theatrical public wanted that object to be.

In saying that imitations tell us something about how a society under- stood the work imitated, I am largely rejecting another model of how theatrical works relate to their predecessors. In the 1950s Irving Ribner argued that Greene's *Alphonsus, King of Aragon* and the anonymous *The Wars of Cyrus* were "replies" to *Tamburlaine*.[8] As though London theaters were pages of a learned journal, Ribner sees playwrights trying to correct Marlowe's erroneous ideas about Providence and advance sounder and more orthodox notions. Perhaps Greene and Marlowe did disagree about politics and human nature. But it is unlikely that Greene thought it more impor- tant to advance an intellectual debate than he did to get a good price from the players. Moreover, an acting company which was making money on a play, or observing its rivals doing so, is more likely to want to produce a play that resembles the popular success than one which shows it really didn't deserve to succeed. High-grossing disaster movies are followed by other

---

8. Irving Ribner, *"Tamburlaine* and *The Wars of Cyrus," JEGP*, LIII (1954), 569–573, and "Greene's Attack on Marlowe: Some Light on *Alphonsus* and *Selimus," SP*, LII (1955), 162–171.

disaster movies, not by films about skillful Commissioners of Public Safety.

Who are the sons of *Tamburlaine*? That distinguished man of the theater, Ancient Pistol, at his first entrance in *King Henry IV, Part II* spouts a resonant jargon echoing not only *Tamburlaine*, but also Green's *Alphonsus King of Aragon* (1587), Peele's *Battle of Alcazar* (1589), the anonymous *Locrine* (1591), and (perhaps anomalously in this company) *The Spanish Tragedy* (1587?).[9] With the help of more recent historians the relevant canon emerges.[10] Of the 38 extant plays for the public theater first performed in England between 1587 and 1593, 10 show clear debts to *Tamburlaine*. In addition to those already named, they are *The Taming of a Shrew* (1589), Greene's *Orlando Furioso* (1591), *The Wars of Cyrus* (1588), Lodge's and Greene's *A Looking-Glass for London and England* (1590), Lodge's *Wounds of Civil War* (1588), *Selimus* (1592), and Shakespeare's *Henry VI* plays.[11] Some of these plays make no effort to imitate Marlowe's characters, plot, or ideas, but simply echo his verse style. After discussing them briefly, I will go on to *Wounds of Civil War* and *Alphonsus*, which mimic Marlowe's new hero and seize upon stage effects such as displays of crowns, treading on captive monarchs, and chariots drawn by kings in ways that suggest that such moments contributed greatly to *Tamburlaine*'s popularity. In *Wounds* and *Alphonsus* characters who act like *Tamburlaine* are hard to judge, though certainly not unambiguously admired. But

9. A. R. Humphreys, ed., *The Second Part of King Henry IV*, The Arden Shakespeare (London, 1966), notes to II.iv.153–180.

10. John Bakeless, *The Tragicall History of Christopher Marlowe* (Cambridge, Mass., 1942), I, 238–273.

11. I rely on the chronology and lists of Alfred Harbage, *Annals of English Drama, 975–1700*, rev. S. Schoenbaum (London, 1964). Claims of indebtedness to *Tamburlaine* are my own responsibility, but are thoroughly conventional. In this essay I don't discuss *The Wars of Cyrus* because I restrict myself to plays for adult actors; nor do I discuss *Henry VI* because I have no space to deal with the complexities of Shakespeare's relationship to Marlowe. Neither play would modify the conclusions I draw here. The relationships among the *Henry VI* plays and *Tamburlaine* are admirably discussed by David Riggs in *Shakespeare's Heroical Histories: Henry VI and Its Literay Tradition* (Cambridge, Mass., 1971). Riggs argues that Shakespeare preserves "the theatrically viable stage business and rhetoric of heroical-historical drama while placing it in a richer context of ethical and political values" (p. 84).

within three or four years after the first performance of *Tamburlaine*, other imitations appear which make clear that overreaching ambition and self-display deserve blame, not praise. Peele's *Battle of Alcazar* and the anonymous *Locrine* and *Selimus* all employ choruses or other framing-devices, morality-play allegorical figures, contrasting groups of characters, dialectical debates, and self-revelatory soliloquies, alone or in combination, as ways of controlling audience response more precisely and effectively than does Marlowe.

At a time when Henslowe's diary reveals the continuous popularity of *Tamburlaine*, these plays invite their audiences to condemn characters for bursting the restraints of conventional beliefs and codes of conduct. Of course, these authors may have misunderstood Marlowe, or may have disagreed with him. But there is a strong likelihood that their plays reflect a popular understanding of *Tamburlaine*, whether or not that understanding was what Marlowe would have desired. Indeed, taken together, all the early imitations of *Tamburlaine* suggest that Marlowe's audience, and therefore his imitators, wanted to be entertained by his splendid rhetoric and glamorous stage effects without having to yield to the discomfort of unconventional ideas. Caging their father, *Tamburlaine*'s weak sons help build edifices which both display and restrict his heirs.

I

A new verse style is one of Marlowe's obvious successes in *Tamburlaine*: classical allusions; polysyllabic "high astounding terms," especially in the form of place names, personal names, and classical references; emphasis on precious, exotic objects and vivid physical sensations; and hyperbolical comparisons and assertions. Writers of comedies and morality plays bearing little other resemblance to Marlowe's work pick up some of his verbal tricks, but do so in ways that tell little or nothing about what besides its vivid language their authors thought audiences admired about Marlowe's play. The anonymous *The Taming of a Shrew* uses Tamburlaine-like rhetoric indiscriminately—sometimes apparently mockingly, as Ferando (Shakespeare's Petruchio) wooes his Kate, and at other times with apparent seriousness, as when romantic lovers speak in scenes where no suggestion of mocking is plausible. [12] Martial rather than domestic, Robert Greene's comedy *Orlando Furioso* could make serious use of Marlowe's ideas, but Greene chooses not to do so. Marlovian rhetoric is an added gimmick for dramatizing a braggart villain whose greatest debt is to the *miles gloriosus*. Similarly, Greene uses heightened Marlovian language to help render Orlando's madness. [13] But there is no connection between Marlovian rhetoric and Marlovian ideas in *Orlando*; though the new style is used for more sharply defined artistic effects than it is in *A Shrew*, it is nonetheless principally a mode of decoration. Like Orlando, Lodge's and Greene's morality play *A Looking-Glass for London and England* embraces *Tamburlaine*'s verbal hyperbole while treating its heroic aspirations as at best repugnant, at worst a joke. [14] The play owes to *Tamburlaine* some effective tricks of language and theatrical turns, but the ethical challenge of Marlowe's new hero is not felt at all. The play depends for its appeal on new *coups de theatre* and utterly conventional ideas. These three plays provide no comfort for anyone who wants to argue that *Tamburlaine*'s popularity arose from audience approval of overreaching ambition. But neither do they offer any illumination about how his contemporaries came to grips with the challenge implicit in such ideas.

In Lodge's *Wounds of Civil War* (1588), a Roman history play, Scilla has seized dominion over Rome in retaliation for the choice of Marius, his rival, as general against Mithridates; *Wounds* tells the story of unsuccessful attempts to unseat him. [15] Startlingly, though Marius dies and Scilla

---

12. For a superficially "mocking" usage, see vii.63–64; for a "straight" usage, see x.1–6, in Geoffrey Bullough, *Narrative and Dramatic Sources of Shakespeare*, vol. I (London, 1957). Full lists of Marlovian echoes in *A Shrew*, appear in *The Taming of a Shrew*, ed. F. S. Boas (London, 1908), pp. 91–98, and in Bakeless, *Marlowe*, II, 251–253.

13. Robert Greene, *The History of Orlando Furioso*, Malone Society Reprints (Oxford, 1907). See, for example, I.i.260–264; IV.ii.1172–1173; IV.ii.1180–1181; V.ii.1600–1604.

14. Thomas Lodge and Robert Greene, *A Looking-Glass for London and England*, Malone Society Reprints (Oxford, 1932), i.30.

15. Whether Thomas Lodge's *The Wounds of Civil War* (1588) immediately preceded or immediately followed *Tamburlaine* is still a matter of controversy. N. B. Paradise, *Thomas Lodge: The History of an Elizabethan* (New Haven, Conn., 1931), pp. 128–142, argues that a writer with Lodge's sensitivity to new styles could not possibly have written a play with so much potential for being like *Tamburlaine*, yet so unlike it, had *Tamburlaine*

triumphs over all his rivals and is eventually named dictator, he resigns his title when he hears of the death of Marius's son and makes his own peace with death. The play's resemblance to *Tamburlaine* is plain enough. Act III, scene iii, begins with "Enter *Scilla* in triumph in his chair triumphant of gold, drawn by four Moors before the chariot." [16] In Act I, scene i, civil war begins as the Senate "rise and cast away their gowns, having their swords by their sides" (l. 242, s.d.). This transformation by doffing garments parallels Tamburlaine's grand gesture as he casts aside his shepherd's weeds and reveals himself as a warrior and potential conqueror of Asia. Scilla makes captive kings draw his chariot (III.iii.67 ff.) and treads on the neck of his enemy, Carbo (V.i.52). Like Tamburlaine, he manifests his power in his gleaming eyes and locates its source in his aspiring mind. No matter how brilliant the glory of a throne of power and its guarding furies, "Tut, Scilla's sparkling eyes should dim with clear / The burning brands of their consuming light, / And master fancy with a forward mind" (II.i.10–12). Marius calls him "the scourge of Asia," and just before the play's end Scilla characterizes his achievement:

> . . . the man that made the world to stoop,
> And fettered Fortune in the chains of power,
> Must droop and draw the Chariot of Fate
> Along the darksome banks of Acheron.
>
> (V.v.315–318)

already appeared. W. A. Armstrong in 1958 disagreed, showing more parallels between the two plays than had earlier been adduced, and claiming that Lodge modified his two sources, Appian's *Roman History* and Plutarch's lives of Marius and Sulla, in order to make the play a critique of the end of *Tamburlaine* ("*Tamburlaine* and *The Wounds of Civil War*," *N&Q*, CCIII [1958], 381–383). The most recent editor of *Wounds*, Joseph W. Houppert, in 1970 presented the evidence for both views and took an agnostic position (*The Wounds of Civil War*, Regents Renaissance Drama Series [London, 1970], pp. xviii–xx). Most recently, Charles W. Whitworth has tried to revive Paradise's case for Lodge's priority ("*The Wounds of Civil War* and *Tamburlaine*: Lodge's Alleged Imitation, *N&Q*, CCXX [1975], 245–247). I believe Lodge to be imitating Marlowe, not vice versa; Marlowe's contemporaries would not have hailed his work as they did had it not seemed to them something new, rather than an evolutionary step beyond Lodge, and the failures to fulfill Tamburlainean potentials which Paradise finds so puzzling are, we shall see, characteristic of the group of plays I am discussing, the rest of which can be dated as *Tamburlaine's* successors.

16. *Wounds*, ed. Houppert, III.iii, opening stage direction. Subsequent quotations from *Wounds* come from this edition.

But Scilla, a conqueror like Tamburlaine, also poses Tamburlaine-like problems for a reader or viewer who wants to know how to judge this Titan. Should we admire his mighty deeds and vaunting speech or should we condemn them? Deciding is made difficult because Lodge usually presents his rival, Marius, quite sympathetically. He is the legitimate choice as general, Scilla a usurper; when the Minturnians capture Marius he speaks to his jailer with dignity about the pains as well as pleasures of high estate; a murderer brought in to kill him is so stirred by the noble look in his eyes that he spares his life (III.ii). If Marius is noble, perhaps Tamburlainean Scilla is a monster—but Scilla's self-assessment before he dies is the work of no monster (though it is arguably quite inconsistent with his character as earlier presented). Marius himself can turn a Marlovian phrase as though he, too, had the potential to be a frightening conqueror.

Neither Marius nor Scilla is a satisfactory focus of value in *The Wounds of Civil War*. One of Scilla's followers, Mark Anthony, has the potential to play that role; his concern, expressed in a number of speeches, is for the health of Rome rather than the triumph of faction. Anthony's murder by Marius's followers helps shift our sympathy toward Scilla, but Scilla's behavior, until his strange repentance at the play's end, makes him even less satisfactory than Marius as a paragon of Roman ideals. While it is likely that Lodge intended us to endorse the stoic acceptance of fate evinced by Scilla before his death, such an affirmation from a character heretofore celebrated for seizing dominion cannot be persuasive. Marius could have been a more effective foil for Scilla than any character is for Tamburlaine, but Lodge doesn't exploit the opportunity for clarification. Lodge and his audience seem to have been interested in claims of rising beyond human limitations for their rhetorical magnificence without clearly sorting out whether or not the intellectual substance of such claims deserves endorsement or condemnation.

Embedded in *The Wounds of Civil War* is not just a Marlovian conqueror play but a Shakespearean history play in which the stability of the realm rather than the triumph of a single hero commands the playwright's imaginative energies. *Gorboduc* could have provided a model for such a play, but without characters of much imaginative force. But Lodge in 1588 didn't know how to shape a satisfactory plot for an aspiring hero.

Thus, the play ultimately leaves us in confusion about what judgment it wants us to make about the events and characters it portrays. But Lodge's decision to write the play suggests that he believed his audience wanted heroic rhetoric and stage spectacle, and that he was prepared to give them those Marlovian commodities whether or not they were consistent with any political or ethical vision implicit in the tale he was telling.

Robert Greene's *Alphonsus, King of Aragon* (1587), even more than *The Wounds of Civil War*, tries to create Tamburlainean heroes apparently without being aware of any of the new and disturbing ideas presented in Marlowe's play. The play tells of Alphonsus's rise from low estate to the crown of Aragon by his superlative martial and rhetorical skills, but takes care to let us know from the first that Alphonsus is the legitimate son of the rightful king, doing nothing more shocking than recovering what is rightly his own. Once he has attained the throne of Aragon Alphonsus says it is too base for him; he bestows it on an underling and seeks the rule of the Turkish empire, whose emperor, Amurack, has undertaken to support Alphonsus's former ally, now rival, Belinus. To Alphonsus's repertoire of Tamburlaine-like tricks Amurack adds atheism. The play ends with Alphonsus married to Amurack's lovely daughter Iphigina and established as heir after her father's death, all as a result of some extraordinary manipulations of events by Alphonsus's father Carinus and a sorceress named Medea.

Clearly, *Alphonsus* is romance, not true heroic play; the prologue says the story will be told "in the maner of a Comedie." [17] But both Alphonsus and Amurack speak in ways recognizably indebted to *Tamburlaine*. Amurack cheers his supporters by assuring them that their foes are "not mightie Tamberlaine" (1573), and his attacks on Mahomet parallel Tamburlaine's burning of the Koran. As Belinus crowns Alphonsus he says he has a "conquering mind" (l. 498); despite his royal birth, Alphonsus says his glory arises from his glorious deeds (ll. 539–541). Alphonsus enters with a procession of tributary kings walking beneath a canopy with a crowned king's head at each corner. He boasts to Amurack, "I clap vp Fortune in a cage of gold, / To make her turne her wheele as I thinke best"

---

17. Robert Greene, *Alphonsus King of Aragon*, Malone Society Reprints (Oxford, 1926), 1. 110. Subsequent quotations come from this edition.

(ll. 1614–1615). Presumably Greene expected his audience to enjoy this Tamburlainean posturing and speechifying as an entertaining phenomenon in its own right. But the play in no way advocates seizing control of one's own destiny. Greene has surrounded his narrative by a series of choruses spoken by Venus and four Muses. Venus first describes Alphonsus as "that man of *Ioue* his seed, / Sprung from the loines of the immortall Gods" (ll. 24–25); she wants to tell his story and laments that no Virgil is available. She meets Melpomene (the Muse of tragedy), Clio (history), Erato (lyric poetry), and Calliope (epic poetry); the first three scorn Calliope because so few poets have lately sought her aid. But Calliope undertakes to aid Venus in telling Alphonsus's story. (Were *Alphonsus of Aragon* a more thoughtful play, one would be tempted to say that by this opening chorus Greene intended to contrast his own "epic" poetical practices with the recent flourishing of tragedy in the hands of Kyd and Marlowe, histories such as *The Famous Victories of Henry V,* and lyric poetry by writers such as Sidney.) As prologue to Act II, Venus speaks of how Alphonsus begins "to climbe / Vnto the toppe of friendly Fortunes wheele" (ll. 378–379). And at the start of Act V, Venus makes clear that the power of God and the Fates, far greater than the strength of heroic Alphonsus, brought about his triumph over his Turkish adversary.

Venus flatly contradicts Alphonsus's claim that he makes Fortune turn her wheel as he thinks best. Moreover, the climactic marriage between Alphonsus and Amurack's daughter Iphigina results not from any skill on Alphonsus's part but from the persuasive influence of Medea. This enchantress in Act III lulls Amurack into a prophetic sleep in which he dreams of his daughter's marriage to his hated rival. When Amurack in consequence banishes his wife and daughter, Medea explains to them the vanity of trying to evade the dictates of destiny:

> In vaine it is, to striue against the streame,
> Fates must be followed, and the gods decree
> Must needs take place in euery kinde of cause.
>
> (ll. 1186–1188)

It is Medea who persuades Alphonsus and Amurack to reconcile their differences at the play's end. The reversal which brings about a happy ending comes about not from any growth in understanding or change of heart by the principal characters, but only by their acceptance of a solution dictated by destiny and eloquently described to them by this clever manipulator.

Thus, by the use of choruses and a plot-manipulating sorceress, Greene creates a clear set of limits to our assent to the overreaching claims of Alphonsus, even while allowing him to attain the happy ending appropriate to a "Comicall Historie" (as the title page describes the play). Irving Ribner argues that Alphonsus should be read as an attack on *Tamburlaine*, which he sees as a play glorifying self-sufficiency and denying the rule of Providence in human affairs.[18] Such a view, I believe, belies the rather casual attitude Greene seems to take toward consistency in *Alphonsus*. The hero is as much of a conqueror as he can get away with being, and the play's happy ending invites us to give him our admiration. At the same time, apparently authoritative spokesmen such as Medea and Venus contradict the hero's own views about Fortune. I suggest that here, as in *Orlando Furioso*, Greene employed the Tamburlainean style as a source of entertaining stage effects rather than as a coherent body of ideas which he expected his audience to assess. Doing so, he implies that there was a less inevitable association in the minds of audiences than Ribner would postulate between *Tamburlaine*'s mode and heterodox or challenging ideas.

George Peele's *The Battle of Alcazar* (1589) is a play filled with confusions, both textual and intellectual. It survives both in a printed text almost surely the result of an abridgment for provincial performance and a theatrical "plot" which preserves dumb shows and indications of scenes no longer extant in the printed version.[19] One cannot say whether confusions in Alcazar about motivation and evaluation of characters result from textual corruption or authorial bungling (though Peele's other work invites the harsher hypothesis). The play provides spectacle and rhetorical effects indebted to *Tamburlaine* and *The Spanish Tragedy*—Peele uses choruses and dumb shows to shape judgments of main characters just as Greene did in *Alphonsus*, and makes more use than Greene of the clarifying potential of

18. Ribner, "Greene's Attack on Marlowe."

19. See W. W. Greg, *Two Elizabethan Stage Abridgements* (Oxford, 1923), and *The Battle of Alcazar*, ed. John Yoklavich, in *The Life and Works of George Peele*, ed. Charles Tyler Prouty, vol. 2 (New Haven, Conn., 1961), pp. 213–373. Subsequent quotations from *Alcazar* are taken from the latter edition.

contrasts between characters. Though *Alcazar* is a tragedy and *Alphonsus* is a comedy, the values attached to Tamburlainean heroism are the same in both plays.

Alcazar tells of the battle between the Moor, Muly Mahamet, and his uncle, Abdelmelec, whose throne he has usurped, for dominion in North Africa. The Moor is aided by Sebastian, King of Portugal, and the swash-buckling Englishman, Captain Thomas Stukley. Abdelmelec dies think-ing his forces are defeated, the Moor betrays Portugal and dies ignominiously while fleeing and cursing his fate, while Stukley and the King die in battle.

Tamburlaine is a vivid presence in *Alcazar*, and even more than in *Alphonsus of Aragon* the Scythian's overreaching ambitions and titanic rhetoric are divided among two characters, the Moor and Stukley. Stukley introduces himself as one "resolvde in all, / To follow rule, honor and Emperie" (II.ii.411–412). Like Tamburlaine, he seeks the sweet fruition of an earthly crown:

> There shall no action passe my hand or sword,
> That cannot make a step to gaine a crowne,
>
> . . . .
> Why should not I then looke to be a king?
> I am the marques now of Ireland made,
> And will be shortly king of Ireland,
> King of a mole-hill had I rather be,
> Than the richest subject of a monarchie,
> Huffe it brave mind, and never cease t' aspire,
> Before thou raigne sole king of thy desire.
>
> (II.ii.452–453, 461–467)

But Stukley's great rival, the Moor, is equally Tamburlainean in his aspirations and his language. Early in the action, when for the moment defeated by Abdelmelec, the Moor describes himself as "soulelesse" (II.iii.500) without his crown. To feed his beloved Calypolis he goes offstage to fight wild beasts single-handed, returning with the raw flesh of a lion on his sword. The Moor's rhythms as he bids Calypolis feast echo Tamburlaine's great speeches to Zenocrate (and are echoed by Ancient Pistol): "Feede then and faint not faire Calypolis" (II.iii.548–561).

With respect to aspiring assertiveness, there's little to choose between

Stukley and the Moor, but choric speeches instruct us to find the Moor monstrous and Stukley a sturdy Briton, admirable for patriotic reasons. The Presenter, costumed as a "Portingall," describes Sebastian of Portugal as "an honorable and couragious king" and his ally as "the barbarous Moore" (I. Prologue 4, 6). When the Moor enters in dumb show with his sons, the Presenter calls them "damned wits" and shows them murdering the Moor's uncle and two young princes. "This unbeleeving Moor . . . Triumphs in his ambitious tyrannie" (I. Prologue 32–34) until vengeance, predicted by the Presenter, strikes him down. Before Act II the Presenter calls the Moor's rival "good Abdelmelec" (II. Prologue 312) and invokes ghosts who cry "Vindicta," Nemesis, and the Furies to aid in revenge against the murderous Moor. Stukley, like the other main characters in *Alcazar* a historical figure, poses a hard problem for Peele. Historically, Thomas Stukley plotted to conquer Ireland and give dominion to the Pope rather than Queen Elizabeth; for a time he was allied with England's great enemy, Philip of Spain. On the other hand, his swashbuckling valor and brave death made him a hero of popular legends and ballads, even as serious historians continued to condemn him.[20] Peele tries to have it both ways in his play. He uses Stukley's announcement of his expedition against Ireland as an occasion for a rebuke by Sebastian which eloquently praises England and Elizabeth (II.iv.670–705). But (for reasons not made clear in the present muddled state of *Alcazar*) Stukley resolves to join forces with Sebastian, and by allying himself with Portugal is also vaguely identified as an enemy of Spain. Stukley's brave death in battle associates him with Sebastian, whom we've been coached to admire, and also helps earn the audience's admiration. And one mustn't forget that any valiant Englishman surrounded by Portuguese, Spaniards, and Moors would have a head start in the affections of an Elizabethan audience. But the most important way that sympathy is maintained for the aspiring Stukley is by contrast with the equally aspiring, but officially vicious Moor.

None of what I have said redeems *The Battle of Alcazar* from confusion. The asserted morality of the play is only tenuously connected to dramatized characters: Sebastian, the King of Portugal, is supposed to be a

20. See Yoklavich's introduction to *Alcazar*, pp. 247–279.

paragon but is nonetheless warring in alliance with the unutterably vicious Moor against the virtuous and noble Abdelmelec; we are meant to accept Stukley's heroism despite his incipient rebellion against England's Queen. The fact that Peele could write such a play, and that it was successful enough to be revived in the late 1590s, shows that the audience which applauded *Tamburlaine* had a powerful appetite for aspiring heroes and was not too picky about their moral status. But the differences between *Alcazar* and *Tamburlaine* show that Peele was trying, not altogether successfully, to combine Marlowe's new hero with traditional strategies for directing the audience's sympathies in ways *Tamburlaine* doesn't attempt. As is true of all the immediate heirs of Marlowe, Peele wants to exploit new sensations while clinging to an undisturbing moral vision.

II

The machinery of revenge tragedy is one element in *Alcazar*'s hodge-podge of new heroism and conventional morality. It is in no way surprising that a popular playwright of the late 1580s should introduce ghosts, cries of "Vindicta, Vindicta," and elaborate speeches about Nemesis, Alecto, and the Furies into his work; Kyd's *Spanish Tragedy* vies with *Tamburlaine* as the most popular play of the decade. Revenge tragedy shares with the heroic play the potential for focusing on a single dominant character, a Tamburlaine or a Hieronimo, and exploring a personality intent on overcoming obstacles and achieving goals not necessarily sanctioned by the rest of society. Unlike Tamburlaine, the hero of a revenge tragedy has a clearly statable limit to his ambition—it's hard to be sure when you've made yourself into a constellation, but easier to know whether or not you've revenged your son Horatio's death. All mortal rivals to a godlike conqueror can seem inadequate to produce powerful dramatic conflict; the revenger is more a man among men, and the obstacles and delays that obstruct his course provide opportunities for dramatizable incidents. A fusion of the two forms is tempting because of the popularity of both, and because the conventions of revenge tragedy have promise to strengthen the structural weaknesses of heroic drama. *Locrine* (1591), printed in 1595 with the tempting initials "W. S." on the title page, is just such a fusion. It began life as a revenge tragedy called *Estrild*, written by Charles Tilney, who died in the fall of 1586.[21] Sometime in the early 1590s a writer whose head was filled with Marlowe and Spenser (conceivably Robert Greene) revised *Estrild* into *Locrine* by rewriting speeches for the play's principal warriors in the new style *Tamburlaine* introduced, revising choruses and dumb shows in language extensively borrowed from Spenser's *Complaints*, and adding a comic underplot (or extensively revising an already existing comic plot) centering on a character named Strumbo, whose actions and speeches often parody the behavior of serious figures in the play. Bibliographical clues and echoes of works by Spenser and Marlowe make it possible to identify those parts of the play that were extensively revised after Tilney's death. The last act of *Locrine* and certain scenes in earlier acts preserve what Tilney wrote.[22]

Locrine tells two stories. The first recounts the war between Locrine, king of Britain (and heir of the Trojan founder, Brutus), and the invading Humber, king of the Huns, during which Humber kills Locrine's brother Albanact. The war against Humber then becomes a battle for revenge, with the Britons spurred on by Albanact's ghost. Humber is duly defeated (though in a puzzling way characteristic of this strange play, he dies by his own hand, and only after a lengthy period of hungry wandering); to the consternation of his wedded wife, Guendolin, Locrine takes as his concubine Humber's former mate, Estrild. The second story then dramatizes Guendolin's war of revenge against Locrine, culminating in the deaths by suicide of Locrine, Estrild, and their daughter Sabren.

The last act of *Locrine* preserves Tilney's *Estrild*. It straightforwardly emphasizes Guendolin's destruction of Locrine and Estrild as revenge for the wrongs they have done her. A speech by the ghost of Corineus, Guendolin's father, provides a fair sample of its style:

> The boysterous *Boreas* thundreth forth reuenge.
> The stonie rocks crie out on sharpe reuenge.

21. Attribution of *Locrine* has been a lively subject of debate since the editors of the Shakespeare Third Folio, presumably enticed by the initials "W. S." on the title page, printed it as Shakespeare's. For an extensive survey of scholarship on *Locrine*'s date and authorship, see Terence P. Logan and Denzell S. Smith, *The Predecessors of Shakespeare* (Lincoln, Nebr., 1973), pp. 259–264.

22. See Peter Berek, "*Locrine* Revised, *Selimus*, and Early Responses to *Tamburlaine*," *RORD*, XXIII (1980), 33–54.

> The thornie bush pronounceth dire reuenge.
> Now *Corineus* staie and see reuenge,
> And feede thy soule with *Locrines* ouerthrow.[23]

The subject matter is English Seneca, the style at best Kyd's in *Spanish Tragedy*. No marks of Tamburlaine appear on this carcass. But in earlier acts, where the reviser has been at work, he has given characters in this old tale out of Geoffrey of Monmouth and *The Mirror for Magistrates* a chance to talk an up-to-date tongue, as though determined to capitalize on a rant that had been winning applause. For example, when Humber arrives in Britain on his mission of conquest, he scorns his opponents' preparation for defense:

> But I will frustrate all their foolish hope,
> And teach them that the *Scithian* Emperour
> Leades fortune tied in a chaine of gold,
> Constraining her to yeeld vnto his will.
>
> (II.ii.471–474)

Humber's rhetoric clearly links him with Tamburlaine, as does his role as conqueror, but an equally strong debt to Marlowe's heroic style is owed by the British champion Albanact. Enraged, he threatens the goddess Fortune who has brought him down:

> Ile passe the frozen Zone where ysie flakes
> Stopping the passage of the fleeting shippes
> Do lie, like mountaines in the congealed sea,
> Where if I finde that hatefull house of hers,
> Ile pull the fickle wheele from out her hands,
> And tie her selfe in euerlasting bands.
>
> (II.vi.865–870)

These overreaching self-assertions, classical allusions, and geographic exotica are all Marlovian, albeit in a clumsy pastiche. But the context in which Humber and Albanact speak makes clear that such self-proclama-

---

23. *The Tragedy of Locrine*, Malone Society Reprints (Oxford, 1908), V.v.2010–2015. I have omitted the stage direction "Sound the alarme" after l. 2012. Subsequent quotations come from this edition.

tion is appliqué, not part of the fundamental conception of either character. Albanact is threatening Fortune though he knows she has already brought him down—his next lines are, "But all in vaine I breath these threatnings, / The day is lost, the *Hunnes* are conquerors" (II.vi.871–872). Within a few lines he thrusts himself through with his sword. Humber for the moment is triumphant, but the fickle wheel of Fortune will soon bring him down as well.

Indeed, beneath the trendy trappings of Marlovian conqueror play and Senecan tragedy of revenge, *Locrine* ultimately emerges as the kind of "tragedy" familiar from *The Mirror for Magistrates* and its medieval predecessors. No man controls his own fate; we all ride Fortune's wheel; all ascent to greatness is followed by a fall. *Locrine* makes little attempt to ascribe rising or falling to special merit or blame; we are expected to sympathize more with British Albanact than with Humber the Hun, but both are equally valiant, and both nonetheless die. Locrine's death, to be sure, results from his infidelity to Guendolin, but the dumb show and prologue before Act V stress a comparison between Guendolin and Medea with her "diuellish charmes" (1779) rather than the justice of her cause. In fact, throughout the play the dumb shows and prologues, which Spenserian imitations show to be part of the revision rather than the Tilney text, minimize whatever sense of individual responsibility or accomplishment is implicit in revenge tragedy and instead stress the vanity and transitoriness of all human achievements. For example, the dumb show preceding Act III shows a crocodile stung to death by a little snake. The prologue, Ate, explains the scene's significance: it shows the fall of one "that did so much in his owne greatnesse trust" (III.i.977).

> So *Humber* hauing conquered *Albanact*,
> Doth yeeld his glorie vnto *Locrines* sword.
> Marke what ensues and you may easily see,
> That all our life is but a Tragedie.
>
> (III.i.978–981)

The reviser who put *Locrine* into its present form seems to have been determined to exploit all the routes he knew to popular success. He has told a perennially popular story (John Higgins's additions to *The Mirror for Magistrates*, which include four poems on the Locrine story, went through five editions by 1620, including one in 1587; Lodge published a poem on the same subject, *The Complaint of Elstred*, in 1593; Spenser told the story in *The Faerie Queene*, Book III, published in 1590). He keeps the ghosts and Senecan trappings of revenge tragedy, and he puffs up his central male figures with Tamburlainean speechifying. But the only way he judges his characters' behavior is to appeal to the general principle that all achievement is vain, all life a tragedy. Whether or not such an opinion be true, it surely operates on a plane of generality so exalted that it fails to encounter most of the moral issues implicit in *Locrine*'s action. I suggest that he does so because he, and perhaps his audience as well, finds the Tamburlainean mode powerfully appealing, but at the same time threatening. *Locrine* muffles its heroes so their brave talk won't be too frightening.

Locrine, like other plays discussed thus far, exploited the new effects of *Tamburlaine* without taking seriously any implications that the play's hero was not bound by the same forces as other men. Characters like Lodge's Scilla, Greene's Alphonsus, or Peele's Moor or Thomas Stukley may from time to time employ catchphrases about ruling fate and suggest that they are exempt from the restrictions of orthodox morality, but the preponderance of evidence in their plays suggests that the writer expected his audience to regard such claims as imitations of theatrical style, which didn't require them to revise their ethical standards. Lodge, Greene, and Peele don't so much disagree with Marlowe as ignore the fact that his play, or their own, raises issues of any complexity. The anonymous reviser of *Locrine*, on the other hand, takes some care to keep potentially troubling ideas out of his play while coaching the audience to assimilate whatever evaluative complexities are present to the *de casibus* formula of *The Mirror for Magistrates* and Spenser's *Complaints*. The author of *Selimus* (1592), quite possibly Robert Greene, appears to have been more conscious than any of the other imitators of Marlowe that the Tamburlainean conqueror posed ethical and dramaturgical problems.[24] Modern critics have had a hard time knowing how to take Tamburlaine; from the confusions and evasions traced in this essay one infers that Marlowe's contemporaries had

24. Kenneth Muir showed that *Locrine* must have preceded *Selimus*. See his letter to *TLS*, 12 August 1944, and "Who Wrote *Selimus*," *PLPLS- LHS*, VI (1949), 373–376. Logan and Smith, *Predecessors of Shakespeare*, summarize scholarship on the relation between the two plays.

difficulties as well. But *Selimus* makes these problems explicit. The play's hero himself discusses them; the play uses parallels and contrasts and employs lengthy soliloquies to help avoid some of the tangles Marlowe created. *Selimus* isn't artistically successful, but more than any other of *Tamburlaine*'s weak sons it points a way out of its own dilemmas.

Selimus, the warrior son of the Turkish emperor Baiazet, kills his father and two brothers, Acomat and Corcut, to seize and maintain the throne. He ends the play triumphant as an epilogue predicts a (nonexistent) Part Two. The deposed Baiazet says his Marlovian namesake was happier than he for being deposed by "the scourge of nations," Tamburlaine, rather than his own son (xix. 1756–1759).[25] Selimus speaks of the sweetness of a crown: "An Empire *Sinam*, is so sweete a thing, / As I could be a diuell to be a King" (ii.435–436). Like Tamburlaine, Baiazet's follower Cherseoli warns that Death stands at his sword point (vi.660–661). Resemblances to *Tamburlaine* aren't only verbal; Selimus's ruthlessness at least matches the Scythian conqueror's, and, with a combination of Senecan and Marlovian sensationalism, the play includes several stranglings, some poisonings, a youth tossed to his death on a forest of spear points, and the hideous mutilation of an elderly royal counselor.

Victorious at the end of the play, Selimus orders his brother Acomat strangled before his (and our) eyes and then muses upon his achievements. Like a weary traveler, Selimus says he's earned the right to tell his story, for he has "trode / The monster-garden paths, that lead to crownes" (xxxi.2520–2521). (I prefer the vivid image suggested by the quarto reading to the linguistically more plausible emendations suggested by W. Bang, the Malone Society editor, "-guarded *or possibly* -guarden.") He then tells of the Egyptian Ibises who devour the armies of swift-winged snakes which threaten to overrun the land. Thus, the Ibises do mankind a good turn, but "From out their egges rises the basiliske, / Whose onely sight killes millions of men" (xxxi.2535–2536). This vignette from natural history applies to his own story:

> When *Acomat* lifted his vngratious hands
> Against my aged father *Baiazet*.
> They sent for me, and I like *Ægipts* bird

25. *The Tragical Reign of Selimus*, Malone Society Reprints (Chiswick, Eng., 1908).

Haue rid that monster, and his fellow mates.
But as from *Ibis* springs the *Basilisk*,
Whose onely touch burneth vp stones and trees,
So *Selimus* hath prou'd a Cocatrice.
And cleane consumed all the familie
Of noble *Ottoman*, except himselfe.

(xxxi.2537–2545)

Tamburlaine called himself the "scourge of God," but Marlowe left his Renaissance and modern audiences in doubt as to whether his hero deserved admiration or scorn. Through his protagonist's own voice, the author of *Selimus* makes that protagonist's villainy manifest. The basilisk, however triumphant he may be, is a monster; Selimus is no new hero transvaluing all old values.

Because Selimus is a self-avowed villain, judgments about him are easier to make than judgments about Tamburlaine. But the author runs the risk that such clarity will make us so hostile to his hero we won't even want to attend to the play. Perhaps in consequence, the plot provides a foil for Selimus—his shrewed, articulate villainy glitters against the sullen, lazy, and violent aggression of his brother Acomat. Acomat decides to seek allies and take up arms to secure his father's throne largely because he's bored with "wantonnesse" and "surfeted with pleasures suquidrie" (ix. 731–735). He captures young Mahomet, the emperor's grandson, and has him thrown to his death on massed spear points. When Baiazet sends his aged counselor Aga as an emissary seeking peace, Acomat (onstage) first tears out Aga's eyes and then cuts off his hands, putting them in the old man's bosom as a souvenir before sending him back to Baiazet. Acomat performs the worst horrors of *Selimus*; when Selimus mounts his own campaign, we thus see him as a scourge and terror, but as preferable to his brother. The contrast with Acomat, along with Selimus's own talkative energy, develops just enough curious concern to keep us from finding Selimus totally abhorrent.

III

The generall welcomes *Tamburlain* receiv'd,
When he arrived last upon our stage,
Hath made our Poet pen his second part.

The Prologue to 2 *Tamburlaine* doesn't prove it a potboiler, but does suggest that it may not have been part of Marlowe's original plan—a suggestion supported by the way Marlowe used up most of his source material in Part One. How does Part Two compare to its heroic father and to the other sons of *Tamburlaine*?

To the extent that plot shapes judgment, Part One is the story of Tamburlaine's unalloyed triumph over all external obstacles, while Part Two shows how "death cuts off the progres of his pomp, / And murdrous Fates throwes al his triumphs down" (Prologue). Death overrules Tamburlaine's desire that divine Zenocrate be his forever and at the end of the play puts a period to his career. The man who held the fates bound fast in iron chains appears to come to his end shackled by his cosmic adversary. In Part One, Tamburlaine's adversaries and foils are clearly of stature lesser than his, or else they ratify his high self-estimation. Mycetes is a weakling, Cosroe and Menander are thunderstruck by the hero's glory, Bajazeth's rhetoric is as cruel as Tamburlaine's own, and his defeat seems to bear out the hero's boasts. Even the Virgins of Damascus blame their death as much on the incompetence of their governor as on the cruelty of their conqueror. But in Part Two Marlowe not only kills his hero, but also creates patterns within his play which might lead to standards by which Tamburlaine's conduct and stature can critically be assessed. In this respect, *Tamburlaine*'s first son is like his non-Marlovian brothers.

Part Two seems to invite the audience to perceive parallels and contrasts between Tamburlaine's career and the careers of his adversaries. For example, Tamburlaine's lowly jail-keeper, Almeda, is seduced by the sweet vision of an earthly crown into freeing Bajazeth's son and heir, Callapine, in return for promotion to status as a tributary monarch. We are clearly meant to see Almeda's social climbing as ludicrous; do his pale aspirations diminish Tamburlaine's? When Tamburlaine first appears on stage (I.iii) he exacts bloodthirsty pledges from two of his sons, though weak Calyphas is content to rest on his father's laurels; then Tamburlaine's tributary kings give him their crowns and receive them again from him. A parallel to this stage spectacle emerges when Tamburlaine's enemies crown Callapine and vow to follow him in destroying "this Thiefe of *Scythia*" (III.i.14). As in some of the plays I discussed earlier, such patterns could clarify our judgment of Tamburlaine himself, but their import is obscure.

Callapine's rhetoric is as inhuman as his opponent's, but Callapine's tributary kings may have more claim to divine sanction than do Techelles, Theridamas, and Usumcasane. Did Marlowe want us to see Tamburlaine as the unworthy conqueror of worthy rivals? as a hero who can impose his will on men equal to him in moral stature, but lacking his strength and imagination? or as a man whose rivals are as foolish and self-deluded as himself?

Perhaps we are to judge characters in Part Two by the degree to which their oaths and boasts are ratified by some power larger than man himself. Certainly, the way the play opens—with a pact between the Christian king Sigismund and Callapine's Moslem ally Orcanes—invites such attention. Urged on by his subordinates, Sigismund breaks his oath to keep peace with Orcanes and then loses in battle to his more honorable rival. If faithless Christians are punished for their oath-breaking, perhaps pagan Tamburlaine rises in our esteem. Or alternatively, the god of Islam may have greater merit than Tamburlaine's classical deities; after all, Tamburlaine sickens and dies as soon as he burns the Koran. But if Allah strikes down Tamburlaine, why didn't he save Callapine and Orcanes from losing to him in battle?

Tamburlaine first encounters limitations to the triumph of his will when his beloved Zenocrate dies. In another apparently parallel action, Tamburlaine's doting attachment to his captive bride may be subtly mocked by the refusal of another fair captive, Olympia, to yield to Tamburlaine's love-struck lieutenant, Theridamas. But the same Olympia subplot shows this admirably constant heroine killing her young son to save him from captivity. If killing a son is allowable, even admirable, for Olympia, then perhaps Tamburlaine's own execution of his effete son Calyphas shouldn't make us regard him as monstrous.

The evidence is tangled, but my point is simple. While the second part of *Tamburlaine* moves beyond the first in incorporating resources that other dramatists working Marlowe's vein employed to clarify moral judgments, Marlowe himself was either unwilling or unable to produce such clarity in 1588. Even Tamburlaine's death is ambiguous. Should we see it as pride's just punishment? the tragedy of wedding unutterable visions to perishable breath? or (as Tamburlaine himself ultimately does) as a deserved apotheosis? The audience is teased with the possibilities of clarification, but no such clarity emerges. As Judith Weil acknowledges, "We must draw our conclusions." Later, she argues for a clear conclusion based on the very obscurity I have just described: "connections that have been at least superficially obscured create a far more powerful satiric resonance than do obvious ones." [26] But surely a satire corroding all characters and action to the same degree is as simpleminded as the judgments in *Locrine* that all is vanity. It is hardly satisfying to think that Tamburlaine receives the same judgment as all his rivals and lieutenants. Further, Weil's case for Erasmian irony is weakened by the strong similarities among Part Two and other early imitations of *Tamburlaine* Part One. Rather than assuming that Marlowe, Lodge, Greene, and Peele are all engaging in satire of extraordinary subtlety, it seems to me more plausible to assume that they are trying with only partial success to gain intellectual control of a genuine theatrical novelty. That the novelty is Marlowe's own invention doesn't make his handling of his hero any more assured. Nor would I want to discount the possibility that Marlowe's own attraction to his hero may partly have subverted his growing dramaturgical skill.

IV

What do *Tamburlaine*'s weak sons tell us about the effects Marlowe intended to produce with his first popular play? As I said at the outset of this essay, they don't enable us to come to any certain conclusions. But they do suggest some considerations which should inform our speculations. They suggest, for example, that morally ambiguous episodes in a heroic play are perfectly compatible with conventional moral and political ideas and can't by themselves be taken as evidence of an authorial intention which is ironic or subversive. They demonstrate that some writers expected audiences to be ready to condemn overreaching heroes, and therefore that Marlowe himself could have entertained such expectations as well. They also demonstrate that if Marlowe wished to create subversive or transforming ethical challenges he was being profoundly original—so original that he found few resources in his theatrical milieu to sustain them, and few if any colleagues who could understand them. Under such

26. Weil, *Marlowe*, pp. 106, 118.

circumstances, it is hardly surprising that the young playwright produced in the two parts of *Tamburlaine* plays with artistic problems as great as their undoubted merits.

Examining imitations of *Tamburlaine* also offers us a useful perspective on the development of Marlowe's brief career as a dramatist. Just as Lodge, Greene, Peele, and "Anon," gradually develop a variety of resources for helping audiences judge vividly rendered characters, so Marlowe himself in his later plays tries to find some way of creating an ethical framework less open-ended than that of *Tamburlaine*. We can trace this development in Marlowe's own work as well as in the works of others. For example the *Jew of Malta*, like *Selimus* (and perhaps influencing *Selimus*), has a hero who explains his own motivations and his own meanings. Like Selimus, the hero of the *Jew* is a Machiavel, a figure indebted to the morality-play vice, and possessed of an intimate relationship to the audience which enables him to be explicit about his own ethical status. [27] T. S. Eliot may be right that the *Jew* is not tragedy but savage farce, but even if the play is farce Barabas is to be condemned despite his vitality, not regarded as a new kind of hero. [28] Just as Selimus has his Acomat to provide the audience with a foil for his villainy, so Barabas has Ithamore. Moreover, in Abigail Marlowe provides a virtuous voice which can ratify the audience's condemnation of her father.

Edward II moves beyond *Tamburlaine* by reducing concentration on a single figure and instead offering a number of well-developed characters whom the viewer can compare with one another. The juxtaposition of Edward, Gaveston, Mortimer Junior, and young Edward enables us to make an essay at assessment by a process of triangulation: clearly drawn weaknesses (as in Gaveston) or virtues (as in the young prince) set limits to our praise or blame of Edward himself. *Doctor Faustus*, on the other hand, is as much a monodrama as *Tamburlaine*, but like Lodge's and Greene's *A Looking-Glass for London and England* it adapts the machinery of homiletic drama to provide an evaluative perspective by nonnaturalistic means. All these plays try to escape from that "terrible fluidity of self-revelation" (to

27. The classic study of the Vice is Bernard Spivack, *Shakespeare and the Allegory of Evil* (New York, 1958).

28. T. S. Eliot, "Marlowe," in *Selected Essays* (New York, 1950), p. 104.

quote Henry James on first-person narration) afflicting a drama as absorbed in a single personality as *Tamburlaine*.

What did the Elizabethan audiences who made *Tamburlaine* such a success admire about the play? Here imitations of Marlowe's play offer us some clear answers to our questions. In every case, we find echoes of Tamburlaine's "high astounding terms." The sheer verbal pleasure of "Marlowe's mighty line" seems to have been as important to those who paid their way into the theaters as it was to the sophisticates who wrote the plays. As so often happens, we are reminded of the Elizabethan delight in rhetoric for its own sake, and of a prevailing sensitivity to language which allows an innovation in poetics to become itself an innovation in dramaturgy. In almost every case, the sons of *Tamburlaine* imitate features of its stage spectacle. *Wounds of Civil War* includes a conqueror who treads on his adversaries and makes captive kings draw his chariot; Alphonsus enters with a procession of crowns and tributary kings; *Alcazar* is filled with Moorish exotics and makes much of the death of multiple kings. Part of the pleasure of all these plays lies in the chance to glimpse the foreign and the strange. However anachronistic and ethnographically inaccurate costumes may have been on the Elizabethan stage, the sheer sartorial display of all these plays must have attracted crowds.

Of course, high astounding terms are best spoken by high astounding speakers. Another constant in most of the imitations is a hero or heroes asserting a power exceeding that of ordinary men. The sons of *Tamburlaine* all make clear that audiences wanted to see that hero on the stage. What the plays don't by any means make clear is that audiences admired the hero. *Tamburlaine* itself is perhaps at one extreme; Part One comes closer than any of its successors to presenting a hero who challenges Elizabethan orthodoxies and demands that audiences entertain the prospect that their conventional ideas are inadequate. *Locrine*, *Selimus*, and *A Looking-Glass for London* are at the other pole; these plays, in very different ways, congratulate their audiences on possessing moral standards superior to those guiding their principal characters. But the over-all pattern that emerges is one of ambivalence. The popular playwrights who imitated *Tamburlaine* seem to have been trying to please an audience which wanted to have it both ways. They wanted the thrill of seeing characters who outraged orthodox notions of social hierarchy and personal identity. They wanted to see

monarchs brutalized, virgins slain, states revolutionized, God himself
dared out of heaven. (I echo Robert Greene's famous comment from his
1588 work, *Perimedes the Blacksmith.* [29])

As well as showing the perennial pleasures of the unexpected, such
desires presumably reflected an awareness of the potential inadequacies of
current social, political, and religious orthodoxies as descriptions of the
state of affairs in London around 1590. A kingdom where men had in fact
risen from the middle classes to great titles and positions near the throne
clearly had the potential to admire as well as invent a Tamburlaine. But
perhaps more than thrills, audiences wanted reassurance. They wanted to
stare into the abyss, but only while roped together. However much
Marlowe may have intended to shock and transform his audience, that
audience seems to have found ways of relishing his language and stage
spectacle while clinging to comforting and conventional ideas. Popular
playwrights, as they assimilated Marlowe's influence, retained many
superficial features of his art while expanding and elaborating those elements implicit in his play which suggested negative judgments of his new
hero.

Faced with audience ambivalence, and perhaps with their own, it isn't
surprising that some playwrights turned to laughter. Laughter, as Freud
reminds us, is a fundamental human resource for dealing with mixed
emotions. Just as festive comedy moves "from release to clarification" (as
C. L. Barber has shown), so the mockery of the Tamburlainean impulse in
some of *Tamburlaine*'s weak sons gives an audience—indeed a culture—a
way of acknowledging the existence of innovative or subversive impulses
without being overwhelmed by them. [30] Similarly, the assimilation of
Tamburlaine to the vice figure in *The Jew of Malta* and *Richard III* represents not only an attempt at clarifying audience judgment, but even more
so a way of acknowledging the ambivalence of audience response. Like the
vice, the Jew and Richard are both the most appealing and entertaining
figures in their plays, and at the same time the representatives of behavior
and ideas the audience abhors and fears. As with the Vice, audience

29. Quoted from Tucker Brooke, "The Reputation of Christopher Marlowe," p. 351.
30. C. L. Barber, *Shakespeare's Festive Comedy* (Princeton, N.J., 1959).

laughter serves to acknowledge discomfort, and allows theatergoers to look on without feeling excessively tainted by subversive impulses.[31]

Finally, *Tamburlaine*'s weak sons offer a vivid example of the process by which genuine artistic innovation is assimilated into a literary and theatrical culture. Let us assume what I believe to be true, though unverifiable: that at least in Part One of *Tamburlaine* Marlowe's intentions were as subversive of ethical orthodoxies as they were innovative in verse and dramaturgy. One is struck by the way his imitators seized upon verbal and theatrical resources appropriate to dramatizing a new hero while ignoring or perhaps even failing to perceive that hero's ethical originality. Lodge, Greene, Peele, and their peers don't run from *Tamburlaine* in shock and horror or try to refute its overreaching claims. Instead, they do something much more insidious. They surround and absorb Marlowe's hero as an amoeba assimilates its prey. Or (to shift metaphors) they offer Marlowe's recipe the sincere flattery of imitation, but then season his ingredients to their own taste to such an extent that we can barely detect the original flavor. At least in this instance, the Elizabethan popular theater and its audience respond to potential challenge with a welcome that largely blunts its real thrust. This pattern, after all, is not unfamiliar in the history of the arts. Cubism turns to Mondrian, and Mondrian turns to wallpaper and kitchen floors. The fragments Eliot shores against his ruins in *The Waste Land* reappear as the glib intercutting of popular films and fiction. Austere and troubling esthetic and moral ideas are recycled into kitsch. This is not to speak bleakly about the afterlife of all artistic innovations, but instead to make a distinction between two kinds of influence. In the years following those I deal with in the restricted scope of this essay, finer artists than Lodge, Greene, and Peele begin to explore the consequences of *Tamburlaine*'s vision of the size and complexity of the secular human personality. *Coriolanus* and *Volpone* (to name two obvious examples) could not be the plays they are without the prior fact of Marlowe. But we cannot trace Shakespeare's and Jonson's responses to Marlowe's originality under the

31. See Robert Weimann, *Shakespeare and the Popular Tradition in the Theater: Studies in the Social Dimension of Dramatic Form and Function*, ed. Robert Schwartz (Baltimore, Md., 1978), pp. 157–160.

narrow definition of "imitation" which has concerned me here. Marlowe
speaks to Shakespeare and Jonson in a way that his immediate imitators
may have found inaudible or unacceptable. Before 1593, these immediate
imitators seem to have felt that the best way to capitalize on the success of
Tamburlaine was by mediating between that play and their audience's
perhaps uneasy, but fundamentally conservative tastes. Not only did
Lodge, Greene, Peele, and their peers "applaud the fortunes" of Marlowe's
heroic play by trying to emulate its popular and financial success, but they
invited their audience to applaud the fortunes of their stage heroes "as they
pleased"—that is, in a manner which tempered thrills with reassurances,
and allowed the pleasures of style without many dangers of substance.

Alice Arden's Crime

CATHERINE BELSEY

I

ON SUNDAY 15 February 1551 Alice Arden of Faversham in Kent procured and witnessed the murder of her husband. She and most of her accomplices were arrested, tried, and executed. The goods of the murderers, worth a total of £184. 10s. 4½d., and certain jewels, were forfeit to the Faversham treasury. The city of Canterbury was paid 44 shillings for executing George Bradshaw, who was also present at the murder, and for burning Alice Arden alive. [1] At a time when all the evidence suggests that crimes of violence were by no means uncommon, Alice Arden's crime was cited, presented and re-presented, problematized and reproblematized, during a period of at least eighty years after it was committed. Holinshed, pausing in his account of the events which constitute the main material of the *Chronicles of England, Scotland and Ireland* to give a detailed analysis of the murder, explains that the case transgresses the normal boundaries between public and private:

1. J. W. Ebsworth, ed., *The Roxburghe Ballads*, Vol. VIII, pt. 1 (Hertford, Eng., 1895), p. 48.

for the horribleness thereof, although otherwise it may seeme to be but a private matter, and therefore as it were impertinent to this historie, I have thought good to set it foorth somewhat at large.[2]

This "horribleness," which identifies Alice Arden's domestic crime as belonging to the public arena of history, is not, I want to argue, a matter of the physical details of the murder, or even of the degree of premeditation involved. On the contrary, the scandal lies in Alice Arden's challenge to the institution of marriage, itself publicly in crisis in the period. Marriage becomes in the sixteenth and seventeenth centuries the site of a paradoxical struggle to create a private realm and to take control of it in the interests of the public good. The crime coincides with the beginning of this contest. *Arden of Faversham*, which can probably be dated about 1590,[3] coincides with a major intensification of the debate about marriage, and permits its audience glimpses of what is at stake in the struggle.

II

There are a great many extant allusions to Alice Arden's crime.[4] It was recorded in the *Breviat Chronicle* for 1551, in the diary of Henry Machyn, a London merchant-tailor, and in Stow's *Annals of England* (1592, 1631) as well as in Holinshed's *Chronicles* (1577, 1587). Thomas Heywood gives it two lines in his 17-canto poem on the history of the world, *Troia Britannica* (1609), and John Taylor in *The Unnaturall Father* (1621, 1630) invokes it as an instance of God's vengeance on murderers. In addition to the play, which ran to four editions between 1592 and 1633,[5] "[The] complaint and lamentation of Mistresse Arden" was printed in ballad form, probably in 1633.

The official record of the murder was given in the Wardmote Book of Faversham, reprinted in Wine's Revels edition of the play, together with

2. Printed in M. L. Wine, ed., *The Tragedy of Master Arden of Faversham*, The Revels Plays (London, 1973), p. 148. I have silently modernized all Renaissance typography. All references to the play are to this edition.

3. Wine argues for a date between 1588 and 1591, *ibid.*, p. xlv.

4. For details see Wine, *Tragedy of Master Arden*, pp. xxxvii-xxxviii.

5. *Ibid.*, p. xix-xxi.

Holinshed's account and the ballad. According to the Wardmote Book, Arden was "heynously" and "shamefully" murdered, and the motive was Alice's intention to marry Mosby, a tailor whom she carnally kept in her own house and fed with delicate meats, with the full knowledge of her husband.[6] The value judgment established here is constant in all the accounts, and the word "shameful" defines the crime in the *Breviat Chronicle*,[7] in Holinshed,[8] on the title page of the first edition of the play, and again in the ballad.[9] What is contested in these re-presentations is not, on the whole, the morality of the murder, but its explanation, its meaning. Specific areas of the story are foregrounded or reduced, with the effect of modifying the crime's significance. The low social status of Mosby, and Arden's complaisance, for instance, both intensify the disruption of matrimonial conventions, and these elements are variously either accounted for or played down. Arden's role in the story differs considerably from one narrative to another. My concern is not with the truth of the murder, not with an attempt to penetrate beyond the records to an inaccessible "real event," not to offer an "authoritative" interpretation of Alice Arden's crime. Rather, I want to examine the implications of the constant efforts at redefinition.

In Holinshed's analysis Arden was a gentleman, a tall and comely person, and Mosby "a blacke swart man." According to the marginal gloss in the second edition of the *Chronicles*, Alice's irrational preference is an instance of the radical difference between love and lust,[10] and her flagrant defiance of the marriage bond accountable in terms of human villainy: "Thus this wicked woman, with hir complices, most shamefullie murdered hir owne husband, who most entirelie loved hir all his life time."[11] But running through Holinshed's narrative is another account of the murder not wholly consistent with this view of Arden as innocent victim, which emphasizes God's vengeance on his greed for property. In this account Arden's avarice, repeatedly referred to in the story, is finally

6. *Ibid.*, pp. 160–161.
7. *Ibid.*, p. xxxvii.
8. *Ibid.*, p. 155.
9. *Ibid.*, p. 169.
10. *Ibid.*, p. 148.
11. *Ibid.*, p. 155.

his undoing. His complaisance is a consequence of his covetousness: "bicause he would not offend hir, and so loose the benefit which he hoped to gaine at some of hir freends hands in bearing with hir lewdnesse, which he might have lost if he should have fallen out with hir: he was contented to winke at hir filthie disorder . . . "[12] After Arden's death, the field where the conspirators had placed his corpse miraculously showed the imprint of his body for two years afterward. This field was Arden's property, and in 1551 he had insisted that the St. Valentine's fair be held there, "so reaping all the gaines to himselfe, and bereaving the towne of that portion which was woont to come to the inhabitants." For this he was bitterly cursed by the people of Faversham.[13] The field itself had been "cruellie" and illegally wrested from the wife of Richard Read, a sailor, and she too had cursed him, "wishing manie a vengeance to light upon him, and that all the world might woonder on him. Which was thought then to come to passe, when he was thus murdered, and laie in that field from midnight till the morning" on the day of the fair.[14] Again the marginal gloss spells out the moral implications: "God heareth the teares of the oppressed and taketh vengeance: note an example in Arden."[15] The murder is thus part of the providential scheme.

These two versions of Arden—as loving husband and as rapacious land-lord—coexist equally uneasily in the play. Here the element of com-plaisance is much reduced: Arden has grounds for suspicion but not certainty. Mosby's baseness is a constant theme, and underlines Alice's irrationality. But what is new in the play is the parallel between Arden's dubious business deals and Alice's. A good part of the plot is taken up with Alice's negotiations with possible murderers. Michael is to carry out the crime in exchange for Susan Mosby. Clarke is to provide a poison, and subsequently a poisoned picture, in exchange for Susan Mosby. Greene gets £10 and a promise of £20 more, with land to follow, for his "plain dealing" in carrying out the murder (I, 517). Greene subcontracts the work to Black Will and Shakebag for £10. Finally, in desperation, Alice increases her offer to Black Will to £20, and £40 more when Arden is

12. *Ibid.*, p. 149.
13. *Ibid.*, p. 157.
14. *Ibid.*, p. 159.
15. *Ibid.*

dead. They leave triumphantly with their gold when the work is completed (XIV, 249). Mosby, too, is part of this world of economic individualism, and there are indications that his motive is not love of Alice so much as desire to come by Arden's money (e.g., VIII, 11–44). He quarrels with Alice in terms of "credit," "advantages," "Fortune," and "wealth" (VIII, 80–92). If the play has any explanation to offer of Alice Arden's crime it is social and economic rather than providential. The event is primarily an instance of the breakdown of order—the rape of women and property—which follows when the exchange of contracts in a market economy supplants old loyalties, old obligations, old hierarchies.

But there are elements of the play which this reading leaves out of account. Some of the dialogue between Alice and Mosby invites a response which contradicts the play's explicit project, defined on the title page, of showing "the great malice and dissimulation of a wicked woman, [and] the unsatiable desire of filthie lust." In these speeches it is marriage which is identified as an impediment to true love, and images familiar from the poetry of the period seem to offer the audience a position of some sympathy with Alice's repudiation of the marriage bond:

> ALICE
> Why should he thrust his sickle in our corn,
> Or what hath he to do with thee, my love,
> Or govern me that am to rule myself?
> Forsooth, for credit sake, I must leave thee!
> Nay, he must leave to live that we may love,
> May live, may love; for what is life but love?
> And love shall last as long as life remains,
> And life shall end before my love depart.
> MOSBY
> Why, what's love, without true constancy?
> Like to a pillar built of many stones,
> Yet neither with good mortar well compact
> Nor cement to fasten it in the joints
> But that it shakes with every blast of wind
> And, being touched, straight falls unto the earth
> And buries all his haughty pride in dust.
> No, let our love be rocks of adamant,
> Which time nor place nor tempest can asunder.
>
> (X.83–99)

The natural and elemental images and the biblical echoes momentarily ennoble Alice's defiance of patriarchy. Early in the play Clarke makes explicit this other face of the crime:

> Let it suffice I know you love him well
> And fain would have your husband made away,
> Wherein, trust me, you show a noble mind,
> That rather than you'll live with him you hate
> You'll venture life and die with him you love.
>
> (I.267–271)

In these instances the play presents Alice Arden's challenge to the institution of marriage as an act of heroism. Alice rejects the metaphysics of presence which guarantees the social enforcement of permanent monogamy, in favor of a free sexuality, unauthorized within the play as a whole, but glimpsed at isolated moments:

> Sweet Mosby is the man that hath my heart;
> And he usurps it, having nought but this,
> That I am tied to him by marriage.
> Love is a god, and marriage is but words;
> And therefore Mosby's title is the best.
> Tush! Whether it be or no, he shall be mine
> In spite of him, of Hymen, and of rites.
>
> (I.98–104)

The ballad, almost certainly derived from the play, redefines the problem yet again. For the first time the woman is the unequivocal subject of the narrative, in contrast to the play, where the title indicates that it is Arden's tragedy rather than Alice's. The ballad reduces the story to two main elements—Alice's love and the series of contracts for the murder. These negotiations are recounted in all their detail within a text of only 192 lines. Arden's rapacity is ignored, and Holinshed's "blacke swart" Mosby becomes a man of "sugred tongue, good shape, and lovely looke" (l. 11). The ballad is a record of contracts made and broken for love. There is no explicit doubt of Alice's wickedness: her "secret dealings" come to light and are duly punished by her death (l. 167). At the same time, a curious formulation, perhaps a slip of the pen, picks up something of the element of ambivalence in the play: "And then by Justice we were straight condemn'd, / Each of us came unto a shameless end . . . " (ll. 165–166).

"Shameless" here is unexpected—appropriate to their (impudent) behavior, perhaps, but not to their (disgraceful) execution. On a reading of the word in use during the fifteenth century, "shameless" could mean "free from disgrace" (OED, 3). Perhaps a parapraxis betrays the unconscious of the text, a world well lost for love, and Alice Arden heroic on the scaffold, exposing herself to death through death.

However that may be, these repeated reinterpretations of the events, reproblematizations of the murder, may be read as so many attempts to elicit a definitive meaning for Alice Arden's crime. In each case this definitive meaning remains elusive, in the sense that each text contains elements not accounted for in its over-all project. I want to argue that what is at stake in these contests for the meaning of the murder is marriage itself, but first I should like to draw attention to the prominence given to parallel cases in the period.

III

The existing historical evidence gives no reason to believe that there was a major outbreak of women murdering their husbands in the sixteenth century. [16] What it does suggest, however, is a widespread belief that they were likely to do so. The Essex county records for the Elizabethan period, for instance, reveal no convictions for this crime, but they list several cases of frightened husbands seeking the protection of the courts. In 1574 a Barnston man complained that his wife, "forgetting her duty and obedience as a wife, had sundry times maliciously attempted to bereave her husband of his life, so that he stand in great fear" both of her and of two men from Dunmow, her "adherents," who haunted his house at night. [17] In 1590 a man called Philpott complained that John Chandler, then living with his wife, had given his consent to Philpott's death, and Rowland

---

16. See, e.g., F. G. Emmison, *Elizabethan Life: Disorder* (Chelmsford, Eng., 1970); C. S. Weiner, "Sex Roles and Crime in Late Elizabethan Hertfordshire," *Journal of Social History*, VIII (1975), 38–60. Weiner gives no instances at all. Emmison lists 131 cases of murder brought before the Essex county courts in the Elizabethan period. In three of these (or possibly two, if the case of the Great Wakering woman mentioned on p. 149 is the same as the one listed on p. 150), women were charged with poisoning their husbands. In each case the woman was acquitted, which implies (since acquittals, except in cases of employers murdering their servants, are rare) that the evidence must have been very slender.

17. Emmison, *Elizabethan Life: Disorder*, p. 162.

Gryffyth deposed that he had been hired to carry out the murder. [18] The records of the ecclesiastical courts in the same county include two cases, both in 1597, of men who refused to live with their wives for fear that they would be murdered by them. [19]

When the crime was actually committed, it seems that notoriety instantly followed. In 1573 Anne Sanders (or Saunders) consented to the murder of her husband, a London merchant, by her lover, George Browne. The case rapidly became as widely known as the Arden murder. It was recorded by Arthur Golding in a pamphlet published in the same year and again in 1577; it was probably the subject of an anonymous pamphlet called "A Cruell murder donne in Kent" published in 1577;[20] the story was told by Holinshed and Stow again; and it was recounted by Antony Munday in *A View of Sundry Examples* (1580). Like the Arden case, the Sanders murder elicited a play, *A Warning for Fair Women* (probably ca. 1590) and a ballad, "The wofull lamentacion of mrs. Anne Saunders, which she wrote with her own hand, being prisoner in newgate, Justly condemned to death."[21] In the ballad Anne Sanders begs all women to be warned by her example; the play, unable to account in any other terms for so scandalous a crime, shows Anne, in an allegorical dumb show instigated by the Furies, suddenly torn between chastity and lust, then pledging herself to Browne in a ceremony which evokes the "sacrament prophane in mistery of wine" between Paridell and the adulterous Hellenore. [22]

In 1591 Mistress Page of Plymouth was executed with her lover and two other men for the murder of her husband. A ballad by Thomas Deloney

18. *Ibid.*, p. 199.

19. F. G. Emmison, *Elizabethan Life: Morals and the Church Courts* (Chelmsford, Eng., 1973), p. 162. Surprisingly, there were only two instances of women protesting that they were similarly frightened of their husbands, and one of these had already been subject to marital violence.

20. Joseph H. Marshburn, "*A Cruell Murder Done in Kent* and Its Literary Manifestations," *SP*, XLVI (1949), 131–140.

21. Hyder Rollins, ed., *Old English Ballands 1553–1625* (Cambridge, Eng., 1920), pp. 340–348.

22. Charles Dale Cannon, ed., *A Warning for Fair Women* (The Hague, 1975), ll. 803–815 s.d. Cf. *The Faerie Queene*, III.ix.30. It is worth noting that, according to Golding's account, Anne Drurie, Browne's accomplice, must have been suspected of poisoning her own husband, since she denied the allegation on the scaffold (see Cannon, p. 224).

appeared at once, recording "The Lamentation of Mr Pages Wife of Plimouth, who, being forc'd to wed him, consented to his Murder, for the love of G. Strangwidge." [23] Here the ambivalences implicit in the Arden narratives are foregrounded to produce a radical contradiction between sympathy and condemnation. The ballad gives a graphic account of the miseries of enforced marriage:

> My closen eies could not his sight abide;
> My tender youth did lothe his aged side:
> Scant could I taste the meate whereon he fed;
> My legges did lothe to lodge within his bed.
>
> (ll. 29–32)

At the same time,

> Methinkes the heavens crie vengeance for my fact,
> Methinkes the world condemns my monstrous act,
> Methinkes within my conscience tells me true,
> That for that deede hell fier is my due.
>
> (ll. 41–44)

In the circumstances it is particularly regrettable that *Page of Plymouth* by Jonson and Dekker, performed by the Admiral's Men in 1599, is now lost, as is *The History of Friar Francis*, produced, according to Henslowe's diary, in 1593/4, though not necessarily for the first time. [24] According to Heywood in 1612, when *The History of Friar Francis* was performed at King's Lynn it had the gratifying effect of inducing an apparently respectable woman in the audience to confess that seven years before she had poisoned her husband for love of a gentleman in precisely the same way as the protagonist of the play. Heywood is here writing in defense of the moral efficacy of stage plays, and it is worth noting that of the three instances he cites of the providential operation of the drama, two concern women murdering their husbands. In the second case it was the method of murder shown on the stage which caused "a woman of great gravity" to

---

23. F. O. Mann, ed., *The Works of Thomas Deloney* (Oxford, 1912), pp. 482–485. I am grateful to Margot Heinemann for drawing my attention to this ballad.

24. H. H. Adams, *English Domestic or Homiletic Tragedy, 1575–1642* (New York, 1943), pp. 193–194.

shriek loudly, and after several days of torment to confess that she had
driven a nail into the temples of her husband twelve years before. She was
duly tried, condemned, and burned. [25]

IV

According to John Taylor, writing in 1621, "*Arden of Feversham*, and
Page of Plimmouth, both their Murders are fresh in memory, and the fearfull
ends of their Wives and their Ayders in those bloudy actions will never be
forgotten." [26] The prominence allotted to these cases, the suspicion which
seems to have been prevalent in Essex in the period, and Heywood's
instances of the salutory effects of stage plays in bringing such crimes to
light, all point to a preoccupation with the possibility of women murdering their husbands which is not accounted for in any of the individual texts
I have discussed. In *Arden of Faversham* Alice Arden defines her problem
specifically in terms of the institutional regulation of sexuality by marriage:

> nothing could enforce me to the deed
> But Mosby's love. Might I without control
> Enjoy thee still, then Arden should not die;
> But, seeing I cannot, therefore let him die.
>
> (I. 273–276)

It is a contest for the control of sexuality in the period which throws
marriage into crisis and precipitates the instability of the institution which
is evident in crimes like Alice Arden's.

The history of marriage in the Middle Ages is a history of an effort to
regulate sexuality by confining it within a framework of permanent
monogamy. From the twelfth century onward the Church gradually
extended its control over marriage, making efforts to contain instances of
divorce and bigamy by urging with increasing insistence the public
solemnization of matrimony after due reading of the banns on consecutive
Sundays. [27] Since at the same time private marriage in the presence of

25. Thomas Heywood, *An Apology for Actors* (London, 1612), sig. G 1^v–2^v.
26. John Taylor, *Works* (London, 1630), p. 140.
27. Michael M. Sheehan, "The Formation and Stability of Marriage in Fourteenth-
Century England: Evidence of an Ely Register," *MS*, XXXIII (1971), 228–263; G. E.
Howard, *A History of Matrimonial Institutions*, 3 vols. (Chicago, 1904), I, 361.

witnesses was held to be valid and binding,[28] it was easy enough to produce just cause or impediment after the event. However, the banns were no guarantee against bigamy, since they were easily evaded by those who had anything to fear. In consequence, the process of taking control was slow and laborious, so that in 1540 it was still the case that bigamy was widespread, and that "no mariage coulde be so surely knytt and bounden but it shulde lye in either of the parties power and arbitre . . . to prove a precontracte a kynnerede an alliance or a carnall knowledge to defeate the same . . . "[29] Many of the cases which came before the ecclesiastical courts depended on such ingenuities, but Michael M. Sheehan finds, after investigating the late fourteenth-century register of the consistory court of the Bishop of Ely, that there at least "the court was primarily a body for the proof and defence of marriage rather than an instrument of easy annulment."[30] The commitment of the court to the stability of marriage above all other considerations may be illustrated by one of the cases Sheehan cites. The marriage between John Poynant and Joan Swan was annulled on the grounds of the husband's impotence. Joan married again, and John took up with Isabel Pybbel. When Isabel became pregnant John prepared to marry her, but the court investigated the matter and found that, since John was apparently not impotent after all, his marriage to Joan Swan should be restored. John protested, claiming affinity within the forbidden degrees between Joan and Isabel, but the court was not impressed, and the original marriage was eventually reinstated.[31]

The Anglican church took over on behalf of the sovereign this effort to control the institution of marriage through the ecclesiastical courts, but not without a struggle which generated a high degree of uncertainty about the nature and permanence of marriage. The introduction of registers of births, marriages, and deaths in 1538 was a move toward population control, but at the same time the Reformation introduced a liberalization

28. Lawrence Stone, *The Family, Sex and Marriage in England, 1500–1800* (London, 1977), p. 31; Howard, *Matrimonal Institutions*, I, 336 ff. Sheehan, "Formation and Stability of Marriage," p. 253.

29. Preamble to 32 Hen. VIII, ca. 38, cited by C. L. Powell, *English Domestic Relations 1487–1653* (New York, 1917), p. 62.

30. Sheehan, "Formation and Stability of Marriage," p. 263.

31. *Ibid.*, p. 261.

of marriage which found a focus in a debate about divorce that remained legally unresolved, apart from a brief interlude during the Commonwealth, until the nineteenth century. [32]

The Catholic church had permitted separation *a mensa et thoro* (from bed and board) for adultery, cruelty, apostasy, or heresy, and divorce *a vinculo matrimonii* on the basis either of impotence or of a prior impediment to valid marriage on grounds of consanguinity, affinity, or precontract. The act of 1540 attempted to abolish precontract as grounds for divorce, but had no practical effect. Meanwhile, most of the newly Protestant states had introduced divorce with remarriage for the innocent party in cases of adultery and desertion. Similar legislation was urged in England, and was incorporated in the *Reformatio Legum Ecclesiasticarum* of 1552. This was defeated in the House of Commons, but the divorce provision had been sanctioned independently, when a commission under Cranmer had approved the remarriage of the divorced Northampton in 1548, a decision that was confirmed by Parliament in 1552. In practice, however, the ecclesiastical courts largely refused to put the law into operation, and in consequence the position of marriage remained extremely confused and controversial for the rest of the century. The divorce debate reached a high point in the 1590s, with the result that in the Canons of 1597 Convocation declared all remarriage after divorce illegal. These were not sanctioned by Elizabeth, but the principle was reiterated in the Canons of 1604 which were approved by James I, though without silencing the controversy. [33]

The importance of the divorce debate lies in its polarization of conflicting definitions of marriage. Broadly, the Anglican position was that marriage was indissoluble, that couples were joined by God for the avoidance of fornication and the procreation of children, and that there was no remedy but patience for marital disharmony and discontent. The position of the radical Protestants is familiar from Milton's divorce tracts, which carry the Puritan arguments to their logical climax. Equally

32. The Cromwellian Marriage Act of 1653 placed the whole matter in the hands of the civil magistrates but gave no indication of the possible grounds for divorce. This legislation was not re-enacted after the Restoration (Powell, *English Domestic Relations*, pp. 99–100).

33. For an account of the legal position see Howard, *History of Matrimonial Institutions*, II, 76–85; Stone, *Family, Sex and Marriage*, pp. 37–41; Powell, *English Domestic Relations*, pp. 61–100; Ernest Sirluck, ed., *The Complete Prose Works of John Milton* (London, 1959), II, 145–146.

broadly, the Puritans held that marriage was a civil covenant, a thing indifferent to salvation, that it depended on consent, and that where this was lacking the couple could not be said to be joined by God, and could therefore justly be put asunder. The Reformers varied in the causes of divorce they were prepared to admit. Only Milton gave real prominence to discord as a cause, while Henry Smith, at the other extreme though still within the pro-divorce lobby, recognized divorce for adultery but vigorously repudiated incompatibility as grounds:

If they might bee separated for discorde, some would make a commoditie of strife; but now they are not best to be contentious, for this law will hold their noses together, till wearines make them leave struggling, like two spaniels which are coupled in a chaine, at last they learne to goe together, because they may not goe asunder. [34]

Not all the Reformers were so optimistic about the couple learning to go together. According to Martin Bucer, whose *De Regno Christi* was addressed to Edward VI when the author was Professor of Divinity at Cambridge, the Church's refusal to permit divorce compelled it to tolerate "whordoms and adulteries, and worse things then these," "throwing men headlong into these evils." [35] "Neither," he argued, "can God approve that to the violation of this holy league (which is violated as soon as true affection ceases and is lost,) should be added murder . . . " [36] John Rainolds, writing in 1597, insists that if divorce is forbidden crimes like Alice Arden's are bound to follow: a husband may be forced to live in permanent suspicion, or worse—

And how can he choose but live still in feare & anguish of minde, least shee add drunckennesse to thirst, & murder to adultery: I meane least she serve him as *Clytemnestra* did *Agamemnon*, *Livia* did *Drusus* as Mrs. *Arden* did her husband? [37]

V

There is some evidence for the bitterness of the struggle. John Dove, who preached a sermon against divorce in 1601, records that many people found his view offensive, "as unseasonable for the time, and unpleasing to

---

34. Henry Smith, *A Preparative to Marriage* (London, 1591), p. 108.

35. Milton's translation, *Complete Prose Works*, ed. Sirluck, II, 447.

36. *Ibid.*, p. 470.

37. John Rainolds, *A Defence of the Judgment of the Reformed Churches* (London, 1609), p. 88.

the auditory." [38] Rainolds wrote his plea for divorce in 1597, but explains in a letter to Pye published in 1606 that the Archbishop of Canterbury at that time "thought it not meete to be printed: as containing dangerous doctrine." He urges Pye to cut out any references to him (Rainolds) in his own argument if he wants to get into print, especially since the Canons of 1604 have hardened the orthodox line. [39] Rainolds's own *Defence of the Judgment of the Reformed Churches* was published in 1609. The archbishop's censorship seems to have been evenhanded, since at about the same time he also discouraged Edmund Bunny from publishing his case against divorce—in order to avoid controversy, on the grounds that he had already "staied" one of the contrary persuasion. [40] Bunny's book appeared in 1610. Later William Whately argued for divorce on grounds of desertion as well as adultery in books published in 1617 and 1624. Whately was brought before the Court of High Commission, and promptly reverted to the Anglican doctrine of the indissolubility of marriage. [41]

Even between the radicals there was considerable sectarianism on this issue. Milton, of course, encountered a good deal of controversy, and was denounced by his fellow Puritans for his divorce pamphlets. [42] And at the very beginning of the debate an interesting piece of sleight of hand shows how delicate the whole issue must have been. In 1541 Miles Coverdale's translation of Bullinger's treatise on marriage was published as *The Christen State of Matrimonye*. Primarily a plea for marriage as a union of minds, and a corresponding repudiation of the Catholic doctrine of celibacy as a way of perfection, this included a chapter recommending divorce not only for adultery but also for "lyke and greater occasions." [43] *The Christen State of Matrimonye* was remarkably popular. Three new editions appeared within five years, and two more before the end of the century. Meanwhile, in 1542, there appeared *The Golden Boke of christen matrimonye* "newly set forth

38. John Dove, *Of Divorcement* (London, 1601), Preface.

39. Reproduced in John Howson, *Uxore dismissa propter Fornicationem aliam non licet superinducere* (Oxford, 1606).

40. Edmund Bunny, *Of Divorce for Adulterie and Marrying againe* (Oxford, 1610), Advertisement to the Reader.

41. William and Malleville Haller, "The Puritan Art of Love," *HLQ*, V (1941–1942), 235–272, 267–268.

42. Christopher Hill, *Milton and the English Revolution* (London, 1977), pp. 131–132.

43. H. Bullinger, *The Christen State of Matrimonye* (London, 1541), fol. lxxvii.

in English by Theodore Basille." "Theodore Basille" was Thomas Becon, and *The Golden Boke* was acutally Coverdale's translation of Bullinger again, with four chapters silently omitted, including the one on divorce.

The contest for the meaning of marriage cannot be isolated from the political struggles which characterize the century between the Reformation and the English revolution. Both sides make explicit the parallel between the family and the state, marriage and the monarchy. "A householde is as it were a little common-wealth;"[44] "A Familie, is a naturall and simple Society of certaine persons, having mutual relationship one to another, under the private government of one."[45] At one extreme Milton argues for liberty within marriage as directly analogous to liberty in the commonwealth:

He who marries, intends as little to conspire his own ruine, as he that swears Allegiance: and as a whole people is in proportion to an ill Government, so is one man to an ill mariage. If they against any authority, Covnant, or Statute, may by the soveraign edict of charity, save not only their lives, but honest liberties from unworthy bondage, as well may he against any private Covnant, which hee never enter'd to his mischief, redeem himself from unsupportable disturbances to honest peace, and just contentment.[46]

And if this position was not made explicit in the radical treatises before 1642, nonetheless it was identified by Anglican orthodoxy as implicit in the Puritan arguments. According to Bunny, divorce can lead only to "disorder."[47] Marriage cannot be dissolved at will any more than can the bond between master and servant, parent and child, "the Prince and the Subject." And for this reason, "the more heed should bee taken, that no such gap should be opened to any, as wherby the looser sort, when they should get their desire in this, should cast about to obtaine the like in

44. Robert Cleaver and John Dod, *A Godlie Forme of Householde Government* (London, 1612), p. 13. The first edition of this popular work appeared in 1598. Cf. William Gouge, *Of Domesticall Duties* (1622), pp. 16–17, cited by Haller, "Puritan Art of Love," p. 246.

45. William Perkins, *Christian Oeconomie, Works* (Cambridge, Eng., 1618), III, 669–700. *Christian Oeconomie* was written in Latin in 1590 and translated by Thomas Pickering in 1609.

46. Sirluck, *Complete Prose Works of Milton*, II, 229.

47. Bunny, *Of Divorce*, p. 161.

other things also of greater consequence."[48] Dove, whose name entirely belies his political position, argues strenuously that,

As when a servant runneth from his M. the chaine of bondage doth pursue him, and bring him back againe to his maister, so when a woman leaveth her husband, the lawe of Matrimony is as a chaine to draw her back againe to her husband . . .[49]

The libertines who believe in divorce pervert the scriptures for their own licentious ends, "Even as others will proove rebellion and high treason out of the scriptures, that the people are above their King."[50] The parallel between domestic patriarchy and authoritarian monarchy is a commonplace of the seventeenth century, and reaches its most notorious formulation, of course, in Robert Filmer's *Patriarcha*, written during the 1640s.[51]

Alice Arden, held in the chain of bondage which is marriage, in a period when liberty is glimpsed but not authorized, is caught up in a struggle larger than her chroniclers recognize. But it may be the political significance of Arden's assassination which causes Holinshed to identify Alice Arden's crime as marking the border between private and public, pamphlet and history.

VI

There is an indication in *Arden of Faversham* that in opting for Mosby in place of Arden, a freely chosen sexuality based on concord in place of the constraints of the institution of permanent marriage, Alice Arden may be committing herself to a form of power more deadly still, and less visible. Mosby's individualism is precisely that:

> Yet Mistress Arden lives; but she's myself,
> And holy church rites makes us two but one.
> But what for that I may not trust you, Alice?
> You have supplanted Arden for my sake
> And will extirpen me to plant another.

48. *Ibid.*, p. 52.
49. Dove, *Of Divorcement*, p. 33.
50. *Ibid.*, p. 51.
51. Gordon J. Schochet, *Patriarchalism in Political Thought* (New York, 1975).

> 'Tis fearful sleeping in a serpent's bed,
> And I will cleanly rid my hands of her.
> But here she comes, and I must flatter her . . .
>
> (VIII.37–44)

The episode could be read as an allegory of the transition to the affective nuclear family, itself a mechanism of regulation more far-reaching but less visible than the repressive ecclesiastical courts. Arden's absolute rights over Alice are clear, and his threats are directed not against his wife but against the man who means to rob him of her, for which he

> Shall on the bed which he thinks to defile
> See his dissevered joints and sinews torn
> Whilst on the planchers pants his weary body,
> Smeared in the channels of his lustful blood.
>
> (I. 40–43)

This overt power and violence give way in Mosby's version of marriage to distrust and surveillance veiled by flattery; in an individualist society of "equals" authoritarian modes of control are replaced by reciprocal fear between partners within the social body. Further, flattery and death are the metaphorical destiny of the wife in the new family. Her standing improves (though always in subjection to her husband) but at the cost of new and more insidious forms of control.

Puritan marriage, founded on consent, is "appointed by God himselfe, to be the fountaine and seminary of all other sorts and kinds of life, in the Common-wealth and in the Church."[52] To this end the family becomes quite explicitly an ideological apparatus, "a schoole wherein the first principles and grounds of government and subjection are learned: whereby men are fitted to greater matters in Church or Common-wealth."[53] In Puritan definitions of marriage and the family as "the Fountain and Seminary of good subjects,"[54] it is made very clear that "the holy and righteous government thereof, is a direct meane for the good ordering both of Church and Commonwealth; yea that the Lawes thereof beeing

52. Perkins, *Christian Oeconomie*, p. 671.
53. Gouge, *Of Domesticall Duties;* Haller, "Puritan Art of Love," p. 246.
54. Sirluck, *Complete Prose Works of Milton*, II, 447.

rightly informed, and religiously observed, are availeable to prepare and dispose men to the keeping of order in other governments."[55] To ensure that the family becomes an adequate model and source of good government, the treatises recommend family prayers, grace before meals, keeping the sabbath, the education of the children and the servants, and the inculcation of the fundamental principles of law and order. The family, separated from the public realm of politics, nonetheless becomes a microcosm of it and, by practice and by precept, a training ground for the ready acceptance of the power relations established in the social body:

For this first Societie is as it were the Schoole, wherein are taught and learned the principles of authoritie and subjection. And looke as the superior that faileth in his charge, will proove uncapable of publike imployment, so the inferiour, who is not framed to a course of Oeconomicall subjection, wil hardly undergoe the yoake of Civill obedience.[56]

The "liberalism" of the Reformers implies a constant scrutiny of marriage for "fitnes of mind and disposition,"[57] since harmony and concord are the precondition of a realm of hearth and home regulated from within. Vigilantly protected from sedition, and isolated from public and political affairs, the family is held in place in the social body as a model of the proper distribution of authority and submission, and thus the fountain and seminary of good subjects.

Read as a political event, Alice Arden's crime was a defiance of absolutism and, in common with the constant reproblematization of such crimes in the period, as well as the great numbers of "divorces" established in the sixteenth century without recourse to the civil or ecclesiastical authorities,[58] it constitutes evidence of the instability of central control at the time. Within a century of Arden's death the absolute power was to have been supplanted and Charles I executed in the name of the liberty of the people of England. The concomitant of this liberty was the construction of the affective nuclear family as an invisible mechanism of correction and control. The chain of bondage had given way to a net of power.

55. Pickering, in Perkins, *Christian Oeconomie*, Epistle Dedicatory.
56. *Ibid.*
57. Sirluck, *Complete Prose Works of Milton*, II, 605.
58. Powell, *English Domestic Relations*, pp. 61–62, 69–70.

VII

The century following Alice Arden's crime was one of crisis—economic, ideological, and political. With hindsight it is possible to interpret many of the events of this period as elements in the social upheaval which found a focus in the civil war of the 1640s. On this reading of the period, the institution most evidently in crisis was the monarchy, but it is also apparent that challenges to authority and authoritarianism were delivered in a number of spheres, many of them more obviously remote from the institution of monarchy than the more explicitly analogous institution of the family. Clearly, such a reading of the history of this period, available to us retrospectively, was only partly accessible in the period itself, and it is this which accounts for the repeated attempts to define and redefine Alice Arden's crime, and which explains why it was so important and so impossible to furnish it with a final meaning. The assassination of Arden is never justified, but it is variously identified as a part of God's providential plan, as a tragedy, as the effect of social and economic change, or as an act of unauthorized heroism, a noble transgression of an absolute law. The re-presentations of the crime are (sometimes contradictory, never neutral) contributions to a discursive struggle for the meaning of resistance to absolutism. *Arden of Faversham* is one of the documents in this struggle, perhaps a relatively complex analysis, but by no means an isolated instance of the attempt to make sense of insurrection.

Meanwhile, the divorce debate, reaching a crisis in the decade which also produced three plays on the theme I have discussed, in the final years of Elizabeth's apparently successful efforts to hold at bay the pressures for social change, is the site of a discursive contest between distinct modes of social control. Its relevance to my argument is not simply that it provides a context for our understanding of the plays, but that it enables us to perceive more sharply what is at stake in this contest. Offering a promise of freedom from the "chain" (the recurring metaphor for authoritarianism) of marriage, the radical position on divorce leads in reality to a new mode of control, no longer centralized and overt, but internalized and invisible. The new family of the seventeenth century, still under "the government of one," remains a place in which power is exercised privately in the interests of public order. Alice Arden's bid for freedom, as the play implies, would have led, had it succeeded, to a new form of subjection, both for the woman within the family and for the family within the state. No text of the 1590s could formulate this point in these terms. Indeed, the explicit identification of the family as a mechanism of social control probably has its tentative beginnings in the nineteenth century. Nonetheless, Mosby's threat that he will subject Alice to surveillance, flattery, and death indicates a glimpse in this text of an issue which is more complex than the simple opposition between authority and freedom, control and consent.

Modern marriage, modern domestic patriarchy, and the modern family as an ideological apparatus were produced in the struggles, dispersed across a range of institutions and practices, of the sixteenth and seventeenth centuries. In this sense the discursive history of Alice Arden's crime is a significant part of the history of the present.

Drama and Society in the Age of Jonson: *An Alternative View*

DON E. WAYNE

M Y TITLE REFERS, of course, to L. C. Knights's book, first published in 1937.[1] It is hardly possible to diverge from Knights's views without acknowledging the extent to which one depends on them. His book remains one of a small handful of significant works in English concerned with the sociology of literature. It is regarded, rightfully, as a classic, and its approach to the social aspects of Jacobean drama has become canonical. But this approach must also be recognized as the product of an earlier moment in the history of thought dealing with the relationship between culture and society. Given recent developments in social theory, in the study of ideology, and in the sociology of knowledge, we need to revaluate the central thesis of Knights's book and the kind of criticism practiced there. The essay that follows is partly concerned with such a reassessment. In the main, however, it is an attempt to redefine the relationship between Jonsonian drama and its sociohistorical context.

Knights acknowledges only one way in which drama and society are related in the age of Jonson; that is, the drama is said to call upon religious

---

1. L. C. Knights, *Drama and Society in the Age of Jonson* (London, 1937).

and popular tradition to criticize bourgeois acquisitiveness and individualism. Indicative of this basic strategy are the titles of his focal chapters on
Jonson's plays: "Tradition and Ben Jonson," and "Jonson and the Anti-
Acquisitive Attitude." In this conception, the Jacobean theater is represented as a place where author and audience are joined in the communal
celebration of a traditional code of behavior and in the censure of those who
violate the code. The formula works well enough in the case of Jonson's
best-known play, *Volpone*. But elsewhere, the relationship between author
and audience is more problematic.

It is significant that the only major play of Jonson's omitted from
Knights's discussion is *Bartholomew Fair*, presumably because of its more
ambiguous treatment of the attitudes and behavior satirized in *Volpone* and
other plays. In a later essay, Knights relegates *Bartholomew Fair* to "the
category of stage entertainments: in them the fun is divorced from any rich
significance . . ." [2] Such a judgment is difficult to comprehend in the
light of more recent studies which have shown this to be among the most
intricate and ironic of Jonson's plays. [3] The moral and aesthetic criteria
that govern Knights's criticism prevent him from perceiving this irony,
and, consequently, from acknowledging the dramatic richness and power
of *Bartholomew Fair*. What makes this lapse all the more serious in my
view is that the source of irony in the play is fundamentally social and
ideological. I shall consider the ideological ambiguity of the play in some
detail later. For the moment, it is sufficient to say that in *Bartholomew Fair*
there is an unmistakable tension between, on the one hand, the traditional
moral doctrine of social obligation according to status, and, on the other,
the more modern principles of rational self-interest and voluntary contractual obligation. [4] The fact that Knights did not recognize such conflict in

2. "Ben Jonson, Dramatist," in *The Age of Shakespeare*, Vol. 2 of *The Pelican Guide to
English Literature*, ed. Boris Ford, rev. ed. (Hardmondsworth, Eng., 1969), p. 314.

3. See, e.g., Jonas A. Barish, *Ben Jonson and the Language of Prose Comedy* (Cambridge,
Mass., 1960), pp. 187–239; Jackson I. Cope, "*Bartholomew Fair* as Blasphemy," *RenD*,
VIII (1965), 127–152; Ian Donaldson, *The World Upside-Down* (Oxford, 1970), pp. 46–77;
Alvin B. Kernan, "Alchemy and Acting: The Major Plays of Ben Jonson," and George A.
E. Parfitt, "Virtue and Pessimism in Three Plays by Ben Jonson," both in *SLitI*, VI, no. 1
(1973), 1–22, 23–40.

4. The distinction between *status* and *contract* societies is generally attributed to the
nineteenth-century legal historian Sir Henry Sumner Maine; see his *Ancient Law*, 8th ed.
(London, 1880), pp. 168–170. While Maine's usage has been effectively repudiated

the play is symptomatic of the limitations of the social theory on which his criticism was founded.

It would be difficult to argue with Knights's central tenet that Jonson's plays exhibit an unremitting critique of acquisitiveness. The deformities of personality that drive Jonson's characters to seek power and self-aggrand-izement in one form or another are ultimately linked to the lust for gold, a disease that is seen to threaten the entire body politic. The "humors" doctrine of characterization is rooted in a tradition of moral philosophy and in Galen's physiology. But it also amounts to a rudimentary social psychology, a technical apparatus for diagnosing the changes that affected English society in the Renaissance; and as such it involves an anticipatory awareness of the phenomenon of alienation in both the Marxian and exis-tentialist senses of the term. Already at a very early stage of capitalist development in England, Jonson recognizes intuitively that the disloca-tion and division of the human subject (the necessary condition of subjec-tivity in the modern sense) are functionally related to historical disjunctions in the social organization of reality. Nor is he alone in this. The literature of the age is filled with a sense of the relationship between social fragmentation and psychological disorder. *King Lear* is the great mythopoeic embodiment of this principle. But in the case of other writers, who lack Shakespeare's "negative capability," the problem is articulated with a deep sense of irony born of the writers' self-conscious anxiety concerning their own place in society. Even the most outspoken critics of the age, who decry the breakdown of hierarchy, who moan the loss of an organic sense of unity and coherence, and who rail against individualism, subjectivism, and acquisitiveness, seem, as Paul Delany puts it, "to oppose in others tendencies which they sensed in themselves." [5]

One reason for this ironic self-awareness is that there is a definite relationship between what these writers criticize and the power they possess to make such criticism. This is an aspect of the literature of the age

---

because of its normative and evolutionist assumptions, the terms continue to be used descriptively in the field of jurisprudence and by social and intellectual historians. See, e.g., Christopher Hill, *Society and Puritanism in Pre-Revolutionary England* (London, 1964), p. 491; the distinction is also implicit in the models of society employed by C. B. Macpherson, *The Political Theory of Possessive Individualism, Hobbes to Locke* (Oxford, 1964), pp. 46–70.

5. Paul Delany, *British Autobiography in the Seventeenth Century* (London, 1969), p. 15.

that Knights tends to ignore. So, while he views Jonson as a social critic, he overlooks the ways in which Jonson is himself implicated in what he criticizes. My point is that the "attitude" of the Jacobean playwrights, Jonson pre-eminently, is far more complex than the phrase "anti-acquisitive" would suggest. While they may be satirizing the acquisitiveness associated with an incipient mercantile capitalism, the dramatists are themselves caught in something of a double bind concerning the place of their own work in this new economic, political, and social context.

The drama of the early seventeenth century does indeed reflect a prevailing sense of social and psychological disorder. These concerns can be related to socioeconomic developments that were transforming England into what C. B. Macpherson calls a "possessive market society," [6] and to the undermining in the Reformation of a universal doctrinal basis for moral judgment and behavior. But the literature of the period also reveals another aspect of the breakdown of feudalism and of the traditional doctrines and behavior patterns associated with the old order. Literature is now becoming a vehicle of the historical individuation of perception and experience that enabled the independence of mind we identify as a characteristic of the modern. At this time we see the first extensive evidence of a pluralization of roles and ideologies in developing Western European societies. In fiction, this tendency is manifested by the emergence of individualized characterization, by a corresponding plurality of authorial voices, personae, and styles, and by an increasing diversification of the social function of literature. Writers and their audiences may still be constrained by institutionalized relationships, but they are also beginning to play a relatively more active and independent role in the historical processes through which social institutions are both sustained and transformed.

Or, at least, they are beginning to imagine themselves as having a more independent and important role. In English literature we see this perhaps as early as Chaucer's *Canterbury Tales* where, for example, in the sequences concerning the Wife of Bath, the Pardoner, and Chaucer himself, the power of storytelling and the power of judgment vested in the audience of pilgrims, and, implicitly, in the reader, are thematized in a way that

6. Macpherson, *Political Theory of Possessive Individualism*, pp. 48, 61–62, 301 n.

makes this collection of tales more complex than its predecessors in the literary tradition. But it is in the Renaissance that this tendency toward individuation, self-assertion, and, at the same time, what has been described as a historical "splitting of the subject" [7] becomes more pronounced. The increasing complexity of social relations in the sixteenth and seventeenth centuries contributed to the developing complexity and diversity of literary discourse, first in the poetry written by Elizabeth's courtiers and, eventually, in the drama produced for a larger, more heterogeneous audience. What follows is an attempt to outline the particular form that such development takes in the work of Ben Jonson. I claim that after his early theatrical triumphs, culminating in *Volpone* (1606), Jonson begins to show signs of a disturbed awareness that his own identity as poet and playwright—and therefore his personal transcendence of the still rigid social hierarchy in which he lived and wrote—depended on the same emerging structure of social relationships that he satirized in his plays.

There is an interesting tension in Jonson's work between, on the one hand, the designation of rampant individualism as the origin of social disorder in Jacobean England, and, on the other, the poet's constant

7. I have deliberately avoided the more familiar phrase "dissociation of sensibility," coined by T. S. Eliot in his widely reprinted "The Metaphysical Poets" (1921) and employed by Knights in "Bacon and the Seventeenth-Century Dissociation of Sensibility," in *Explorations* (1943; rpt. New York, 1964), pp. 108–128, because Eliot's usage is too restrictive historically and is associated with doctrines concerning poetry that are notoriously problematic. The phrase "splitting of the subject," derived from Lacan's interpretation of Freud, occurs in a discussion of the multiple "voices" of the literary text by Guy Rosolato, "The Voice and the Literary Myth," in *The Languages of Criticism and the Sciences of Man*, ed. Richard Macksey and Eugenio Donato (Baltimore, 1970), p. 202. Rosolato's essay has a double impact that is typically Lacanian, i.e., striking speculative insight and maddeningly elliptical argumentation. There is, however, a historical component to his idea that makes it particularly relevant here (pp. 207–208). Another model of such a split in the subject of discourse during the later Middle Ages and the Renaissance—one that is both empirically and dialectically grounded in the idea of language as mediated by social *praxis*—is the "dialogic" or "polyphonic" conception that underlies Mikhail Bakhtin's *Rabelais and His World*, trans. Hélène Iswolsky (Cambridge, Mass., 1968). Bakhtin's study, with its emphasis on the pluralistic discourse of marketplace and carnival in opposition to an official language and culture, is of considerable relevance for an understanding of Jonson's comedies, especially *Bartholomew Fair*.

assertion of his own individuality and independence. One of the more disturbing and strikingly modern aspects of Jonson's plays is the way they point up the dilemma of attempting to distinguish between independence and fragmentation, between freedom and license. This tension is manifested in at least two ways. It appears, first, as an ambiguity in the playwright's relation to the individuals and the society he portrays. As Jonas A. Barish has noted, Jonson seems uncomfortably aware at times of a parallel between the social climbing of the satirized characters in his plays and his own aspirations to a position of status. [8] But there is yet another level at which such tension is evident; this concerns the poet's relation to his audience.

The audacious publication, in 1616, of a volume of poems and plays entitled *The Works of Benjamin Jonson* is generally regarded as a historical index of the literary artist's developing sense of self-importance. At the same time, Jonson's constant fretting about his readers' competency and his intermittent troubles with theater audiences indicate the growing importance of reader and audience response that occurred with the professionalization of literature and its expansion to a widening segment of society. The tension between these two loci of self-assertion and their respective demands for recognition, the one situated in the place of the author, the other in the place of the audience, is constantly present in Jonson's dramatic works. Often, he will incorporate into his texts (usually in a prologue, induction, or epilogue) a representation of the relationship between his own assertion of the place, the authority, the power of the poet and his audience's assertion of its own power to pass judgment. I want to focus now on the implications of such framing devices in Jonson's major comedies, and particularly, in *Bartholomew Fair*.

The pre-eminence of the poet's authority is stated unequivocally in the Epistle to *Volpone*: [9]

8. Barish, *Ben Jonson and the Language of Prose Comedy*, pp. 88–89.

9. Stephen J. Greenblatt, "The False Ending in *Volpone*," *JEGP*, LXXV, nos. 1–2 (1976), 103–104, offers an ironic reading of the Epistle in relation to other framing devices of the play. My emphasis in the present context is somewhat different, though not antithetical. Citations from the plays are to the modernized texts of the Yale editions: *Volpone*, ed. Alvin B. Kernan (New Haven, Conn., 1962); *The Alchemist*, ed. Kernan (1974); *Bartholomew Fair*, ed. Eugene M. Waith (1963). Citations from Jonson's nondramatic works are to *Ben Jonson*, ed. C. H. Herford and Percy and Evelyn Simpson, 11 vols. (Oxford, 1925–1952), with spelling modernized.

For, if men will impartially, and not asquint, look toward the offices and function of a poet, they will easily conclude to themselves the impossibility of any
man's being the good poet without first being a good man. . . . [The poet is he]
that comes forth the interpreter and arbiter of nature, a teacher of things divine
no less than human, a master in manners; and can alone, or with few, effect the
business of mankind . . .

Jonson's confidence here depends in part on the reputation he had already
succeeded in establishing for himself. But it also reflects the special status
of *Volpone* among his plays. For it is the tightest of Jonson's dramatic
works, with the possible exception of *The Alchemist* to which I shall turn in
a moment. Unlike most of the plays that precede or follow it, *Volpone*
shows little authorial intrusion in the action itself. Here the moral is
carried without the intervention of a character like Asper, Crites, Truewit,
or Manly to make sure that the audience grasps what the author would
have it understand. *The Alchemist* and *Bartholomew Fair* are also notably free
of such Jonsonian spokesmen, but neither of these plays has the confident
moral authority or the severity of *Volpone*. Jonson had discovered a formula
whereby he could unite the diverse elements of his audience in judging and
censuring the action on stage. This unity of judgment served to corroborate the author's claim to being the "arbiter of nature," hence of truth and
of public morals. At the same time, the social value of consensus in the
theater was that it provided a plausible sense that there existed a coherent
and absolute moral foundation in English society for grounding such
judgment.

Of course, the thematic and structural unity of *Volpone* and its apparent
ethical consistency depended on something of a red herring, that is, the
displacement of all vice and corruption to an Italian setting. The unity of
judgment on the parts of author and audience, and the credibility of an
absolute moral standard rendered possible by the play, depended on the
scapegoating of the Italians. Thus, writes William Empson:

London was jealous of Venice, as an aggressive leader of international maritime
trade, because London wanted to do that on a bigger scale. "Terrible pigs, that
tyrannous Council of Ten; they never think of anything but money." Jonson
could rely upon getting this reaction even from business men in his audience,
while most of the audience were enjoying the play as a satire upon business
men. [10]

10. William Empson, "Volpone," *HudR*, XXI, no. 4 (1968–1969), 654.

This is, however, a pretty tenuous basis for a reciprocity of judgments in the theater or for the moral sanctioning of a sense of community. As a theatrical event and experience, *Volpone* did not enable an affirmative mode of identification between the author and his audience. At the most, it permitted a sense of common purpose and of social order based on a strictly negative appraisal of a certain kind of acquisitive behavior that was conveniently displaced elsewhere.

Jonson could not have been satisfied by such a formula no matter how sublime his handling of it, and no matter how successful it may have been in the theater. He was far too concerned to expose folly and corruption in his own society, and to instruct his own countrymen "in the best reason of living" (another phrase from the Epistle to *Volpone*) to be content with a form of dramatic satire that depended on characters who were stereotypical Italian thieves and mountebanks. The plays that follow are located in a domestic setting. But, curiously, they lack the moral certitude that informs the theme and structure of *Volpone*. Whether or not Jonson consciously recognized a flaw in the ethical foundation on which he claimed to rest the "offices and function of a poet" is by no means clear. Certainly he continued to proclaim the high moral purpose of playing in the theater, and the absolute Truth on which the good was founded. In the *Discoveries* he could declaim grandly, citing the appropriate *locus classicus*, "*Veritas proprium hominis*":

> Truth is man's proper good; and the only immortal thing, was given to our mortality to use. . . . For without truth all the Actions of mankind, are craft, malice, or what you will, rather than Wisdom. Homer says, he hates him worse than hell-mouth, that utters one thing with his tongue, and keeps another in his breast. Which high expression was grounded on divine Reason. For a lying mouth is a stinking pit, and murders with the contagion it venteth. Beside, nothing is lasting that is feigned; it will have another face than it had, ere long . . .
>
> (ll. 531–542)

The word "feigned" refers to dissimulation or dissembling here. Poetry is, of course, another kind of feigning altogether, one carried out in the service of Truth and goodness. In the *Discoveries* Jonson managed to keep the distinction clear:

I could never think the study of Wisdom confined only to the Philosopher: or of Piety to the Divine: or of State to the Politicke. But that he which can feign a Commonwealth (which is the Poet) can govern it with Counsels, strengthen it with Laws, correct it with Judgments, inform it with Religion, and Morals, is all these.

(ll. 1032–1038)

But the pragmatics of the actual social context in which Ben Jonson had assumed the offices and function of a poet made it increasingly difficult for him to maintain such a neat distinction between poetic feigning and dissembling in the theater.

The Alchemist (1610) is in certain respects even more closed in structure than *Volpone*. Its action, as Ian Donaldson has observed, takes place almost entirely in a single interior setting, a house in London, the restrictiveness of which "has an unsettling effect upon the characters of the play, and, in turn, upon the audience itself." [11] The conclusion in which Lovewit, the returned master of the house, dispenses a mild and sympathetic justice, releases much of the tension and anxiety that has accumulated in the earlier scenes. I want to suggest, however, that this apparent relaxation only masks a deeper underlying tension in the play and in the relationships it sets going in the theater.

At the end of *The Alchemist*, Lovewit and his butler Jeremy, who has disguised himself throughout most of the action as Face, remain alone on stage. Lovewit has taken possession of the treasure which was accumulated in his absence by Face and his accomplices. He has also acquired, thanks to Face's devices, a rich widow, Dame Pliant. Lovewit recognizes Face's hand in his good fortune, and he acknowledges this by the offer of an exchange in kind:

LOVEWIT
. . . That master
That had received such happiness by a servant,
In such a widow, and with so much wealth,
Were very ungrateful if he would not be

11. Ian Donaldson, "Ben Jonson," in *English Drama to 1710*, ed. Christopher Ricks (London, 1971), p. 299.

> A little indulgent to that servant's wit,
> And help his fortune, though with some small strain
> Of his own candor.
>
> (V.v. 146–152)

What is thus legitimated here at the play's conclusion is not a judgment and an action founded on an ethical absolute, but one founded on the exigencies of power, self-interest, and reciprocal exchange.

Having announced his intention to reward Face, Lovewit gives his man another order: "Speak for thyself, knave." The injunction is paradoxical; Face is still a "knave," and he is still subject to a master's order. Yet he is enjoined to speak for himself. And, to a degree, his new fortune is indeed an expansion of his freedom. But that freedom depends on his ability to be other than what he might be if he did not have to serve masters; he must dissemble, and continue to dissemble in order to maintain his new-won freedom. Thus though he is permitted to speak for himself, he must continue to speak for others, to imitate others, to be a player and wear another's face. Now, he comes forward to speak the epilogue. He stands at the edge of the stage where the narrow line between play and audience has marked, up until now, the possibility of there being a limit to excess, a limit to all the dissembling that has gone on in the play. It is a boundary that has served to this point as the index of a norm for real *being* instead of mere playing at being, a norm upon which judgment in the theater can be shared by the author and his audience. Face's words are like nothing that we have heard in *Volpone*:

> LOVEWIT
>   Speak for thyself, knave.
>   FACE
> [Advancing] So I will, sir.
>
>   Gentlemen,
> My part a little fell in this last scene,
> Yet 'twas decorum. And though I am clean
> Got off from Subtle, Surly, Mammon, Dol,
> Hot Ananias, Dapper, Drugger, all
> With whom I traded; yet I put myself
> On you, that are my country; and this pelf
> Which I have got, if you do quit me, rests,
> To feast you often, and invite new guests.
>
> (V.v. 157–165)

Implicit here is the drafting of a new contract to replace the "indenture tripartite / 'Twixt Subtle, Dol, and Face" (V.iv.131–132). Face refers to the feigning and the trading that have gone on in the previous scenes. But the speech refers as well to what goes on in society, and this includes relationships in the theater. The tone here is festive, light, even frivolous. Yet behind the frivolity lies a message that is disturbingly serious. Face has "traded" not only with all the gulls whom he mentions; he has also "traded" with his master Lovewit, and now he is trading with the audience. His speech implies that all is only dissembling and trading, and that this being the case it is perfect decorum for the one who trades best to be "clean / Got off . . ." Now he works a deal with his audience and his "country" that would require them to become accomplices in his future confidence games. The device may be viewed simply as a clever joke, and a good-natured manipulation of the audience's identification with the place of Lovewit in the play.

But we must remember that Face performs the role of an Epilogue here; clearly he speaks for the playwright and for future plays by his hand. The narrow line between the play and the audience seems suddenly, in these final words, to have dissolved. Jonson is standing before us as much as Face, and he is speaking not about relations among characters in a play but about his own relation to his audience, a relationship that has a social function not only in the theater but in the world at large. There is a confession implied here, a suggestion that we too have been traded with; but there is also an indication that there is only the possibility of trading between us. Unlike the closure maintained in *Volpone*, where we are able to join complacently in the final act of moral censure, the last scenes of *The Alchemist* leave us in an ambiguous position. It will not suffice to explain this ambiguity away, as one critic has recently done in a passing reference to *The Alchemist*, by asserting that the comic genre "seeks something that might be called 'emotional closure' rather than a strict psychological or moral justice . . ." [12] Descriptively the statement may be valid, but it does not explain the inconsistency between Jonson's theory and his practice as a comic dramatist after *Volpone*.

---

12. Nancy Lindheim, review of *Sir Philip Sidney: Rebellion in Arcadia*, by Richard C. McCoy, *Seventeenth-Century News*, XXXIX, no. 1 (1981), 6.

The opening up of the closed play-world at the end of *The Alchemist* is a momentary vision of the possible truth behind the "Truth" that Jonson so confidently espoused elsewhere. We may recall here the passage quoted earlier from the *Discoveries*, to the effect that "Truth is man's proper good . . ." and that "a lying mouth is a stinking pit . . .," and consider now with some irony the last words of that passage: ". . . nothing is lasting that is feigned; it will have another *face* than it had, ere long . . ." At the end of *The Alchemist* there is at least a momentary speculation that truth can only be "feigned," that there is only feigning, and that the "good man" can only be another Face. This admission threatens to undermine the poet's assumption of moral authority. However, Jonson keeps his footing, as did Face himself, by making us acknowledge our complicity in the assertion that comes in the epilogue. This time, the judgment which we corroborate and share with the author is a judgment of him and of ourselves; and since we are not likely to be too harsh on ourselves we allow him to get off as well, to return "to feast [us] often, and invite new guests." Face's epilogue to the play is as much a straight business deal between the dramatist and his audience, the negotiation or renegotiation of a contract.

The implied metaphor is literalized at the beginning of Jonson's next great comedy, *Bartholomew Fair* (1614).[13] In the Induction a "scrivener" comes onstage to read certain "Articles of Agreement indented between the spectators or hearers at the Hope on the Bankside, in the county of Surrey, on the one party, and the author of *Barthol'mew Fair* in the said place and county, on the other party . . ." The agreement stipulates "that every man here exercise his own judgement, and not censure by contagion, or upon trust, from another's voice or face that sits by him, be he never so first in the commission of wit . . ." The device is a cranky bit of satire; but it also constitutes an acknowledgment, however grudgingly, of the growing power of audiences in the public theaters, and an appeal

---

13. The importance of legal imagery in this play is emphasized by Ray L. Heffner, Jr., "Unifying Symbols in the Comedy of Ben Jonson," in *English Stage Comedy: English Institute Essays, 1954*, ed. W. K. Wimsatt, Jr. (New York, 1955), pp. 74–97, rpt. in *Ben Jonson: A Collection of Critical Essays*, ed. Jonas A. Barish (Englewood Cliffs, N.J., 1963), pp. 141–146; Jackson I. Cope, in the essay cited previously, discusses the theme of litigiousness and relates it to the traditional iconography of *Ate* or *Discordia* (pp. 144–146).

that they judge the scene with the same independence of mind the author imagines himself to have used in creating it.

In *Bartholomew Fair*, as Barish has suggested, a certain solidarity is struck between the author and his audience, motivated in part by the attacks of Puritans and civic leaders on the fleshly temptations of fairs and theaters. But it is a tenuous solidarity at best. The legalistic device of the "Articles of Agreement" reflects the weakening in the early seventeenth century of a reliable order of shared assumptions, embodied in popular tradition, religious ritual, and dogma, upon which to base moral and aesthetic judgment in the public playhouse. The feigned necessity of a contract mediating the relationship between independent parties to a literary or theatrical communication focuses, at the plane of the aesthetic, what is becoming a fundamental problem in all aspects of social life. With individuals acquiring a relatively greater sense of personal independence, and with the breakdown of a universal, authoritative belief system, it now becomes difficult—especially for those who eschew the too stringent spiritual community of the Saints—to sustain a sense of collective identity. The implication, not very hidden in *Bartholomew Fair*, is that patterns of spiritual and moral conduct have become blurred. In the Induction Jonson repeatedly puns satirically on the *"grounded* judgments and *understandings"* of the groundlings in the pit at the Hope. Yet despite the intended irony, *Bartholomew Fair* acknowledges that a regrounding of the social order is indeed under way in England, and the play offers an account of the principles upon which the new system of social organization will be constituted.

While the action of the play deals with this state of affairs in a more tolerant and open manner than is customary for Jonson, the contract read at the outset is typically severe. It includes an ironic deflation of the doctrine of "free-will" and a parody of what is viewed as the arbitrary rationality and the strictly quantitative equity of commercial law:

It is further agreed that every person here have his or their free-will of censure, to like or dislike at their own charge, the author having now departed with his right: it shall be lawful for any man to judge his six pen'orth, his twelve pen'orth, so to his eighteen pence, two shillings, half a crown, to the value of his place; provided always his place get not above his wit . . . . marry, if he drop but sixpence at the door, and will censure a crown's worth, it is thought there is no conscience or justice in that.

Once again, as in Volpone's hymn to his gold, Jonson rails against the symptoms of incipient capitalism, representing as a perverse confusion of categories the reduction of all value to a universal equivalent in money.

And, as in *Volpone*, this madness is represented as a debasement of human into animal nature. Beginning with his earliest "humors" comedies, Jonson had sought to comprehend contemporary social problems in psychological terms. In *Bartholomew Fair* the related, though somewhat different concept of "vapors" is introduced. The psychology is still primitive. "*Bartholomew Fair*," writes Barish, "reduces all human activity to the gross level of an organic disturbance." [14] To a degree, this reduction occurs in the framing device of the contract as well as in the main body of the play. The effect of the Induction is to extend the old doctrine of "humors" to the audience at the Hope. Among the multiple connotations of the word "grounded" in the jokes concerning the spectators of the pit is its association with the physiological origin of the humors and vapors in the lower regions of the body. The irony of the pun is thus enhanced by the juxtaposition of "grounded" with "judgments," ordinarily identified with human reason. In the text of the contract itself the image we get of the spectators is that they are obsessed by a dominant passion for the power of passing judgment, a passion that obstructs the functioning of the rational faculty upon which true judgment depends. The author continues to assume the magisterial persona of an arbiter, not only of good taste but of public morality as well. Yet now, frustrated in the performance of his rightful social office and function by the incompetence of a debased public, he is forced into a humiliating compromise, a contract that will limit his liability, guarantee his audience's attention for the space of about two and a half hours, and place a curb on the tendency of money to usurp the place of wit in validating judgment. The power of the audience is acknowledged. But the poet, forced to endure such frustration and humiliation, gains his revenge in the contempt with which the audience is treated in the last clauses of the contract:

In witness whereof, as you have preposterously put to your seals already (which is your money), you will now add the other part of suffrage, your hands. The play shall presently begin. And though the Fair be not kept in the same region that

14. Barish, *Ben Jonson and the Language of Prose Comedy*, p. 219.

some here, perhaps, would have it, yet think that therein the author hath observed a special decorum, the place being as dirty as Smithfield [the place near London where the actual Bartholomew Fair was held annually], and as stinking every whit.

The immediate reference for this "special decorum" is the fact that the Hope Theater was also used for bear-baiting contests and may well have stunk from the constant presence of animals within its confines. But another implication of these lines is that the public theater is a place where animals (i.e., members of the audience who have fallen below their human natures) are as readily found as at the fair.

The self-conscious metadrama of the Induction and the disdain for the audience implied there are compounded further by the fact that for another performance of this play Jonson wrote a separate Prologue and an Epilogue. These were addressed to James I before whom *Bartholomew Fair* was acted on the day following its first performance at the Hope (31 October 1614). The Epilogue is especially interesting in comparison with the contract of the Induction:

> Your Majesty hath seen the play, and you
>   Can best allow it from your ear and view.
> You know the scope of writers, and what store
>   Of leave is given them, if they take not more,
> And turn it into license.
> . . . .
> This is your power to judge, great sir, and not
>   The envy of a few. Which if we have got,
> We value less what their dislike can bring,
>   If it so happy be, t'have pleased the King.
>   (ll. 1–5, 9–12)

In contrast to the parodic treatment of the theater audience's desire to judge and to censure in the Induction, and to the milder comedy with which Justice Adam Overdo's "warrant" is treated in the body of the play, here in the Epilogue the final "power to judge" is treated seriously and is vested in the king. The identification of that power with the monarch is not especially significant in itself. It is conventional for a play presented at court. It is also typical of Jonson to claim "the scope of writers" who have the judgment not to "turn it into license," and to identify that authorial capacity for aesthetic and moral judgment with the king's juridical power in relation to his subjects.

But what is especially interesting here is that in connection with the same play we have two very different kinds of framing devices, addressed to different audiences and different social classes. And in each case there is exhibited a deep preoccupation with the author-audience relationship. The address to the king and to the court mediates and helps to sustain the self-image Jonson puts forth in relation to the audience of the playhouse. The place of the author is finally privileged in opposition to that of the theater audience by an identification of his own judgment with the "power to judge" of the king. In this way, the place of the king, the highest earthly place, functions as more than just that of another audience of the play; it is the place of final authority, and as such it is the locus of the voice of the Father, the voice that *author-izes* (if I may be allowed the pun) the writer's voice even as it limits its scope.

Yet despite these efforts to sustain the authority of the poet in the speeches which frame *Bartholomew Fair*, the moral force that animates the "anti-acquisitive attitude" here is far less stable and consistent than it was in *Volpone*. This difference cannot be explained as a response to different audiences since *Volpone* was first played by Shakespeare's company at the Globe, where the social composition of the audience was probably not too different from that at the Hope.[15] Jonson's satiric treatment of the play-goers in the opening of *Bartholomew Fair* is complicated by the main action which follows, and the attitude that drives this play is in the end more ambiguous than the phrase "anti-acquisitive" would allow.

Underlying the bitterness of the contract as a satiric device is a deeper acknowledgment of the general shift that was under way at this time from an idea of community founded on doctrinal tradition to one based on market relations and contract law. It is significant, for example, that at roughly the same time that the Elizabethan and Jacobean drama reaches its apogee, contract law is established on a firmer footing in England. In 1602, a momentous decision in *Slade's Case* brought to culmination a gradual process whereby the mercantile notion of contract had been encroaching on the common law through the evolution of the action of

15. Alfred Harbage, *Shakespeare and the Rival Traditions* (1952; rpt. New York, 1968), p. 27.

assumpsit. The case brought with it, too, a considerable degree of confusion; for the distinction between debt and deceit, between contract and tort, was now, and for some time thereafter, obscured if not obliterated. [16] We can detect a similar type of confusion in the dramatists' representation of moral and contractual obligation. In *Bartholomew Fair* the "Articles of Agreement" point ironically to the increasing reliance on arbitrary regulation (contract law), in the absence of the more spontaneously recognized mechanisms of social control provided by a coherent and viable system of belief. Contractual obligation, enforced by an arbitrary, impartial, and impersonal authority, is satirically acknowledged as the way of containing the threat of anarchy in a society where the only consistent value appears to be that of the marketplace. But despite the fact that the "Articles of

16. The issues in *Slade's Case* are too complex to rehearse in detail. I have relied principally on the following: Theodore F. T. Plucknett, *A Concise History of the Common Law*, 5th ed. (Boston, 1956), pp. 637–651; H. K. Lücke, "Slade's Case and the Origin of the Common Counts," *Law Quarterly Review* (1965), pp. 422–445, 539–561, and (1966), pp. 81–96; S.F.C. Milsom, *Historical Foundations of the Common Law* (London, 1969), chap. 12; J. H. Baker, "New Light on Slade's Case," *Cambridge Law Journal*, XXIX (1971), 51–67, 213–236; and A.W.B. Simpson, *A History of the Common Law of Contract* (Oxford, 1975), pp. 281–315. The case brought to a head a controversy between the courts of Common Pleas and King's Bench concerning the respective boundaries of the actions of debt and of *assumpsit*, an action on the case associated with trespass and deceit. The intensity of the Common Pleas judges' opposition to any blurring of these judicial boundaries can be heard in the following pronouncement (quoted in Baker, p. 231) from another case in the same year: "Cleerly the action will not lye, for the debt is hereby not changed and these new devises of accions of the case cannot be mainteined. For there ought to be no accions of the case but grounded upon some fraud, for so are the words of the writt, 'machinans [defraudare] etc.' What fraud is here committed?" While there has been a recent difference of opinion among legal historians as to whether the conflict between the courts was motivated primarily by economic self-interest or by intellectual concerns (see Baker, "New Light on Slade's Case," pp. 215–216; Simpson, *A History of the Common Law of Contract*, pp. 293–294), there is less disagreement concerning the effects of the decision in *Slade's Case*. These included the culmination of a process whereby *assumpsit* was extended into the area of law served by the action of debt. To my knowledge, Plucknett's assessment of the confusion created by this decision remains unchallenged in the recent debate: "two generations later we still find the learned Vaughan, C. J., lamenting that *Slade's Case* was 'a false gloss' designed to substitute *assumpsit* for debt. So it was; on principle, the decision is indefensible, for it obliterates the distinction between debt and deceit, between contract and tort" (*A Concise History of the Common Law*, p. 647; cf. Milsom, *Historical Foundations of the Common Law*, p. 304, and Baker, "New Light on Slade's Case," p. 227).

Agreement" are satiric in intent, the author reveals himself to be implicated in his own satire and in the new contractual basis of social obligation.

In contrast to its frame, the play itself sheds a very different light on the
contemporary preoccupation with authority, hierarchy, freedom, and
license. But it also tends to reinforce the idea of a contractual basis to
society. Where the attitude in the Induction is ironic, even caustic, in the
play's conclusion we detect a more conciliatory tone. A sense of community is restored not by means of a coherent theological, moral, or legal
code of behavior, but rather through the recognition that the desire for
pleasure and the consequent "frailty" of the flesh are universal conditions
among the descendants of Adam. In this respect, *Bartholomew Fair* is
"more radical than its author." [17] Where Jonson ordinarily distances himself from his audience, resting his claim to special status on his superior
learning, and representing the poet as combining the social functions of
priest and judge, in this play such roles are satirized and the satire inevitably touches the satirist himself.

Compared to most of Jonson's earlier plays, *Bartholomew Fair* has no
clear ethical foundation; it is more open, more inclusive, more ambiguous;
its action is sprawling, its cast of characters enormous, its overall effect
more fragmented and confusing. Jonson halfheartedly continues to support
the social and ethical norms espoused in the earlier plays. But the absurd-
ity of Troubleall's insistence on having Justice Adam Overdo's "warrant"
before he will perform even the most basic functions such as eating has a
rippling effect that touches every aspect of the play. At the most, what
Bartholomew Fair urges is tolerance where all is vanity, even the vigilant
enforcement of law and order and of public morals. If couched in serious
terms this would have been a dangerous message to place on the stage; but
the confusion and the light-hearted humor of the play most likely tended
to distract attention away from its lack of moral certainty and from its
potentially subversive content.

This is about as close as Jonson ever gets to anything like an egalitarian
conception. Yet despite his retention of hierarchy as a necessary principle
of social order, there is in the conclusion of *Bartholomew Fair*, as Barish
maintains, a striking sense of solidarity in the theater: "One might sug-

17. Barish, *Ben Jonson and the Language of Prose Comedy*, p. 235.

gest, finally, that with this play, in which the reformers are reformed by the fools, Jonson confesses his own frailty and his own flesh and blood. Though he continues to satirize popular taste, he now—momentarily at least—identifies his own interests with it." [18] Barish's statement explicates a logic that underlies the relationship between the author, his characters, and his audience in the denouement of the play. But once this logic has emerged dramatically, it is contagious, affecting (or infecting) relationships within the larger framework of the Induction, and of the Prologue and Epilogue addressed to the king.

In the Epilogue, Jonson may indeed be seeking legitimation of his own authority through an identification with the king's "power to judge." But this authorization is more or less tainted by the play's satirical undermining of Justice Overdo's warrant and of the tutor Wasp's authority: "Nay, then the date of my *Authority* is out; I must think no longer to reign, my government is at an end. He that will correct another must want fault in himself" (V.iv.97–99). This is not to say that Jonson intentionally subverts the authority of majesty here, but only that his attempt to locate himself in a direct line of descent from that absolute locus of power is vitiated by the play's message that all human beings, regardless of their place in society, are flesh and blood and therefore subject to frailty. The Epilogue shows Jonson still claiming, as he did in the Epistle to *Volpone*, "the impossibility of any man's being the good poet without first being a good man." But as Barish suggests, the logic of the comic resolution in *Bartholomew Fair* conveys a sense of authorial self-irony that is lacking in the earlier plays.

Perhaps more than any other play of Jonson's, *Bartholomew Fair* lends itself to modern pragmatic, existential, or even absurdist interpretations. This is not necessarily anachronistic, for the play contains within its theme and structure the rudiments of such modern conceptual paradigms. Alvin B. Kernan writes in a brief but probing study that "Jonson's only answer to the vision of ultimate emptiness is the provisional one of accepting your own limitations and realizing that no warrant confers very much authority. Perhaps, in the long run, good sense and natural instinct are the surest and only warrants the world provides. . . . Even in the theater life gets its

18. *Ibid.*, p. 238.

business done and satisfies its needs by a reasonable adjustment of interests." [19] The statement is fine as a description of the relativistic ethic that
seems to govern this play, but it needs to be put in historical perspective.
For behind all the apparent uncertainty and the "vision of ultimate emptiness" of *Bartholomew Fair* is the model of a new ideology. It is not an
ideology that Jonson necessarily espoused in theory, but it does appear in
his text. Instead of a social order based on fixed, hierarchical ranks and
relations determined by the warrant of authority (whether terrestrial or
divine), the play depicts a world in which, as Kernan suggests, men are
urged to rely for the ordering of their affairs on "good sense and natural
instinct" in arriving at a "reasonable adjustment of interests." But what
does it mean to state the play's ethic in these terms? Such phrases are not
anachronisms when applied to *Bartholomew Fair*; but neither do they come
to us already full of an inherent meaning that is timeless and universal.
They refer to concepts with a history that is rooted ideologically in doctrines which Jonson's own drama and poetry helped to promulgate.

It is probably not just coincidence that some of the most perceptive
readings of *Bartholomew Fair* point to the emergence of the idea of rational
self-interest in the denouement as a key to the meaning of the entire play.
Kernan refers to a "reasonable adjustment of interests" among the characters. Barish implicates the author and the audience as well when he
writes that Jonson "now—momentarily at least—identifies his own
interests with" popular taste. Such assertions have a historical basis to
them. As Albert O. Hirschman has recently demonstrated, the term
"interest" underwent important changes in meaning in sixteenth- and
seventeenth-century writings that provided what Hirschman calls "political arguments for capitalism before its triumph." In place of the old
connotation of avarice, a new conception arose of *interest* as the one human
passion that had positive social value. It was argued that given the impossibility of effectively repressing the passions through reason, a relatively
harmless passion had to be pitted against the more unruly ones in order to
contain their destructive effects. The traditional dichotomy between
reason and the passions was thus attenuated by the introduction of a third
term, the "countervailing passion" of *interest*. This countervailing strategy

19. Kernan, "Alchemy and Acting," p. 22.

became, in turn, the foundation of the social-contract doctrine.[20] Jonson does not contribute directly to this semantic and ideological redefinition; but the comic resolution of *Bartholomew Fair* is a dramatization of the same basic principle.

What is perhaps most remarkable about *Bartholomew Fair* is that some of the very ideas that we take to be self-evident, immutable truths concerning society and human nature, truths which we assume to be pragmatic rather than doctrinaire, were first encoded as part of our own governing ideology in this play and in contemporary works like it. Despite the satire on contracts in the Induction to *Bartholomew Fair*, it is finally the idea of contract that emerges as a solution to the problem of maintaining order in society. By replacing the warrant of authority with a new basis of social order that amounted to a rational compromise, in Kernan's words "a reasonable adjustment of interests," Jonson's play contributed to the contemporary redefinition of the notion of interest and, consequently, to the idea of a social contract.

At the same time, in this early dramatization of the concept that the only effective social control is that of rational self-interest, we can see the emergence of another modern phenomenon, the problem of alienation. In *Bartholomew Fair* the cry of the vendors, "What do you lack? What do you lack?" becomes a refrain that has ontological as well as economic connotations. But unlike *Volpone*, which moralizes on the alienated condition of human beings driven by the pursuit of money and power, *Bartholomew Fair* attempts to provide an alternative to that condition within the limits of the new contractual system of social organization acknowledged in its conclusion.

For there is another side to the ideology of rational self-interest as it is dramatized in this play. It is evident in the conviviality with which the complex and tumultuous action is resolved. Jonson avoids a thoroughly cynical reduction of human relations to market relations and of ethical principles to the impersonal mechanisms of contract law. Justice Overdo's genial invitation, "home with me to my house, to supper," is a gesture

20. Albert O. Hirschman, *The Passions and the Interests: Political Arguments for Capitalism Before Its Triumph* (Princeton, N.J., 1978), pp. 14–42. See also Felix Raab, *The English Face of Machiavelli: A Changing Interpretation 1500–1700* (London, 1964), pp. 157–158, 233.

that bespeaks the happier side of the emerging middle-class ideology, the side Dekker had celebrated fifteen years earlier in the more grandiose bourgeois hospitality of Simon Eyre. But where the homely virtues of the middle classes are extolled with unambiguous mirth in *The Shoemakers' Holiday*, Jonson can manage only a resigned acceptance of the new order and of his own complicity in it. The Saturnalian conclusion of *Bartholomew Fair* compensates for the felt loss of a coherent moral code based on traditional, feudal conceptions of hierarchy, status, and *noblesse oblige* by offering a momentary vision that is as close as Jonson ever comes in his satires to an image of utopia, a vision of society in which mutual respect and tolerance are fundamental to the "interests" of all members.

To the extent that this is something of a utopian image, it is conveyed poetically by the reference to "home" which occurs twice in the closing few lines of the play, first in Overdo's invitation to supper, then in Cokes's response: "Yes, and bring the actors along, we'll ha' the rest o' the play at home." Cokes is referring to the puppets whose play has been disrupted by the Puritan, Zeal-Of-The-Land Busy. But his words have broader implications. As Barish points out, in the mouth of Cokes, "the archetypal puppet" among men, these final words "carry the human comedy indefinitely forward into the future."[21] Though Cokes is a satirized character, the context of his line does not allow for a satiric reading. If Jonson is being ironic, it is an irony of pathos rather than one of mockery and censure. In fact, Jonson shows uncharacteristic sympathy and a capacity for tolerance in his benign treatment of human folly here. Of course, a certain amount of self-interest may be involved, since the play is a comic defense of plays and playwrights. But there is also a deeper sense to the repetition of the word "home" and to its prominence as the final word spoken in the play. Jonson employs the same phrase "at home" in other, more solemn contexts in his writing. It is a figure that connotes the *integer vitae* as in:

> Nor for my peace will I go far,
>   As wanderers do, that still do roam,
> But make my strengths, such as they are,
>   Here in my bosom, and at home.
>   (*The Forest*, IV, 65–68)

---

21. Barish, *Ben Jonson and the Language of Prose Comedy*, p. 238.

The phrase, or an equivalent such as the verb "dwells," which concludes one of Jonson's best-known poems, "To Penshurst," occurs as a *leitmotif* in his poetry. [22] The frequency of such imagery suggests a habitual association of integrity and plenitude with the idea of home. With this in mind we can look back at Bartholomew Cokes's call for the relocation of the pleasures of the stage to the home and realize that it is more than just a continuation of Cokes's exuberant but mindless pursuit of pleasure. It is a recognition and an assertion of the mitigating, compensatory function, of aesthetic play in a world in which Jonson and his contemporaries had begun to find it increasingly difficult to feel "at home."

A psychoanalytic study might have much to say about Jonson's dwelling on such domestic imagery; but in the present context, it makes more sense to view this preoccupation in the work of a major writer of the period as indicative of a sociocultural and historical problem rather than a personal one. This problem and the centrality of the figure of "home" in the contemporary orientation to its solution is admirably summed up by Christopher Hill:

> The forces of distruption had gone too far. Economic processes were atomizing society, converting it from a hierarchy of communities to the agglomeration of equal competing individuals depicted in *Leviathan*. . . .
> The economic tension of the community in process of breaking up is focused on the household, in transition from a patriarchal unit of communal production to a capitalist firm. . . . Neither a peasant hut nor the travelling household of the great noble nor the celibate community of the monastery was favourable to home life: that was developed by the middle class in town and country, whose houses began to replace churches as the centres of social life. . . . So, especially in towns, new, voluntary communities arose, independent of the parish. These new select groups were united by community of interest rather than by geographical propinquity or corporate worship. For a short time men could even envisage bringing about fundamental reform in the State via reform in the household. [23]

But household reform, the conviviality of the "new, voluntary communities," and the spirituality of the new sects built on the principle of

22. Other poems in which these terms figure in this way include: "To Sir Robert Wroth," *The Forest*, III, 13, 94; "An Epistle to Master John Selden," *Underwood*, XIV, 30; "An Epigram to My Muse, the Lady Digby, on her Husband, Sir Kenelm Digby," *Underwood*, LXXVIII, 8.

23. Hill, *Society and Puritanism*, pp. 487–488.

the covenant were bound up inextricably with the same economic "forces of disruption" to which Hill refers at the beginning of the above quotation. To the extent that institutions were sought to contain the atomizing effects of capitalist development, which meant containing voluntarism itself, the solutions arrived at tended to be based on the notion of contract. Thus, Hill writes of "contract communities" replacing "status communities." The household became the fundamental social unit of the "contract community," as is evident from the frequent parallels drawn in the sixteenth century between the patriarchal family and the state, and in the seventeenth, between the marriage contract and the social contract. Patriarchy in the family was the common basis of argumentation in conflicting doctrines concerning the foundations of state and society. [24] This being the case, it is not surprising to find Jonson employing the image of "home" in such different contexts as "To Penshurst," where social order is conceived in terms of degree and obligation according to prescribed doctrine, [25] and at the end of *Bartholomew Fair*, a comedy focused on the middle classes, where society is viewed as the product of a compromise, "a reasonable adjustment of interests," a social contract.

While it may be true that this shift from "status" to "contract" was grounded in a tradition—the Old Testament doctrine of the covenant between God and Israel—it is important that we not confuse contemporary rationales of observable transformations in seventeenth-century English society with the actual phenomena of social and political change. [26] When Knights writes of the dramatists working in an "anti-

24. See Hill, chap. 13; and Keith Thomas, "Women and the Civil War Sects," *Past and Present*, no. 13 (1958), rpt. in *Crisis in Europe 1560–1660*, ed. Trevor Aston (Garden City, N.Y., 1967), p. 332.

25. There are, in fact, contractual elements in poems of praise like "To Penshurst," especially where the relationship between poet and patron is concerned. I have discussed this question from a related perspective in "Poetry and Power in Ben Jonson's *Epigrammes*: The Naming of 'Facts' or the Figuring of Social Relations?" *RMS*, XXIII (1979), 79–103.

26. Hobbes buttresses the "Principles of Reason" on which he would ground his contractual model of society by the "Authority of Scripture," which provides the precedent of "the Kingdome of God, administered by Moses, over the Jews, his peculiar people by Covenant" (*Leviathan* [1651], ed. C. B. Macpherson [Harmondsworth, Eng., 1968)], chap. 30, p. 378; cf. chaps. 35 and 40). J.G.A. Pocock, "Post-Puritan England and the Problem of the Enlightenment," in *Culture and Politics from Puritanism to the Enlightenment*, ed. Perez Zagorin (Berkeley, Calif., 1980), pp. 97–99, argues that a common ground of the political theories of Hobbes and of Harrington was their interpretation of Israel as a theocracy—"a republic to Harrington, a monarchy to Hobbes"—founded by covenant.

acquisitive tradition inherited from the Middle Ages" he adopts the moralistic and conservative rationale of the playwrights themselves. In so doing, he neglects to distinguish between an ideological "conservatism" that appears to connect the morality of these plays to a medieval popular tradition and contrary indications which, if not always manifested overtly in the plays, are, nonetheless, embodied in the professional and commercial form of the new theaters.

Curiously, Knights does acknowledge such tensions in the work of lesser, more naïve playwrights like Dekker and Heywood. [27] But his treatment of Jonson is less dialectical. No doubt, that is partly because the tensions or contradictions between traditional morality and the emergent ideologies associated with capitalist development in England are not as obvious in Jonsonian drama. But Knights is too observant a critic in other respects to have missed this facet of Jonson's plays were it not for his deeply held conviction that the great drama of the period has an uncompromising moral unity and coherence which draws on and elaborates a solid and stable "sense of community." As Francis Mulhern has recently shown, the theme of "community" was a central and constant concern of *Scrutiny*, the journal with which Knights was closely associated and where portions of *Drama and Society in the Age of Jonson* first appeared. [28] In one sense, the moral conviction that drives Knights's reading of Jonson is a replica of the nostalgia and the longing that we find, at times, in Jonson's own works. Knights employs words like "tradition," "community," and "neighborliness" throughout his book in a way that is virtually the equivalent of Jonson's "at home." Indeed, the association is given by Knights himself in one characteristic sentence: "His [Jonson's] classicism is an equanimity and assurance that springs—'here at home'—from the strength of a native tradition." [29] The phrase in single quotation marks alludes to the same poem I have cited above. But where Knights shares Jonson's nostalgia, he lacks the seventeenth-century poet's capacity for self-irony.

The difference here is itself susceptible to historical and sociological analysis. Knights, F. R. Leavis, and the other Cambridge intellectuals who founded *Scrutiny* in the 1930s could imagine themselves as part of an independent "critical minority," whose task it was to oppose the alienation

27. Knights, *Drama and Society*, chap. 8.
28. Francis Mulhern, *The Moment of "Scrutiny"* (London, 1979), pp. 58–63.
29. Knights, *Drama and Society*, pp. 187–188.

of life and of language in modern commercial and industrial society by bearing witness to the moral, "organic community" of the past. [30] Ben Jonson was understandably attractive as a literary exemplar of the "culture" Knights and his colleagues sought to defend and as a precursor of their high-minded purpose. But Jonson could not have imagined himself to be engaged in such an enterprise with the same compelling belief in his own detachment from society's economic infrastructure. He might try to do so in the *Volpone* Epistle which, significantly, was written for a university performance. But he was not a university man. As an intellectual and a social critic, his situation was an ironic one. The "anti-acquisitive" culture to which he contributed was intimately bound up with the emerging commercial society of Jacobean England.

Capitalism was indeed on the rise, as it had been for some time. But it had not yet triumphed to the point where a sufficient surplus capital existed to sustain a large-scale educational apparatus, one that could produce not only a technically trained managerial elite but a cultural elite as well who could imagine themselves to be morally superior to and independent of the new economic order. Despite his constant efforts to represent himself as an intellectual rather than a mere playwright, as a poet in the most dignified sense of the term rather than one writing under a system of patronage in which flattery was obligatory, Jonson could not easily blind himself to the manner in which his claim to special status was dependent on the emerging commodity system of economic and social exchange. Acquisitiveness was only one aspect of the new system, an aspect that the moralist could confidently look upon with disdain; but contract was another, and the kind of social relationship it legitimated entailed a form of alienation from which it was more difficult to stand aloof.

The development of Jonsonian drama from *Volpone* to *Bartholomew Fair* is an index of Jonson's increasing awareness of this dilemma. Knights's focus on only the one side of capitalist development—accumulation, or in his more ethically loaded term, "acquisitiveness"—coupled with his need to view Jonson as an unwavering traditionalist, prevented him from recognizing the deeper significance of *Bartholomew Fair*. He was undoubtedly right in pointing out that earlier critics had overestimated the importance

30. Mulhern, *The Moment of "Scrutiny,"* pp. 33, 76–78.

of Jonson's classical erudition in evaluating his plays. But the alternative view of tradition which he proposed was, in its own way, limited. It was an oversimplification to represent Jonson as merely drawing on a traditional sense of community in order to construct a bulwark against the growing tendency of commodity exchange and the contractual regulation of such exchange to encroach upon fundamentally human relationships. Such a view depended on an eclipsing of the ambiguity and tension that provide the rich intellectual and psychological texture of Jonsonian drama. Indeed, it led to the dubious exclusion of *Bartholomew Fair* from among the more important of Jonson's plays.

Though *Drama and Society in the Age of Jonson* remains a landmark in the sociology of literature, its governing conception of the relations among the categories alluded to in its title—drama, society, history, and the psychology of the author-audience relationship—is too narrowly drawn. Knights's demand for a consistent moral "attitude" as the criterion of Jonson's greatness as a dramatist resulted in a flattening of the social and ideological terrain mapped in the plays. Conservative as he may have been in principle, Jonson demanded a status that was unacknowledged in the traditional social and cultural system from which England was then emerging. In using the theater as a space for negotiating that demand he provided his audiences with a model of the society which they themselves were already in the process of creating. Thus, despite his classicism and his traditionalism, Jonson looked ahead as much as he did backward in time. His work, together with that of other Elizabethan and Jacobean dramatists, marks a significant change in the sense that playwrights and their audiences had of their relation to history and to their society. [31]

31. I am grateful to colleagues at the University of California, San Diego, and particularly to Page Du Bois, Louis Montrose, and Michael Parrish for suggestions and criticisms that were helpful to me in the writing of this essay.

"This For the Most Wrong'd of Women": A Reappraisal of The Maid's Tragedy

WILLIAM SHULLENBERGER

A REAPPRAISAL OF *The Maid's Tragedy* is in order. T. S. Eliot's assessment of Beaumont and Fletcher seems to have so determined the critical climate in which the play is received [1] that even a sympathetic critic like Michael Neill, who demonstrates the imagistic coherence of the play, nevertheless concludes his closely argued essay with a mystifying recantation:

Beaumont and Fletcher have suffered more than most from neglect of the principle that criticism should move towards, rather than from, evaluative comparisons. An attempt to set that right need not, of course, involve any radical change in our assessment of their worth as dramatic poets, but it ought to enhance our respect for their virtues as theatrical craftsmen. [2]

1. "Looking closer, we discover that the blossoms of Beaumont and Fletcher's imagination draw no sustenance from the soil, but are cut and slightly withered flowers stuck into sand. . . . The evocative quality of the verse of Beaumont and Fletcher depends upon a clever appeal to emotions and associations which they have not themselves grasped; it is hollow. It is superficial with a vacuum behind it; the superficies of Jonson is solid." T. S. Eliot, *Selected Essays* (New York, 1950), p. 135.

2. Michael Neill, "'The Simetry, Which Gives a Poem Grace': Masque, Imagery, and the Fancy of *The Maid's Tragedy*," *RenD*, III (1970), 135.

131

It is hard to establish the basis for the tenuous distinction between "dramatic poets" and "theatrical craftsmen," but a survey of the criticism suggests that the basis is in the moral assumptions of the critics. Irving Ribner provides a convenient summary of the faults of Beaumont and Fletcher as "dramatic poets": their plays represent "the triumph of theatrical over philosophical substance . . . There is no real quest for moral certainty in their plays, only the facile reduction of artificially contrived paradoxes, with no attempt to resolve moral issues."[3] Everywhere one looks, one finds the playwrights fixed on the disparaging side of dichotomies: craftsmanlike rather than poetic, theatrical rather than philosophical, sensationalistic rather than morally serious.

Certainly the moral order represented in *The Maid's Tragedy* is not very reassuring; in *Philaster*, at least, there is a sort of fidelity, and there is luck. But the pattern of disintegration enacted in *The Maid's Tragedy* calls into question the dichotomizing morality by which it has been assessed: in a world where everything one counts on proves quixotically deceptive, where can one draw the distinction between theatrical and philosophical substance? How can Ribner be so sure that Beaumont and Fletcher's dramatic manipulations do not disguise a desperate quest for some kind of certainty? If the play questions its critics' moral assumptions, then the very faults which they have identified—rhetorical bombast rather than "philosophical substance," a plot continually flaunting the laws of probability, a stable of Jacobean stereotypes lost in endless charades and transformations, a sensationalistic pitch to a jaded audience[4]—may be studied as dramatic strategies which provide points of interpretive entry to a rich, complicated, entertaining, and ultimately coherent drama. The play's glaring theatricality and its inability to settle the crises it dramatizes do not signal the lack of poetic integrity, but a loss of innocence. In the grotesque world of the play, people, ideals, passions, the very world order, not only prove false; they turn into their opposites.[5] Ribner is wrong:

3. Irving Ribner, *Jacobean Tragedy: The Quest for Moral Order* (London, 1962), pp. 16–17.

4. See Ribner, *Jacobean Tragedy*; Clifford Leech, *The John Fletcher Plays* (London, 1962); Robert Ornstein, *The Moral Vision of Jacobean Tragedy* (Madison, Wis., 1960).

5. On the theater of the grotesque, see Stephen Wigler, "If Looks Could Kill: Fathers and Sons in *The Revenger's Tragedy*," *CompD*, IX (1975), 206–225.

there are dozens of attempts to resolve moral issues in *The Maid's Tragedy*, and they all prove disastrous.

Of the play's critics, John F. Danby has come closest to measuring its pulse. He writes, "Beaumont and Fletcher's work indicates the collapse of a culture; an adult scheme is being broken up and replaced by adolescent intensities."[6] "Adolescent intensity" renders accurately the passions which ravage the characters in their "monadic self-enclosure."[7] It suggests that the energies set loose in the play, like the headstrong urges of adolescence, have not yet been curbed and stabilized in relatively coherent patterns of identity. But if culture itself supplies patterns of identity, the collapse of culture noted by Danby provides the playwrights little information about how to account for and to master the ungovernable energies they have summoned to the stage. For *The Maid's Tragedy* tells of a crisis in the Renaissance world order through the imagery and ideology of that culture; but the imagery and ideology, subject to the profound stress of the play, prove inadequate to comprehend the emerging forces which threaten dissolution. The play's "sensationalism" seems the inevitable effect of the psychic material of sexuality and aggression which it represents. Formerly repressed, or secured within a controlling moral and ideational order, such material seems shocking or titillating as it emerges from the debris of that order. That the lurid glow of *The Maid's Tragedy* has not dimmed suggests not its moral inadequacy, but its representation of our own anxieties. In its strange desolation, its disruption of a whole culture's sustaining images of order, and the departure of centric personalities from its stage, the play foreshadows not only much of modern drama but the very world stage of modern life.

I wish, then, to examine the "faults" of *The Maid's Tragedy* as geological or structural, rather than moral "faults": they mark the points of stress where the dramatic order is at the verge of collapse. The play is a Jacobean nightmare whose excesses reveal the crisis of the soul in a patriarchal culture acutely aware of its own unstable purchase on political and metaphysical authority.[8] In the play, kingship is threatened, and with king-

6. John F. Danby, *Poets on Fortune's Hill: Studies in Shakespeare, Sidney, Beaumont and Fletcher* (Port Washington, N.Y., 1966), p. 165.

7. *Ibid.*, p. 170.

8. For the formation of this insight, and for a great deal else in this essay, I am indebted to Bonnie Alexander.

ship the ordered hierarchy which, in the Renaisssance, is at once macrocosmic and microcosmic, natural, social, and personal. This order is threatened from within, by a kind of libidinal explosion whose epicenter is the king himself. Andrew Gurr writes, "If any title could summarize the major concerns of the play it is one of Thomas Rymer's alternatives, *The Lustful King*. The whole action of the play stems from the initial circumstance of the King's having made Evadne his mistress."[9] By tracing the way in which the action of the play completes and fulfills the premises and plot of its opening masque, I shall draw attention toward the king and Evadne as the central figures, the focal points of a dramatic conflict which is political, psychological, and mythic. This conflict is not so much resolved as the tensions building it are released, through the bloody catharsis of the play's fifth act. Although the king is dead, kingship survives. Yet although kingship survives, its myth of sanctity does not. The play seems in retrospect a rehearsal for the Civil Wars; it demystifies the central myth of monarchy.

I

The mythic theater of the masque is the play's own point of departure. Masques "teach, they celebrate virtue, they persuade by example; they lead the court to its ideal self through wonder," according to Stephen Orgel. "As models of the universe, as science, as assertions of power, as demonstrations of the essential divinity of the human mind . . . [masques] are the supreme expressions of Renaissance kingship."[10] If kingship, the cosmic order which underwrites it, and the psychological structure it mirrors are subject to the deep stress of events in *The Maid's Tragedy*, the first place to look for signs of cracking is in its wedding masque. One does not have to probe beneath its surface for evidence that something is out of joint.

The first lines of the play offer a parody of Orgel's interpretation of the genre as the Renaissance court's idealized image of itself, or Enid

---

9. Andrew Gurr, "Critical Introduction," *The Maid's Tragedy* (Berkeley, Calif., 1969), p. 3.

10. Stephen Orgel, *The Illusion of Power: Political Theater in the English Renaissance* (Berkeley, Calif., 1975), pp. 57–58.

Welsford's description of its sophisticated play of aesthetic and erotic exuberance:[11]

LYSIPPUS
Strato, thou hast some skill in poetry:
What think'st thou of a masque? Will it be well?
STRATO
As well as masques can be.
LYSIPPUS
As masques can be?
STRATO
Yes, they must commend their king, and speak
In praise of the assembly, bless the bride and groom,
In person of some god: they're tied to rules
Of flattery.[12]

Ventured by one who "has some skill in poetry," this remark goes undisputed. If it does not represent Beaumont's own attitude toward the masque, the remark at least indicates that the courtly audience may have held the genre in less reverence than its modern interpreters have accounted for. Strato's in-joke here is a deflating outline of the structural principles of masques with which Orgel and Welsford have acquainted us. Yet even this remark is scant preparation for the breakdown of the genre which follows. The consequences of the masque's collapse will run deep into the structure of the play.

The conventional masque symbolically masters the chaotic energy of figures of disorder through the triumph of a hierarchy which is at once mythic, political, and psychological. The head of the mythological hierarchy is a god who represents order, light, and reason. In the wedding masque, the appropriate figure is Hymen, "regarded not merely as 'the god who sits at wedding feasts,' but also as the god of marriage regarded as a social function, and even as a mystic symbol of national unity or of the harmony of all men with one another."[13] As the masque opens out in the

11. Enid Welsford, *The Court Masque: A Study in the Relation Between Poetry and the Revels* (New York, 1962), pp. 374–406.

12. Beaumont and Fletcher, *The Maid's Tragedy*, ed. Howard B. Norland (Lincoln, Nebr., 1968), I.i.5–11. Subsequent references to the play, identified by act, scene, and lines, will be indicated parenthetically in the essay, and will refer to this edition.

13. Welsford, *Court Masque*, p. 397.

closing gesture peculiar to its genre, to include its audience in the harmonious vision, the mythic hierarchy itself defers to the king, as its true head, the sovereign witness who is, as Orgel points out, the source of its energies and the resolver of its dissonances.[14] Imagistically associated with the sun, the king is the human representative of the Deity, the human sign of that divine presence which secures all things in its vast design. As the masque unfolds into courtly song and dance, it realizes dynamically the spiritual harmony which charges all existence.

Although Hymen is invoked in the third song of the masque in *The Maid's Tragedy*, the god does not appear to culminate its rites. The two figures which control the performance are a somnolent Night, and Cynthia, whose function as "patron of generation and childbirth" is "not so much as alluded to."[15] Night calls upon her to "Produce a birth, to crown this happy hour" (I.ii.151), and to summon her own mortal lover, Endymion, to share in the generative ritual. Cynthia refuses, protesting that the fable of her passion for Endymion was spun out by drunken poets (ll. 159–161). Nevertheless, she agrees to assist with the mythic elevation of the lovers for whom the masque has been prepared. When Cynthia promises to "give a greater state and glory, / And raise to time a nobler memory / Of what these lovers are" (ll. 161–164), we hear the echo of Strato's ironic prologue. The action of the play will deepen the irony.

Assuming the role of stage manager, Cynthia summons Neptune and the ranks of lesser gods to provide the appropriate spectacle. Night, the "great queen of shadows" (l. 136), settles back as the drowsy royal witness of the revels. That Night is the presiding divine presence, and a Cynthia who has rejected her own generative aspects is the divine mover of the entertainments, must strike a jarring note. Night's presence evokes the world of primordial darkness. Hesiod renders her the second child of Chaos, and Milton represents her as the sable-vested consort of Chaos, ruling the intermediate space between creative existence and the frozen wastelands of Hell.[16] The spectacle which Night oversees in *The Maid's*

14. Orgel, *Illusion of Power*, p. 52: "Thus the ruler gradually redefines himself through the illusionist's art, from a hero, the center of a court and a culture, to the god of power, the center of a universe . . ."

15. Neill, "Masque, Imagery, and the Fancy," p. 117.

16. Hesiod, *The Poems and Fragments*, trans. A. W. Mair (Oxford, 1908), p. 35. Night's progeny include Doom, Fate, Death, Sleep, Blame, Woe, the Fates, Nemesis, Deceit, Love, and Strife. Night appears in *Paradise Lost*, II.894–897.

Tragedy is less a turmoil than the "eternal Anarchy" invented for her by Milton. Yet a masque instigated by a figure mythically associated with original darkness, chaos, and conflict may be unable to fulfill the generic requirements of light, harmony, and generation.

In the masques of which Welsford gives an account, the dominion of Night is presented largely through the action of the antimasque, whose forces are eventually either dispelled or structured by the larger, luminous patterns of the masque, controlled by the King / Sun. This representation of an idealized ordering of psychic forces performs the kind of wish fulfillment which Freud considered one of the functions of literature: the threatening energies of the unconscious were invoked and given play, then banished or mastered by the organizing powers of consciousness. The masque in *The Maid's Tragedy* nominally follows this pattern of mastery. Cynthia and Night divest themselves of authority in the presence of "a greater light, a greater majesty" (I.ii.274), the Rhodian king. Daylight arrives to supplant the hierarchies of darkness who vanish "into mists" and "into day" (l. 278). But the masque ends abruptly at this point. It fails to confirm in dance and in song the moral order of which the king is the keystone. On the command of the king, the courtly spectators vanish into the darkness of a wedding night over which Hymen has lost his benevolent and fructifying sovereignty.

Nature hateth emptiness. In the absence of Hymen, the erotic and aggressive forces which are to ravage the characters in the play take control of the masque. Neill has traced the darkening ambiguities of the "night" imagery in the play; night becomes the chaotic realm where impulses toward love and aggression so intertangle as to translate the masque's promise of epithalamium into the grim foreclosure of epitaph.[17] The speech of Night herself forecasts this movement. The mood of masque and play is set by Night's introductory words, filled with apocalyptic antagonism toward the daylit realm: "Our reign is come, for in the raging sea / The sun is drown'd, and with him fell the Day" (I.ii.112–113). This antagonism is reiterated at the end of the masque. This nocturnal sovereign yields her authority with little magnanimity:

> Oh, I could frown
> To see the Day, the Day that flings his light

17. Neill, "Masque, Imagery, and the Fancy," pp. 126–127.

> Upon my kingdom and contemns old Night!
> Let him go on and flame! I hope to see
> Another wild fire in his axletree,
> And all fall drench'd.
>
> (I.ii.266–271)

Her attitude toward the values whose imagistic and mythic center is the sun, and whose social center is the king, is not merely subversive, but murderous. Her lines allegorically foreshadow the action of the play: the wild fire of the king's lust brings all the principal characters to ruin.[18]

The mythic antagonism expressed by Night poses a threat not only to the solar hierarchy of the play's universe, but to the social and psychological structures which ideally mirror that hierarchy. Both kingship and reason are challenged by their negatives, by libidinal forces which can only identify themselves through disruption. The most immediate representation of this antagonism is in the sexual dispute, the hostility which charges the play. Each scene of the drama rides out a deep tension between characters who nervously parry, seeking to penetrate veils of disguise, not merely to discover another's identity, but by discovering to master it, to convert it into an identity forged by the seeker. Sex and aggression are violently interfused; with the slightest change in emotional valence, one turns into the other. The second song of the masque plays with this deadly confusion:

> Hold back thy hours, dark Night, till we have done;
>   The Day will come too soon.
> Young maids will curse thee if thou steal'st away,
>   And leav'st their blushes open to the day.
>   Stay, stay, and hide
>   The blushes of the bride.
>
> Stay, gentle Night, and with thy darkness cover
>   The kisses of her lover.

---

18. The conflict between a primordial goddess and a solar god is an archetypal drama which recurs in the different mythologies of the world. It seems to me no coincidence that this mythic contention surfaces in a drama which rehearses the cosmic anxieties of its period. For further description of this mythological background, see Joseph Campbell, *The Masks of God: Occidental Mythology* (New York, 1971), pp. 75–87.

> Stay and confound her tears and her shrill cryings,
>   Her weak denials, vows, and often-dyings;
>   Stay and hide all,
>   But help not though she call.
>
> (I.ii.223–234)

The song takes a frightening turn in the second stanza: the "gentle Night" is summoned to conceal an act of sexual violence, as the coy curses of the maids turn to what sounds like a desperate plea for help. The stanza may be a conventional enough version of Jacobean wit, but the wit uneasily conceals the sexual antagonism of the statement.

Perhaps the second song was too cynical a statement about sexual love to close the round of singing and dancing and lead into the masque's final movement. A second quarto of the play adds a third song, with introductory dialogue, to the original 1619 quarto.[19] The additions seem to bridle the sexual thrust of the second song, and to restore the epithalamial note appropriate to the occasion:

> To bed, to bed! Come, Hymen, lead the bride,
>   And lay her by her husband's side;
>   Bring in the virgins every one,
>   That grieve to lie alone,
> That they may kiss while they may say a maid;
>   Tomorrow t'will be other, kiss'd and said.
>   Hesperus, be long a-shining,
>   Whilst these lovers are a-twining.
>
> (I.ii.242–249)

But the invocation to Hymen is merely formal and superficial. Only the first two lines, and the last two (where the identity of "these lovers" includes, but is not restricted to, the married couple) may be construed as hymeneal. The song is not so much a celebration of married love as a playful description of lust masquerading as innocence. The conventions again prove inadequate to bind the energies unleashed in the masque.

This brings us to Boreas, the offstage villain whose escape brings the masque to an abrupt close. Boreas represents the spirit of disorder which

19. Norland discusses the variant texts in his introduction to the edition of *The Maid's Tragedy* cited in n. 12, pp. xxii–xxviii. The Q2 addition of lines 235–249 in Act 1, scene ii, is noted on p. 20 of this edition.

the traditional masque ultimately masters in its ritual. Among the anthro-
pomorphic deities of the masque, Boreas is characterized as more beastly
than human or divine: "Only Boreas, / Too foul for our intentions as he
was, / Still keep him fast chained" (I.ii. 174–176). There is little evidence
that the spirit of the North Wind was regularly vilified in the Renaissance.
The Greeks had credited him with minor rapes, but this is nothing
exceptional among the Greek deities. But his emblematic representation
may have appealed to the playwrights: "Boreas had a rough beard and grey
wings, his feet ended in serpents' tails, and he carried a leafless branch
covered with icicles."[20] The iconic association with age and impotence
hides a sinister sexuality, the serpents' tails growing out of his feet.
Clifford Leech notes the sexual implications of his escape,[21] and as we enter
the emotional maelstrom of the drama proper, we can recognize Boreas's
secret presence. The fiction of the masque and the reality of the court
always interpenetrated in Jacobean England, but the masque of *The Maid's
Tragedy* opens into the world of its court in a unique way. Boreas, the
spirit of sexual anarchy, passes through the veil between the masque and
the play which contains it, to become an active yet unnamed menace to
the courtly spectators of the masque. The masque leaves two dramatic
loose ends. One is the realization of Night's apocalyptic fantasy, the acting
out of her murderous rage against the sun. The other is the chaining of
Boreas, the containment of the chaotic energies he personifies. In a brilliant subterranean dramatic conceit, the dramatists tie these loose ends
with a single climactic action, Evadne's binding and murder of the king.

II

The success of the conceit depends on our recognition of the Rhodian
king's identity both with the sun, as center of a constellation of spiritual
and social values, and with Boreas, the grotesque yet powerful threat to
those values. The conceit also depends on identification of Evadne with the
menacing power of the masque's dark goddesses. The action of the play
supports these identifications. The king is virtually without personality in
the play; the stress is upon his symbolic identity as keystone of the social

20. Orgel, *Illusion of Power*, p. 25.
21. Leech, *The John Fletcher Plays*, p. 122.

order, and upon his dramatic function as the subverter of this order. The king's failure becomes not merely a symbol of the social disorder of the play, but the center of those shock waves which disturb the moral and emotional poise of all the characters. He infects the court with lust, greed, and deceit, undermining the order of which he is supposed to be keeper. His office thus links him to the solar hierarchy, but his actions betray that status, and rank him with the slimy Boreas of the masque. Yet even with his corruption exposed, the king retains enough mythic authority to paralyze the other male characters of the play. His ritual murder is accomplished not by the chief soldiers of his court, who have the cause and the power to do so, but by Evadne, whose conscience is not constrained by the taboo against regicide which inhibits the men. Only Evadne is not mesmerized by "that sacred name, / 'The king'" (II.i.305–306), and her death-strokes enact Night's revenge against the masculine hierarchy of the solar god even as they drive to the heart of the corruption of the dramatic universe.

Failing to pursue the ambiguous lead proposed by the title of the play, critics tend to neglect Evadne and turn to the central male characters, Amintor and Melantius, to account for the play's twisted plotting. But these characters prove too unstable and shifting to provide the psychological focus and the dramatic momentum and coherence which the conventional Jacobean Revenger provides. Instead, Amintor and Melantius are almost clinical studies of avoidance, and their failure finally to act provides evidence of the ideological and psychological power of the trope which locates the king at the center of the cosmic and political order. Amintor is rendered an emotional cripple, and Melantius, although nominally the Revenger who uses Evadne as the instrument in his plot against the king, is nevertheless transformed from a bluff and bloodthirsty warrior into a Machiavellian whose murder plot will keep his own hands clean. Amintor's confused impotence and Melantius's scheming are symptoms of a common dread of regicide.

Amintor especially is baffled by the king's double identity. Honor requires Amintor to murder the man who has cuckolded him even before he has been married, but the same honor paralyzes him with the thought of raising a hand against his king:

> As you are *mere man*,
> I dare as easily kill you for this deed
> As you dare think to do it. But there is
> Divinity about you that strikes dead
> My rising passions; as you are *my king*,
> I fall before you and present my sword
> To cut my own flesh, if it be your will.
>   (III.i.243–249; emphasis mine)

It is easy enough to make Amintor a source of ridicule, a kind of small change Hamlet, as Robert Ornstein does:

Are we really asked to admire the vacillating Amintor, who is as obtuse as he is sensitive, who speaks of honor but is totally absorbed in his own vanity, and whose royalism is as instinctive a reflex as a knee-jerk? All the evidence would suggest that Amintor is a pitiless and, at times, comic study of immature, unstable egotism. Yet unless we accept Amintor's "nobility" at face value, the emotional structure of the play apparently collapses, since he is the mover of Evadne's, Melantius', and Aspatia's passions.[22]

Like Ribner, Ornstein pursues a "moral vision," so he can afford a few cynical lines on a youth who cuts so melodramatic and unheroic a figure. If we grant the parodic element in Amintor's indecisiveness, we must acknowledge as well its psychological basis. How old is Amintor? Nineteen, perhaps? He has already been in wars, and knows the strange closeness of men who have killed together. He returns from the glory of battle to discover that his honors are hollow, that his bride has already cuckolded him, that he has been chosen to wear the horns by the king. Inadvertently, Ornstein is right on one point: the emotional structure of the play does collapse. The play is about the collapse of emotional structure, and about the terror of passion released when the old taboos do not hold. Amintor is no knee-jerk royalist. He tries to ward off madness by invoking and prostrating himself before the one power on earth which might maintain the stability of a world he discovers in collapse. The last vestiges of his belief—perhaps the last vestiges of his sanity—guard the notion that "in the sacred name, / 'The king,' there lies a terror" (II.i.305–306). The word "king" serves him as a talisman to control his rage, to translate his

---

22. Ornstein, *Moral Vision of Jacobean Tragedy*, p. 177.

thoughts of murder into self-laceration, or, in the emotional patterning of the play, to translate "anger" into "grief." Amintor is torn apart by the double image of the king: the Boreas of flesh and appetite and betrayal, the divinely appointed representative of order. At the same time that he feels the impulse to kill, Amintor feels the force of a prohibition backed by divine authority.[23]

The bluff warrior Melantius, unlike his tortured companion, is a man of few words, and the words he does speak repeatedly claim that his actions speak louder than words:

> these scratch'd limbs of mine
> Have spoke my love and truth unto my friends
> More than my tongue e'er could. My mind's the same
> It ever was to you; where I find worth
> I love the keeper till he let it go,
> And then I follow it.
>
> (I.i.21–26)

Melantius's guiding principle, "worth" or "honor," is free-floating, not bound to any man or title. Melantius claims the right to choose, at any time, whom he will fight for. He presents the character of another "unstable egotist," considerably more dangerous than Amintor because he knows his own strength, knows that even the king can claim no more authority over him than he is willing to concede. In these lines Melantius also reveals a lethal confusion between sexuality and bloodshed, which becomes more explicit when he balks at the invitation to the masque: "These soft and silken wars are not for me: / The music must be shrill and all confus'd / That stirs my blood, and then I dance with arms" (I.i.42–44).

The confusion truly becomes shrill and stirs his blood when Melantius learns that his sister's chastity is stained. He takes it as a personal and

---

23. It can be argued that Amintor and Melantius are both afflicted by the oedipal dilemma writ large in a political context. Both feel murderous rage toward an all-powerful father figure whose death is forbidden. The rage is provoked by the father figure's sexual sovereignty over a woman whom both Amintor and Melantius wish to possess. The prohibition is strengthened by the trope which identifies the king with the Sun and the Deity; thus Amintor's rage baffles him as a threat to the cosmic order: "fall I first / Amongst my sorrows, ere my treacherous hand / Touch holy things. But why? I know not what / I have to say" (III.i.255–258).

familial disgrace that his sister should be whored by the king: "My worthy
father's and my services / Are liberally rewarded! King, I thank thee! / For
all my dangers and my wounds thou hast paid me / In my own metal:
these are soldiers' thanks!" (IV.i. 127–130). Yet he turns his rage upon
Evadne rather than the king, and in his confrontation with her forces
repentance from her. The violent loathing and simultaneous fascination
with his sister's sexuality expressed in the confrontation scene (IV.i)
resembles the bedroom scene of *Hamlet* and the sexual threats against the
Duchess of Malfi by her brother, Duke Frederick: the passion for family
honor scarcely veils the seething patterns of family romance.[24]

Melantius is stung by the horrible fascination which Evadne's whore-
dom forces upon him: she is not chaste, therefore not untouchable, as
brothers come to believe that their sisters should be. The consummated
marriage of his sister to his bosom friend Amintor would have been a
doubly satisfactory solution to Melantius's unacknowledged incestuous
wishes, for not only would Amintor, whom he looks upon as a virtual
younger self, have proved a perfect substitute for him in Evadne's arms.
Evadne, in her own turn, would have functioned as a perfect surrogate for
the consummation of his desire for Amintor; he had hinted as much when
he congratulated Evadne on her nuptial choice: "You look'd with my eyes
when you took that man; / Be happy in him" (I.ii. 108–109). But that
imagined consummation is ruined by the revelation of Evadne's whore-
dom.

In facing the ruin of the family honor, Melantius exposes the mystique
of virginity upon which he had suspended the family honor; in the disintegration of that mystique, his passion for honor becomes confounded with
his fascination with his sister's sexual passion. Such fascination takes the
form of denial, but the ambiguities of Melantius's dialogue with Evadne
are telling. Each time she rebuffs his questions, the incestuous fury
mounts. Here is a sequence of Melantius's responses:

---

24. The incest motif is so frequent and deliberate in Jacobean drama that the confrontation between Melantius and Evadne cannot avoid referring to that motif. But the evidence
for reading the confrontation's incestuous potential is intrinsic as well as extrinsic, as I
attempt to demonstrate.

> I am as far from being part of thee
> As thou are from thy virtue; seek a kindred
> 'Mongst sensual beasts, and make a goat thy brother:
> A goat is cooler. Will you tell me yet?
> . . . .
> Work me no higher. Will you discover yet?
> . . . .
> Force my swoln heart no further; I would save thee.
>   (IV.i.63–66, 76,78)

Loathing and lust reach a climax in the single obscene threat, "This sword shall be thy lover!" (IV.i.99). The play's fatal mixture of sexuality and aggression will exceed this outburst only in Evadne's murder of the king. Melantius's histrionics are effective: he forces Evadne into a penitent chastity, which eases the sexual threat she represents. In a strategic act of cunning, Melantius plots to complete his sister's penitence with an act of blood which will relieve him not only of the anxiety which Evadne must henceforth arouse in him, but of the man responsible for the family disgrace, and the psychic turmoil it engenders.

There is a profound discrepancy between Melantius's original conception of revenge and his actual plot:

> But from his iron den I'll waken Death
> And hurl him on this king; my honesty
> Shall steel my sword, and on my horrid point
> I'll wear my cause, that shall amaze the eyes
> Of this proud man and be too glitt'ring
> For him to look on.
>   (III.ii.191–196)

In light of this vaunt, Melantius's actual response is as difficult to account for as Amintor's schizophrenic vacillation. As Melantius enters the sexual combat zone of the play, he experiences a marvelous influx of guile. His murder plot is a two-pronged strategy designed to remove himself from the site of the crime. First, we have seen, he brutalizes his sister into compliance; second, he dupes his aged antagonist, Callianax, into yielding control of the city's fortifications to him. If the confrontation with Evadne displays Melantius's brutality, the banquet scene, where he ruthlessly

manipulates both the king and Callianax, reveals his Machiavellian potential. Here Melantius shows that he can use words as treacherously as the
next fellow; he can not only overpower the king, he can outflank him as
well.

The inane little altercations between Melantius and Callianax which
have threaded the plot (I.ii; III.ii.) now make sense. Whatever sympathy
we might have felt for Callianax because of his daughter's heartbreak has
steadily eroded, as we discover him to be a querulous old fool and a
coward. In a single stroke, the banquet scene exposes the king as no more
clever or daring than Callianax. The scene may be read two ways: either
the king is fooled by Melantius, or he is faced down. In either case, the
hapless Callianax is backed into a corner where he has no choice but to turn
the fort into Melantius's hands.

Yet in a matter of such personal and familial honor, why does Melantius
resort to duplicity rather than the power of the sword in which he takes
such pride? The possible motives are manifold, yet each in itself seems
insufficient. Evadne must do penance for her own sins, wash her stains in
the blood of the king. The moral exactitude of such a motive would be
surprising, for Melantius seems to have little patience with moral
economy. This leads to a cruder cause for his plot. He must cover his own
tracks: "To take revenge and lose myself withal / Were idle, and to
'scape, impossible, / Without I had the fort . . ." (III.ii.289–291). Here
Melantius betrays his own potential as a Revenger who would readily
throw himself into the breach his own act opens. What better way to
protect himself than to force his sister to kill, while he stands on the walls
of the fort backed by a small army, "And with a loud voice calls those few
who pass / At this dead time of night, delivering / The innocence of this
act" (V.i.141–143). One can imagine him beginning his proclamation of
innocence even before Evadne bloodies her knife. The strategy works:
Lysippus delivers him a blank check in return for his promise not to
"unbuild / This goodly town" (V.ii.58–59).

But this deal forces the question: if Melantius has the strength to take
the town apart, why an elaborate charade to protect himself and declare an
innocence which none believes but which all must consent to? The deep
motive for Melantius's indirection and for Amintor's paralysis is the same:
the king is taboo, a kind of living totem, a sign of cosmic and social

coherence, and the incalculable power of the Diety stands behind him. Although Melantius is too proud to soliloquize his anxiety as Amintor does, the authority of the king forces Amintor to blunt his rage, and channel it into the subversive design of a murder from which he can escape direct responsibility.[25]

Evadne thus appears to be merely the sacrificial pawn in Melantius's strategy. When the murder is discovered, Strato advises, "Never follow her, / For she, alas, was but the instrument" (V.i.137–138). Why, then, does she emerge as the most awesome figure in the play? The murder of the king is itself a measure of her power: she commits a crime which the patriarchal warriors of the drama implicitly dread, and in the act of murder, Evadne assumes herself some portion of the mystique which had rendered the king inviolable. As Freud explains the dynamics of the violation of the taboo, "any one who has violated such a prohibition assumes the nature of the forbidden object as if he had absorbed the whole dangerous charge."[26] Amintor's response to her after she comes to him to confess and to exult in her crime is a mixture of dread and panic, and Evadne's death must come by her own hand because no one else in the play can approach her.

Yet Evadne's power has been implicit from her first appearance in the play, and it comes from a source independent of the murdered king: she radiates a sexual authority which she refuses to curb or shame. The men's responses to her indicate how disarming her sexual presence is. Amintor lightly tosses off his vows to Aspatia for the promise of losing his "lusty youth" (I.i.141) in Evadne's arms. The king devises the elaborate charade of her marriage to provide a cover for his possession of her, and when he senses that possession is endangered by her marriage, he erupts in violent jealousy (III.1.122 ff.). The threat of her illicit sexual satisfaction drives

25. Freud's writing on the nature of the taboo explains why the thought of regicide has such a paralyzing effect on the warriors of this play: "Originally the punishment for the violation of a taboo was probably left to an inner, automatic arrangement. The violated taboo avenged itself. Wherever the taboo was related to ideas of gods and demons an automatic punishment was expected from the power of the godhead." Freud makes clear that psychic connection between the magical "inner, automatic arrangement" for punishment, and what we call guilt. *Totem and Taboo*, trans. A. A. Brill (New York, 1946), p. 29.

26. *Ibid.*, p. 31.

Melantius into his murderous hysteria. Sexual power is the key to her independence of, and defiance of, the men who imagine they control her. Not only can she assert to Amintor, "I do enjoy the best, and in that height / Have sworn to stand or die" (II.i.293–294). She defies the king on the same terms:

> I swore indeed that I would never love
> A man of lower place, but if your fortune
> Should throw you from this height, I bade you trust
> I would forsake you and would bend to him
> That won the throne. I love with my ambition,
> Not with my eyes.
>
> (III.i.178–183)

The hierarchy holds no mystique over her; she values it insofar as it helps her to secure her own place. Yet her situation involves a curious and ultimately fatal split in consciousness. An independent, sexually aggressive woman, she is utterly dependent on the masculine hierarchy for her status in the court. In choosing the king for her lover, and vowing to have no one less than a king, she binds herself to the power of place in the patriarchal system. That system, she knows, has no mythic authority other than the conventions it proposes to perpetuate itself; it is merely a distribution of power. Yet in placing herself as a dependent within that system, she implicitly consents to its authority, and sets herself up for its judgment on her sexual audacity, when the balance of power shifts and she finds herself without the support of the king.

The instrument of moral retribution proves to be her own conscience. In the turbulent confrontation scene, Melantius converts Evadne to a path of penance that must lead to the murder of the king. Repudiating her sexual aggressiveness, she submits to the moral judgment of which she was once openly contemptuous. This psychic reversal may seem improbable to the modern reader schooled in psychological realism, but the stress which produces her conversion is vividly suggested. It is her brother, whose own libido has fueled his war-making prowess, who brings the message of her crime home to her, in the deadly erotic threat, "This sword shall be thy lover!" (IV.i.99). That the consequence of sexual activity might be death is sufficient to force Evadne into a kind of negative chastity, in which fear and guilt drive the libido back on itself in outrage. The claim of family, that primary organization of psychic energy, the original patriarchal hierarchy, is the snare in which Melantius catches Evadne. He couples his death threat with the specter of their blood father to tear Evadne from her liaison with the king:

EVADNE

Let me consider.

MELANTIUS

      Do, whose child thou wert,
Whose honor thou hast murdered, whose grave opened,
And so pull'd on the gods, that in their justice
They must restore him flesh again and life,
And raise his dry bones to revenge this scandal.

(IV.i.88–92)

If we allow for the foreshortening and resulting intensification of temporal and psychological process demanded by the Jacobean dramatic economy, we may find Evadne's reversion to the docile feminine place in the structure of the family not only dramatically effective but psychologically compelling.

Evadne now accepts and conforms to the masculine terror of unbridled sexuality in women: "Sure I am monstrous, / For I have done those follies, those mad mischiefs, / Would dare a woman" (IV.i.183–185). Her conversion involves a repudiation of this "monstrous" sexuality; she views herself as a fallen antitype of Eve, seduced by the "devil king" (IV.i.263; Melantius's phrase).[27] Her conformity does not render her less awesome, however, for under the pressure of guilt and fear engendered by Melantius's threats, her erotic power assumes a different form of "monstrosity," as it changes valence into the murderous rage mythically expressed by the goddess Night in the masque. Michael Neill has pointed out that the imagery of Night invests Evadne as she hurries to her fatal task.[28] The path of what she takes to be her expiation leads her to the most monstrous of crimes, regicide. Mythic motive here merges with the motive of personal revenge to transform Evadne's part as instrument in Melantius's scheme into a role of tragic consequence, and Evadne's

27. The name Evadne is an abbreviated acronymic combination of the names of Adam and Eve, and her fall in a vague way mirrors their original seduction from paradise.

28. Neill, "Masque, Imagery, and the Fancy," pp. 127–128.

heightened consciousness in the midst of her commitment to the crime enlarges and complicates her character in a way unmatched by any other character in the play:

> The night grows horrible, and all about me
> Like my black purpose. Oh, the conscience
> Of a lost virgin, whither wilt thou pull me:
> To what things dismal as the depth of hell
> Wilt thou provoke me? Let no woman dare
> From this hour be disloyal, if her heart
> Be flesh, if she have blood and can fear. 'Tis a madness
> Above that desperate fool's that left his peace
> And went to sea to fight; 'tis so many sins
> An age cannot repent 'em, and so great
> The gods want mercy for. Yet I must through 'em;
> I have begun a slaughter on my honor,
> And I must end it there.
>
> (V.i. 13–25)

The moral confusion of this soliloquy is itself eloquent, as is the tragic clarity of will which closes it. The revenging "conscience of a lost virgin" provokes Evadne to what she knows to be an act of unimagined evil. Yet that conscience is so powerful that Evadne considers her true sin, the "slaughter on her honor," the original betrayal of her chastity. The murder of the king will end the slaughter, and the torments of conscience; it is less a crime to her than a violent and cleansing repudiation of the greater crime of promiscuity.

Evadne ties the king to the bed and rouses him. At first the king is pleased by what he takes to be a new love game, yet he soon realizes that its consummation will be fatal. Indifferent to the aura of the king's name and office, Evadne calls him to account for her ruined virtue, and for the lost honor of her family:

> Thou art a shameless villain,
> A thing out of the overcharge of nature,
> Sent like a thick cloud to disperse a plague
> Upon weak catching women, such a tyrant,
> That for his lust would sell away his subjects,
> Ay, all his heaven hereafter.
>
> (V.i.90–95)

Like Boreas of the masque, "a thing out of the overcharge of nature," the king embodies for her the lust which has corrupted all love and honor and afflicted all the central characters of the play. In this ritual love-death scene, Evadne completes the archetypal intentions of the masque: the binding of Boreas, and the destruction of the solar king.

If the binding promises a conclusion to the tragedy, a containment of the nearly exhausted drives which have pushed the characters beyond the pale of human sanity, the murder does not signal what we might project from the mythic patterns of the masque. Night has her moment's vengance in Evadne's act, but it is only a brief glory, a momentary interruption in the patriarchal structure of power. Yet the replacement of the old regime by a new one does signal more than a smooth transition in power. For the murder of the king represents a deathblow to the idea of order which sustained the monarchic idea in the Renaissance. No divine power, offended by the death of a legitimate monarch, exacts revenge; the world does not collapse when its symbolic keystone is destroyed. So the magic of the myth which bound King to Sun to Diety is broken. The values of the new regime are secular and pragmatic, resting not on the assurance of divine right, but on the uneasy balance between soldier and diplomat.

Melantius is the key figure in the new dispensation. Lysippus, brother of the dead king, does not hesitate to give Melantius a pardon for which he can write his own terms. Yet Melantius has not foreseen the full cost of his coup. When he enters the corpse-strewn stage in the final scene, his grief is all for Amintor: "Here lies my sister, father, brother, son, / All that I had" (V.iii.268–270). This is one of the most appalling and pathetic responses of a play torn by extremities of feeling. The honor of the family had been the manifest motive for Melantius's betrayal of the king. He had so overpowered Evadne with the sacred claims of family that she came to believe that her crime was the act of a saint. Melantius now discards "family" into the pile of outworn ideals which love and honor occupy. None of the old securities or stabilizing values endures the general wreck of world order.

Ornstein hints at the perversity of Melantius's devotion to Amintor.[29] What is perverse about that devotion is not that it is homosexual, since it is the deepest and most constant emotional commitment of the play—

---

29. Ornstein, *Moral Vision of Jacobean Tragedy*, p. 179.

except perhaps Aspatia's devotion to the pleasures of her grief. What is perverse is the way that this emotion becomes so all-consuming that Melantius is indifferent and utterly ruthless to all the other characters, including Amintor himself, finally, whom Melantius does not trouble to warn of his intrigue.

But there is something about Melantius's final gestures which subverts even the ultimacy of his passionate attachment to Amintor. He attempts to stab himself—unsuccessfully, for he is quickly disarmed by other, lesser men. His is the only suicide attempt which fails. Deprived of weapons, he threatens to starve himself. Are these protests mere charade? If he truly intended to kill himself, could he not have overpowered the guards who restrain him? Will he starve himself, or eventually accept the post of chief of staff under Lysippus? If he should starve himself, it would be the final effect of the shock waves generated by Boreas in the play. If he should live to fight again, it would secure the new secular ordering of power in the court of Rhodes.

III

Critical response to The Maid's Tragedy tends to deny that it has a tragic focus: "It is not a tragedy in the usual sense; it has no single great figure brought low by Fortune's wheel or Aristotle's peripeteia."[30] The play's title appears to refer to Aspatia, who is surely no tragic hero. Danby tries to establish her moral prominence in the drama: "Aspatia represents the large and immovable continent of the traditional morality from which the 'wild island' of Beaumont's dramatic world detaches itself."[31] Danby's description of Aspatia is misleading on two counts. First, "traditional morality" is no continent in the drama, but a swamp of quicksand. Second, Aspatia's pathetic story does not frame the play, as Danby claims; it runs alongside the play, irrelevant to the rest of the story. The most self-absorbed character in the play, Aspatia has not the slightest awareness of the intrigues in which all the other characters are tangled. She is the self-conscious artist who weaves out her history as an emblem of the

30. Gurr, Introduction to The Maid's Tragedy, p. 4.
31. Danby, Poets on Fortune's Hill, p. 205.

forsaken woman. In perhaps the most admired and frequently cited lines in the play, she compares herself to Ariadne:

> Suppose I stand upon the sea breach now,
> Mine arms thus, and mine hair blown with the wind,
> Wild as that desert, and let all about me
> Tell that I am forsaken. Do my face
> (If thou hadst ever feeling of a sorrow)
> Thus, thus, Antiphila: strive to make me look
> Like sorrow's monument; and the trees about me,
> Let them be dry and leafless; let the rocks
> Groan with continual surges; and behind me
> Make all a desolation.
>
> (II.ii.68–77)

The critical admiration of this passage indicates how seductive the rhetoric of self-pity can be. Its extreme beauty almost makes the reader lose sight of its artificiality. This passage is sheer pose, in which Aspatia wishes to gather herself and her audience into the artifice of eternity she has designed. It will be a mournful artifice, "sorrow's monument," yet it will be a monument of pathos, not of tragedy. As Antiphila remarks to Callianax, "It is the lady's pleasure we be thus / In grief she is forsaken" (II.ii.92–93). The emotional circuit dictated here between character and audience opposes the cathartic flow of tragedy. Whereas tragedy produces pleasure for its audience through the grief of its protagonist, Aspatia wishes to please herself by producing grief in her audience. If she does represent the "traditional morality" of the play, she represents it as a parodic icon, and it is not her experience of suffering, however vividly she tries to represent it, with which the audience can sympathize.

Aspatia's self-absorption is a powerful repression of the same libidinal anarchy which afflicts all the characters. In her extensive fantasy identification with Ariadne, she rewrites the myth to "make the story, wrong'd by wanton poets, / Live long and be believ'd" (II.ii.58–59). Her misprision of the myth fixes Theseus the betrayer in the web of art at the moment when she would have him destroyed by the elements:

> Antiphila, in this place work a quicksand,
> And over it a shallow smiling water,

And his ship plowing it, and then a Fear:
Do that Fear to the Life, wench.

(II.ii.54–57)

Aspatia's grief is the shallow smiling water over quicksand, a quiet surface hiding an engulfing rage. Both the speeches of Aspatia cited above reveal her apocalyptic motivation, her desire to obliterate everything outside herself. Not only is the male betrayer frozen in the moment of terrified recognition of his death; the whole landscape is left desolate in Aspatia's monument to herself. She can only act out her rage, however, when she hides the passive, virginal, suffering feminine in masculine disguise. Her brother's clothes permit Aspatia the psychological room to harass Amintor. She mounts no defense or attack in the ensuing sword fight, and takes Amintor's blows like embraces (V.iii.101–104). She has suffered the same confusion of love and violence as all the other characters, yet the consummatory act of aggression she permits herself in male clothes is Chaplinesque rather than heroic: it is a kind of vaudeville miming of what she wishes to do.

Aspatia, then, reveals in an oblique and parodic way the rage against the masculine hierarchy which begins to haunt the play with the first words of Night in the masque. *The Maid's Tragedy* is a tragedy of maids in the generic sense, for both the central women characters are destroyed by masculine court intrigues. Aspatia and Evadne are inverse images of each other. Aspatia is the passively suffering abandoned woman who dresses like a man as if male clothing brings with it aggressive behavior. Evadne is the sexually aggressive woman who determines the fate of men, until she is brainwashed into a docile yet murderous femininity. If the idea of monarchy is the secret motive which determines the action or inaction of Melantius and Amintor, the idea of maidenhood or maidenhead is the tragic crux and the driving obsession for Aspatia and Evadne. "The loss of virginity is like a breakdown in universal logic":[32] Aspatia's grief sanctifies in perpetuity the maidenhead she wishes she had lost, Evadne murders for a maidenhead she wishes she could recover. Yet whereas Aspatia's story

32. Angus Fletcher, *The Transcendental Masque: An Essay on Milton's Comus* (Ithaca, N.Y., 1971), p. 218.

attempts to write itself as a moral icon, a fable of grief fixed beyond time, Evadne's story is marked by tragic action and tragic change.

Evadne seems not only to stand at the human center of the play's thematic and dramatic entanglements, but to undertake, alone among the characters, the tragic pilgrimage from passion to perception. In binding and murdering the king, Evadne gives a human shape and voice to the primal anger of the goddess Night. She focuses the chaotic energies of lust and aggression in a consummatory act which ensures their ultimate exhaustion and containment; she thereby completes the actions anticipated in the mythic theater of the masque. Unaffected by the anxiety over regicide which restrains the men, she commits an ultimate sacrilege against the Renaissance world order. What is most striking about her murder of the king is that it produces no cosmic repercussions. Evadne's murder of the king does not throw the time out of joint; it gives a symbolic deathblow to the myth which had sacralized the figure of the king.

Furthermore, Evadne epitomizes the dissolution, under the stress of passion so intense as to be hallucinogenic, of stable forms of identity. Of the central quartet of characters, none arrives at the end of the drama without being stripped of every certainty. The other three all recoil from the signs of a world coming apart: Amintor into a pathetic vacillation between revenge and self-pity, between the commitment to honor and the commitment to appearances; Melantius into malevolently focused hysteria; Aspatia into the blind pleasure of her grief. Evadne alone endures the flux of absolute feeling to approach the tragedy of perception in the midst of the dramatic chaos.

Her passage into the full desolation of reality comes late. When she murders the king, she strikes a blow for herself as "the most wrong'd of women" (V.i.111). Yet her revenge is not enacted for herself alone; it is a symbolic gesture performed for Amintor, for her brother, even for "all you spirits of abused ladies," whom she has invoked to "Help me in this performance" (IV.i.170–171). The murder of the king is thus, in dramatic context, an act of tragic courage: daring, representative, and necessary. But the way of passion which leads Evadne to the crime involves an immense and pathetic delusion. "One does not get a second chance at being a virgin";[33] yet when she returns to Amintor, the king's blood still smoking on her hands, she believes her tragic expiation has purified her: "Am I not fair? / Looks not Evadne beauteous with these rites now?" (V.iii.118–119). Her pleas to Amintor to take her to bed reveal the glazed-over consciousness of one whose trauma has delivered her from ordinary reality. Were her story to end here, Evadne would appear to be another victim of Boreas, a character torn apart by the dramatic maelstrom. Yet Amintor's appalled rejection of her casts her into full recognition of her circumstances: her crime, its consequences, her fate.

In the midst of the carnage, the vaudeville deaths of Amintor and Aspatia, the suicide vaunts of Melantius, Evadne's self-murder is striking for its clarity of will. Like other tragic heroes, she has been so thrust beyond the dimensions of ordinary human experience that she has already stepped outside of life. She chooses death without bitterness: "Amintor, thou shalt love me now again. / Go, I am calm. Farewell, and peace forever. / Evadne, whom thou hatest, will die for thee" (V.iii.169–171). Suicide can only be problematic when considered an act of tragic courage, yet in the emotional anarchy of the play's conclusion, such a choice may be the only possible act of integrity.

"Here I swear it, / And all you spirits of abused ladies, / Help me in this performance" (IV.i.169–171). This is a maid's tragedy, and Evadne is the lost maid who performs it. In the half-light given off by the destruction of a coherence-giving arch of beliefs whose keystone, the king, had been the very cause of its collapse, and in the specter of as yet incomprehensible forces rising out of that destruction, Evadne stands with a double mask. She appears monstrous because she is the human conductor of much of those terrifying forces, violating the sacred prohibitions of the world she inhabits. She appears heroic because she salvages, in the midst of her own defeat, an integrity of commitment which is the only aspect of being human that a grotesque and appalling world cannot destroy.

33. *Ibid.*, p. 213.

Massinger's The City Madam *and the Caroline Audience*

MARTIN BUTLER

I N HIS SEMINAL STUDY *Drama and Society in the Age of Jonson* (1937), L. C. Knights represented Jacobean and Caroline "city comedy" as the reaction of a society with a deeply rooted conservative world-view to the changes and new economic forces that threatened to overturn all its old hierarchies of social degree and moral value, a pattern which would seem to be epitomized by Massinger's *The City Madam*. The downfall of Massinger's avaricious citizen Luke Frugal and the humiliation of Luke's proud sister-in-law and her daughters provoke the quasi-authorial moral that there should be "In their habits, manners, and their highest port, / A distance 'twixt the city and the court" (V.iii.154–55),[1] and most critics agree to find in Luke and Lady Frugal "representatives of the early Stuart trading class whose hunger for financial power and social prestige is, Massinger feels, endangering the social integrity of the upper class—the aristocracy and minor gentry which form the basis of traditional society."[2] Massinger shows this traditional society avenging itself on those who defy

I am grateful to the British Academy for a "Thank-Offering to Britain" Research Fellowship that has enabled me to research and write this paper.

1. All references are to the text edited by Colin Gibson in *The Selected Plays of Philip Massinger* (Cambridge, Eng., 1978).

2. A. G. Gross, "Social Change and Philip Massinger," *SEL*, VII (1967), 330.

its norms, and at the close "the framework of the hereditary class system is reasserted" while Luke Frugal "is rendered ineffectual and Sir John and his wife repent."[3] *The City Madam* is the anti-acquisitive play *par excellence*.

However, there is also a widely held feeling that city comedy's inherent conservatism represents a *failure* to come to terms with social change, that Massinger was on the wrong side of a historical process which within a decade would render any attempt to keep the city in its place absurdly irrelevant, and that the quality of his insight was unequal to his situation. One writer, noting a split in the play between the "characters of the trading class whose ambitions were very much part of the social world to which they belong" and Massinger's "traditional, Christian analysis of the difficulties these ambitions create," describes his "fear and hatred" of these developments as "definite impediments to his understanding."[4] Another, more crudely, describes this as merely "the distaste of the son of an old retainer family for the vulgar bourgeois."[5] To put it another way, Massinger wrote as the servant of the fashionable and exclusive Caroline audience, and could only be horrified by the forces that would eventually destroy the court's social and political hegemony, but his arguments exerted no authority in the intractable "real" world outside the playhouse from which the conditions that enabled both court and theater to exist would soon disappear. As M. C. Bradbrook says, in the heady Blackfriars milieu of 1632—one "increasingly alienated from the city"—Massinger would "find no audience among citizens."[6] The play's narrowness was dictated by the environment for which it was written.

If *The City Madam* really was as "decadent" as this, a "rearguard action on behalf of . . . a decaying or collapsing culture,"[7] it would be an interesting social document but no more. I wish to defend Massinger's intelligence and show that his play is much more "open" than the simplified formula "court versus city" suggests. We may begin by questioning this

3. *Ibid.*, pp. 338, 340.

4. *Ibid.*, pp. 330, 331–332.

5. R. A. Fothergill, "The Dramatic Experience of Massinger's *The City Madam* and *A New Way to Pay Old Debts*," *UTQ*, XLIII (1973), 74.

6. *The Living Monument* (Cambridge, Eng., 1976), p. 102.

7. Terms borrowed from J. P. Danby, *Elizabethan and Jacobean Poets*, 2d ed. (London, 1965), pp. 181–182.

traditional picture of the play's audience as inherently prejudiced, by its elitist social composition, against the city and toward the court.

I

Colin Gibson[8] has paralleled Sir John Frugal's career with that of Sir William Cokayne, an erstwhile apprentice of the Skinners' Company who rose to become alderman, sheriff and Lord Mayor of London (1619), the governor of the London companies' Ulster colony (1612), and, through trading ventures with the Eastland Company and the East India Company, one of the richest citizens of his day. He was a prominent example of citizen stock moving into the nobility, earning a knighthood, and gaining aristocratic promotion for his son, Viscount Cullen (1642), and daughters. What Gibson overlooks is that Cokayne was related to at least one well-known theatergoer. Sir Aston Cokayne, author of three plays and friend of many dramatists, including Massinger (for whom he supplied commendatory verses), belonged to a Derbyshire gentry family representing the elder branch of the stock from which Sir William descended.[9] The connection was fairly remote; nevertheless, Sir Aston's *Chain of Golden Poems* (London, 1658) includes an epigram to *"the Lady* Mary Cokaine, *Viscountess* Cullen," Sir William's daughter-in-law (p. 186). Moreover, Sir William's widow, herself the daughter of a Master of the Ironmongers' Company, remarried Henry, Earl of Dover, for whom Thomas Heywood wrote private theatrical pieces in the 1630s. Dover's son, Viscount Rochford, who in 1630 married his own stepsister, Abigail Cokayne, was the dedicatee of Nathaniel Richards's tragedy *Messallina* (1640). [10]

Such links between wealthy citizenry and theatergoing circles were by no means exceptional, as may be illustrated in the city connections which would be taken for granted by the Essex gentleman and diarist Sir

8. "Massinger's London Merchant and the Date of *The City Madam,*" *MLR*, LXV (1970), 737–749.

9. "Pedigrees Contained in the Visitations of Derbyshire 1569 and 1611," *The Genealogist*, N.S. VII (1891), 70–72; G. E. Bentley, *The Jacobean and Caroline Stage*, 7 vols. (Oxford, 1941–1968), III, 166–167.

10. G. E. Cokayne, *Some Account of the Lord Mayors and Sheriffs of the City of London During the First Quarter of the Seventeenth Century* (London, 1897), pp. 83–89; T. Heywood, *Pleasant Dialogues and Dramas* (London, 1637; dedicated to Dover), pp. 242–247.

Humphrey Mildmay, who in several ways was a representative Caroline playgoer. [11] One companion Mildmay took to the theater was his brother-in-law Sir Christopher Abdy, the son of a lawyer, but also a member of a leading London merchant family governing the Clothworkers' Company. Sir Christopher's uncle Anthony was Master of the Clothworkers (1632), an alderman and sheriff, and held high office in the East India Company, Levant Company, and Virginia Company. [12] The Abdys were rising to county importance in Essex, and had commercial and blood ties with other powerful city dynasties. Sir Christopher's aunt came of the wealthy Cambell family. Her father and brother were both lord mayors; the former founded a charity school, and the latter, Sir James Cambell, was colonel of the trained bands and president of St. Thomas's Hospital (1629–1642). An ironmonger, he had interests in the East India Company, the French Company, and the Merchants of the Staple, and left £50,000 in charitable bequests in his will. Another brother was sheriff (1630) and father of a baronet. [13] A cousin of Sir Christopher matched into another distinguished city family, the Soames. His wife's grandfather, an Elizabethan lord mayor, died worth £46,000; her father, Thomas Soames, traded with India, Russia, the Adriatic, and the Levant, was sheriff (1635) and colonel of the trained bands. In 1640 he was elected MP for the city on the radical platform. [14] He has particular interest for us since it was to him that the playwright Nathaniel Richards dedicated his *Poems Sacred and Satirical* (1641).

Another brother-in-law of Humphrey Mildmay was John Bennet, himself the father of Henry Bennet who wrote verses for Killigrew's *Prisoners and Claracilla* (1640). John Bennet was the son of a diplomat, but also an offshoot of citizen stock. His great-uncle, Sir Thomas, a mercer, was an alderman until his death (1627), and had been lord mayor (1603). He was governor of the Irish Society, and as president of Bridewell and

11. See Bentley, *Jacobean and Caroline Stage*, II, 673–681, for Mildmay's diary.

12. *Publications of the Harleian Society*, XIV, 627; V. Pearl, *London and the Outbreak of the Puritan Revolution* (Oxford, 1961), pp. 288–289; G. E. Cokayne, *Complete Baronetage*, 5 vols. (Exeter, 1900–1906), II, 98; III, 34, 55.

13. Pearl, *London and . . . Revolution*, pp. 294–295; Cokayne, *Some Account of the Lord Mayors*, pp. 41–45.

14. Pearl, *London and . . . Revolution*, pp. 191–192; Cokayne, *Complete Baronetage*, II, 98.

Bethlem Hospital he controlled two of the best-known city institutions; his son was raised to a baronetcy.[15] His second son, an alderman and mercer, died in 1626 leaving a widow reputedly worth £20,000; her suitors in 1628–1629 included Sir Edward Dering, a regular visitor to the London theaters.[16] Bulstrode Whitelocke, a face so familiar in the Blackfriars that the coranto he composed for Shirley's *Triumph of Peace* (1634) was played whenever he "came to that house (as I did sometimes in those dayes)," married the daughter of another Thomas Bennet, Mildmay's brother-in-law's uncle, also an alderman and sheriff (1619). A second daughter married Sir Gamaliell Capell, cousin to Mildmay on his mother's side.[17] Finally, another Bennet widow married Sir Thomas Shirley, father of Henry Shirley the dramatist (d. 1627); the same match made her aunt to Jane Crofts, newly the wife of Sir Humphrey Mildmay.[18]

Mildmay had connections with two other city families. In 1635 he accompanied to a masque Joan, wife of Sir John Coke, secretary of state. Her father was Sir Robert Lee, merchant tailor and former mayor (1602), who had interests in the Levant company; her first husband, William Gore, had been sheriff (1615) and died in 1624 on the point of becoming mayor.[19] Finally, Mildmay's brother Sir Henry Mildmay, a courtier and Master of the Jewel House, married in 1619 a daughter of Alderman Halliday, mercer, sheriff (1617), and chairman of the East India Company. On his marriage King James gave Mildmay "as they say, two manors worth £12,000, to make his estate somewhat proportionate to his wife's." Her mother, also the daughter of a mayor, married after the alderman's death Robert Rich, the puritan Earl of Warwick.[20]

---

15. V. Barbour, *Henry Bennet, Earl of Arlington* (London, 1914), pp. 1–4 (this confuses Sir Thomas with his nephew, Thomas); Cokayne, *Some Account of the Lord Mayors*, pp. 16–18, 65–67.

16. L. B. Larking, *Proceedings, Principally in the County of Kent* (London, 1862), pp. xiv-xxxiii; M.A.E. Green (ed.), *The Diary of John Rous* (London, 1866), p. 34; T.N.S. Lennam, "Sir Edward Dering's Collection of Playbooks," *SQ*, XVI (1965), 145–153.

17. Bentley, *Jacobean and Caroline Stage*, I, 40; Cokayne, *Some Account of the Lord Mayors*, pp. 65–67; *Publications of the Harleian Society*, XIII (1878), 32, 171.

18. E. P. Shirley, *Stemmata Shirleiana*, 2d ed. (London, 1873), pp. 235, 271.

19. Cokayne, *Some Account of the Lord Mayors*, pp. 12–15, 73–74.

20. T. Birch, *The Court and Times of James I* (London, 1849), II, 152; Cokayne, *Some Account of the Lord Mayors*, pp. 78–80.

These families were among the city's elite, immensely powerful, and influential dynasties that controlled the livery companies, constituted the aldermanic bench, and, as the people most extensively engaged in commerce, dominated the great trading organizations. Often they were men of deep Puritan conviction; Thomas Soames, for example, entered parliament as a fierce court opponent, and Sir James Cambell held "earnest and zealous prayer with his family all the dayes of the weeke."[21] With the Abdys, Cambells, Soameses, and Bennets, we are in the heart of London's big business world.

II

It has long been recognized that the small citizen was a minor quantity in the audience of the Caroline "private" theaters. Jonson's *Magnetic Lady* (Blackfriars, 1632) scorns "the [faeces], or grounds of your people, that sit in the oblique caves and wedges of your house, your sinfull six-penny Mechanicks";[22] in the praeludium to Goffe's *Careless Shepherdess* (Salisbury Court, 1638) the citizen, Thrift, leaves for a less fashionable theater; Henry Peacham's *Art of Living in London* (1642) includes a cautionary fable about gallants taking advantage of a citizen's wife who sat in a playhouse box.[23] But it is clear from my evidence that the theaters' fashionable tone did not mean that they had lost contact with the city and that the greater citizenry, the "acquisitive" classes whose families were rising to supply the ranks of the aristocracy, were excluded from the audience. Massinger would have expected a not insubstantial proportion of his Blackfriars audience of 1632 to have had close links with, or even to have been, people who would consider themselves more "city" than "court." Indeed, one of his own patrons had married the daughter of a lord mayor.[24]

21. E. Browne, *A Rare Pattern of Justice and Mercy* (London, 1642), p. 38; cf. Pearl, *London and . . . Revolution*, pp. 191–192.

22. In *The Works of Benjamin Jonson, The Second Volume* (London, 1640), pp. 5–6.

23. The presence of small citizens is suggested by the prologue to Davenant's *Platonic Lovers* (Blackfriars, 1635), which says that " 'Bove half our City audience would be lost, / That knew not how to spell [the play's title] on the post." *The Works of Sir William Davenant* (London, 1673), p. 384; the Blackfriars prologue to Habington's *The Queen of Aragon* (London, 1640), which mentions the presence of "wife of Citizen" in the audience (sig. A2^v); and the epilogue to Brome's *Court Beggar* (Phoenix, 1640), which addresses ladies, knights, citizens, and country gentry in turn.

We must not read the real feeling of class antagonism between gentleman and Cheapside shopkeeper that we find in the lower-class Jacobean comedies of (say) Middleton onto the world of Massinger, but allow for the greater ease with which interaction occurred between the gentry and the more established commercial families in the Caroline period. These aldermanic families were respected businessmen whose affairs involved continual contact with the theatergoing gentry class and drew them into dependence on the crown rather than into opposition to it. They needed commercial privileges and protection which only the king could grant; conversely, the government needed their specialist business expertise, and many magnates became trusted intermediaries between Whitehall and the city.[25] Their interests harmonized with those of the gentry; as city fathers, they held positions carrying great trust and prestige. Their life-style was gentlemanly. One merchant family in the 1630s visited the court at Greenwich, played bowls, viewed the king's flagship, feasted daily "with thir relations and acquentance, which were then many in London," and made an entertainment on their Hertfordshire estate for

the Earl of Salisbury and his Countesse, the Lord Cranborne his son, with the rest of his sons and daughters, and the Lord Norris, and several other persons of honor, where thir was all varieties that England could afford, for viands and severall sorts of wines, and cost, as I was informed, one hundreth and fortie pounds.[26]

Before one could become an alderman, a property qualification of £10,000 was required; a sheriff or mayor might disburse £4,000 in expenses of office.[27]

Moreover, it was quite normal for younger sons of gentry families to be apprenticed into trade. In a mock petition of 1641 the London apprentices claimed their "blouds are mingled with the Nobility, although it were our fortune to be younger brothers."[28] Sons of gentlemen constituted 15 percent of those apprenticed in London in the years 1630–1660; the

24. See D. S. Lawless, "Sir Warham St. Leger," *N&Q*, CCXXIV (1979), 411–412.

25. For example, Anthony Abdy (Pearl, *London and . . . Revolution*, p. 288). See also R. Ashton, *The City and the Court 1603–1643* (Cambridge, Eng., 1979), pp. 2, 12, 28.

26. R. Davies (ed.), *The Life of Marmaduke Rawdon* (London, 1863), pp. 24–25.

27. R. G. Lang, "Social Origins and Aspirations of Jacobean London Merchants," *Economic History Review*, XXVII (1974), 44–45.

28. *The Petition of the Women of Middlesex* (London, 1641), sig. A4[r].

Oxindens, a Kent family of similar status to that of Sir Edward Dering, had two sons apprenticed in the 1620s and 1630s.[29] Sir John Frugal's apprentices are explicitly described as gentlemen's sons ("Are you gentlemen-born, yet have no gallant tincture of gentry in you?" [II.i.51]). Critics have treated them simply as citizens[30] or as evidence of the gentry's decline at the hands of citizen affluence,[31] but they reflect a quite ordinary form of interaction between the two classes.

So the interpretation of the play as consistently anti-citizen is tricky, and we must carefully distinguish the sort of citizen the Frugals represent. Firstly, to discriminate between Jacobean and Caroline city comedy, Sir John Frugal is not the small Cheapside tradesman of Middleton's plays (for example), but offers huge dowries for his daughters (II.ii.1), and his business is all on the Exchange (I.iii.114). His apprentices "are no mechanics, / Nor serve some needy shopkeeper, who surveys / His everyday takings" (II.i.52–54), but clerks and factors. Sir John has indeed risen, but the details are deliberately left vague, and curiously little sense of the actual *acquisition* of status surrounds him. He rose through his "industry" (I.iii.50, IV.iv.71), necessitated because his inheritance was passed over in favor of Luke, who dissipated it (I.iii.138)—it is as though he has, so to speak, regained his status. This is in striking contrast with, for example, Dekker's *Shoemaker's Holiday*, in which Simon Eyre is a fellow of shoemakers even when lord mayor. There is a real dynamic emphasis on Eyre's achievement of new rank, emphasized by a strong feeling of social (and moral) dislocation when he semi-legally "borrows" an aldermanic robe to clinch the business deal that makes his fortune. Whereas Simon Eyre climbs to high status, Sir John seems to be entitled to it.

Secondly, to adopt Robert Ashton's distinction between those businessmen "whose interests were confined to orthodox commodity trade, and those who dabbled extensively in domestic concessions, such as customs farms, licenses and patents of monopoly,"[32] Sir John has no domestic

29. S. R. Smith, "The Social and Geographical Origins of the London Apprentices," *The Guildhall Miscellany*, IV (1973), 199. D. Gardiner (ed.), *The Oxinden Letters 1607–1642* (London, 1933), pp. 39–42, 189–190.

30. See, e.g., Gibson's note on V.ii.6.

31. See, e.g., Gross, "Social Change and Philip Massinger," p. 333.

32. *The City and the Court*, p. 28; cf. pp. 16–28.

concessionary interests. Concessionaires established intimate—occasionally spectacular—relationships with the court by acting, usually in association with favored courtiers, as the operators of the crown's economic controls, implementing government economic policy while exploiting to their private profit fiscal devices or privileges which the crown rented or granted as rewards to them. It is just this distinction that separates Sir William Cokayne from the other citizens I have mentioned, for he held a large variety of concessions from the crown. He was purveyor to the English forces in Ireland, belonged to a syndicate renting (for £150,000 a year) the Great Farm of Customs, held a monopoly for the transportation of tin, and had money out on loan to the king. He also promoted the infamous King's Merchant Adventurers' Company (1614), a scheme to profit the king and stimulate the dyeing industry, but also designed to enable Cokayne and his fellow racketeers to take over the privileges of the cloth trade. This collapsed disastrously, plunging the cloth industry into a huge depression, and earning Cokayne great opprobrium.[33] Cokayne was wholly a creature of the crown, and it is this sort of courtly monopolist, capitalizing for a huge personal return on government favors, that Massinger attacked violently in *A New Way to Pay Old Debts*.[34] *A New Way* and *The City Madam* are often treated as if they made the same points, but Sir John Frugal's activities are delineated as wholly regular and carefully distinguished from such notorious preferential enterprises.

Sir John is presented primarily as a merchant trading to India and the East; the Red Indians also link him with ventures to America.[35] Secondarily, he is a usurer dealing with the nobility and smaller citizens. These were operations characteristic of men like the Abdys, Bennets, and Cambells, large magnates with considerable reserves of capital to manipulate, who were engaged in commerce, in the widest sense, rather than in

33. Gibson, "Massinger's London merchant," pp. 740–742; F. C. Dietz, *English Public Finance 1559–1641*, 2d ed. (London, 1964), pp. 159, 334; J. F. Wadmore, *Some Account of the Worshipful Company of Skinners* (London, 1902), p. 173; Ashton, *The City and the Court*, pp. 105–106; M. Prestwich, *Cranfield: Politics and Profits under the Early Stuarts* (Oxford, 1976), pp. 113, 163–170.

34. Based on the activities of Buckingham's client, Sir Giles Mompesson.

35. Cf. I.i.20, II.i.70–72.

manufacture.[36] Less is said of Sir John's participation in the administrative side of civic life. However, the question of the serious commitment of the city fathers to the maintenance of social and moral discipline is raised fairly explicitly in the scene in which the rebel apprentices so to speak re-enroll in the service of Luke, the anti-type of the good master ("We'll break my master to make you," one says [II.i.139]), and in the brothel scene (III.i) in which representatives of municipal coercion, the magistrate and constable, are ironically transformed into a libertine and musicians. Similarly, the list of "services and duties" (II.ii.99) that Frugal's daughters make for their suitors, usually regarded as an anticipation of Restoration "bargain scenes," is perhaps more appropriately interpreted as a mock indenture, another inversion of civic authority (Sir Maurice refers to Anne's conditions as "my apprenticeship" [II.ii.102]). In general, the context of *The City Madam* is aldermanic. Sir John is expected to "wear scarlet" (I.ii.143) and when Luke comes into wealth his debtors

> see Lord Mayor written on his forehead;
> The cap of maintenance, and city sword
> Borne up in state before him.
>
> (IV.i.70–72)

III

In view of the usual opinions about *The City Madam*, it cannot be emphasized enough that this picture of the world of a great citizen is painted in considerable detail and is largely sympathetic. It is difficult to maintain the view that this is an anti-citizen play when we consider the dignity in which Massinger invests Sir John Frugal. Tradewell's first description of him strikes the dominant note:

> 'Tis great pity
> Such a gentlemen as my master (*for that title*
> *His being a citizen cannot take from him*)
> Hath no male heir to inherit his estate,
> And keep his name alive.
>
> (I.i.11–15; emphasis mine)

36. Cf. Ashton, *The City and the Court*, p. 39.

So it is stressed at the outset that being in trade makes Sir John no less a gentleman, and two acts later Lord Lacy calls him "noble" in a eulogy of his character:

> The noble merchant
> Who living was for his integrity
> And upright dealing (a rare miracle
> In a rich citizen) London's best honour . . .
>
> (III.ii.39–42)

Sir John's first appearance, issuing from his house to intervene in the brawl between the suitors, is calculated to reinforce this impression:

> Beat down their weapons! My gate Ruffians' Hall?
> What insolence is this? . . .
>   If you proceed thus
> I must make use of the next justice's power,
> And leave persuasion, and in plain terms tell you
> *Enter LADY {FRUGAL}, ANNE, MARY, and MILLISCENT*
> Neither your birth, Sir Maurice, nor your wealth,
> Shall privilege this riot. See whom you have drawn
> To be spectators of it! Can you imagine
> It can stand with the credit of my daughters
> To be the argument of your swords? I'th'street too?
>
> (I.ii.76–93)

The distant echo of *Othello* ("Look if my gentle love be not rais'd up!") is appropriate. Sir John, restoring civil order and admonishing the suitors to preserve self-respect, has here an authority which stays with him throughout the play. He is the peacemaker, the responsible citizen, commanding courtier and country gentleman alike, and consorting on equal terms with Lord Lacy. Although his household is disordered, the play charts his personal[37] plan to regulate it, and the final scene endorses his precedence utterly.

Similarly, his business procedures establish him as a prototype for imitation. Luke, admitting that Sir John, as "a citizen . . . would increase his heap, and will not lose / What the law gives him" (I.ii.140–

---

37. Cf. II.iii.1–6.

142), still denies reports that in "the acquistion of his wealth he weighs not / Whose ruin he builds upon" (I.ii.138–139). The following scene shows Sir John collecting his debts with a conscience. He is severe but just toward his debtors, having nothing but contempt for "drones" like Hoist who game and "keep ordinaries, / And a livery punk, or so" (I.iii.13, 7), for an "infidel" like Penury who neglects his family's welfare (I.iii.19), and for the prodigal speculation of Fortune. Nevertheless, at Luke's entreaty, he forbears with them, even though if publicly known it would harm his business prospects. Luke sums up the character of his dealing:

> the distinction
> And noble difference by which you are
> Divided from 'em [other traders], is that you are styl'd
> Gentle in your abundance, good in plenty,
> And that you feel compassion in your bowels
> Of others' miseries (I have found it, sir,
> Heaven keep me thankful for't), while they are curs'd
> As rigid and inexorable . . .
>
> (I.iii.55–62)

Sir John's "affability and mildness" will gain him his debtors' thanks and providential reward (I.iii.64–68, 101–106). Related to mercy in usury is the depiction of Luke as the profligate redeemed from prison:

> I am a freeman, all my debts discharg'd,
> Nor does one creditor undone by me
> Curse my loose riots. I have meat and clothes,
> Time to ask heaven remission for what's past.
> Cares of the world by me are laid aside,
> My present poverty's a blessing to me;
> And though I have been long, I dare not say
> I ever liv'd till now.
>
> (I.ii.127–134)

Although this action was the natural duty of brother to brother, Luke's pious tone (making it a spiritual, as much as an economic redemption) invites us to connect it with the wide range of charitable and religious activities to which puritan businessmen were known to be deeply committed. This can be illustrated from a contemporary eulogy on Sir James Cambell which presents him as "a rare example of Justice moderated by

Mercy."[38] Cambell's business and administrative acumen went hand in hand with his zeal for practical godliness. Though reputed, like Frugal, "a neere, austere and hard man," he was directed by human tenderness:

He was so farre from oppressing any with tedious suits in law, that to my knowledge during the time that I lived with him, he was very unwilling that any should bee cast into prison at his suit, and would rather agree upon a small composition, then take the rigour of the Law against any, though he lost thereby. For I doe not remember that he caused above one or two to be arrested, though he hath had many bad debtors, as his Executors shall find.[39]

Cambell's upright dealing, severe yet humane, followed God's way, for he too is a hard master who expects a just account. At his death the fruits of a just life were reaped, for he was blessed with profits to husband "for the glory of God, and good of others."[40] There follows a long list of his vast bequests, for the sick, the poor, the enslaved, the imprisoned (like Luke), and for public works, cheap loans, and city institutions.[41] It is in relation to such a nexus of thrift and conscience that I believe we are intended to read Sir John Frugal's character.

The first act, then, establishes a strong positive, the representative of which is the citizen and gentleman, Sir John Frugal. Equally, its antithesis is stated in citizen terms. Luke Frugal's behavior—swindling his master and encouraging his apprentices to debauchery and falsification of the accounts (II.i.45–56, 66–67)—is wholly abhorrent from the perspective of the merchant and of the sheriff who shuts down the brothel. Furthermore, although the play principally attacks proud city dames, it by no means refrains from criticizing the court. The scene that establishes Sir John's authority also shows Sir Maurice Lacy, the lord's son, put down by Plenty, the country gentleman, with a satire on the penury of the aristocracy and their neglect of their social responsibilities for the sake of following fashions:

38. Browne, *A Rare Pattern of Justice and Mercy*, p. 37.
39. *Ibid.*, pp. 42–43.
40. *Ibid.*, pp. 44, 66.
41. The whole will is printed in J. Nicholl, *Some Account of the Worshipful Company of Ironmongers*, 2d ed. (London, 1866), pp. 539–542. As well as sums for members of the Abdy family, it includes typically Puritan bequests to lecturers and silenced clergy.

> Though I keep men, I fight not with their fingers,
> Nor make it my religion to follow
> The gallant's fashion, to have my family
> Consisting in a footman, and a page,
> And those two sometimes hungry. I can feed these,
> And clothe 'em too, my gay sir . . .
>   . . . my clothes are paid for
> As soon as put on, a sin your man of title
> Is seldom guilty of, but heaven forgive it.
> I have other faults, too, very incident
> To a plain gentleman. I eat my venison
> With my neighbours in the country, and present not
> My pheasants, partridges, and grouse to the usurer . . .
> I can make my wife a jointure of such lands, too,
> As are not encumber'd, no annuity
> Or statute lying on 'em.
>
> (I.ii.38–60)

Sir Maurice can only reply with a stale jest about country upstarts, and after their abortive duel, Plenty remains on the offensive against courtly complimenting:

> SIR MAURICE [to ANNE]
>   May I have the honour
> To support you, lady?
>   PLENTY [to MARY]
>   I know not what's supporting,
> But by this fair hand, glove and all, I love you.
>
> (I.ii.101–103)

Lord Lacy comes off no better. He is principally a foil to Sir John with whom he disagrees concerning Luke's true nature, and, of course, he is proved spectacularly wrong. There is fine comedy in the scene in which he gives Luke the countinghouse keys, admonishing him to "make good the opinion I held of you, / Of which I am most confident," and exclaiming, "Honest soul, / With what feeling he receives it" (III.ii.105, 121). His disabusal is swift and hilarious, leaving him incredulous as the hitherto deferential Luke makes promises of unparalleled pomp to the women.[42] It

---

42. In this the audience is superior to Lacy, having been alerted to Luke's true nature in II.ii, and possibly as early as I.i.135.

is notable that the formula about keeping decorum between court and city first occurs in Lacy's mouth in this wholly ironic context (III.ii.152); such easy moralizing is speedily deflated. The rest of the play sees Lacy apologizing for his error (even in his final line), and in the penultimate scene he is totally speechless as his erstwhile protégé suddenly turns on him for the recovery of overdue debts:

> I find in my counting house a manor pawn'd;
> Pawn'd my good lord, Lacy Manor, and that manor
> From which you have the title of a lord,
> And it please your good lordship . . .
> I would be loath your name should sink, or that
> Your hopeful son, when he returns from travel,
> Should find you my lord-without-land. You are angry
> For my good counsel. Look you to your bonds. Had I known
> Of your coming, believe it, I would have had sergeants ready.
> Lord, how you fret!
>
> (V.ii.64–80)

The comedy of this clever speech is surely at Lacy's expense, rather than Luke's.

The diatribes aimed at the Frugal women also have a double edge. This is the household Anne Frugal wants:

> my page, my gentleman-usher,
> My woman sworn to my secrets, my caroch
> Drawn by six Flanders mares, my coachman, grooms,
> Postillion, and footmen . . .
>   . . . mine own doctor;
> French, and Italian cooks; musicians, songsters,
> And a chaplain that must preach to please my fancy;
> A friend at court to place me at a masque;
> The private box took up at a new play
> For me, and my retinue; a fresh habit,
> (Of a fashion never seen before) to draw
> The gallants' eyes that sit on the stage upon me . . .
>
> (II.ii.113–124)

This satirizes not just city ambition, but fashionable society in general; its references out of the illusion to those actually watching the play would ensure its significance was felt not only by citizens. Similiarly, Holdfast's lament at citizen extravagance expands into a description of *court* gluttony ("Their pheasants drench'd with ambergris, the carcasses / Of three fat wethers bruis'd for gravy to / Make sauce for a single peacock," etc. (II.i.4–6), the fashionable lasciviousness of the Frugal girls (I.i.133) involves a comparable judgment on bona fide society ladies, and Luke's lengthy rebuke to the women takes full cognizance of the court's "superfluous bravery," "pomp and bravery," and "prodigality" (IV.iv.46, 91,95). In laughing at city pride, the audience also, to a considerable degree, laughs at itself.

Massinger's distinction between court and city cannot, then, be interpreted as a nostalgic, simpleminded defense of the sanctity of rank. The principal point of attack on the women is their violation of rank, but the whole attack is not only made in social terms. The women's first appearance establishes they are guilty of more personal forms of *superbia*. They are vain, easily flattered (I.i.83), and lascivious (I.i.133); they love rare fashions (a characteristically Puritan charge), extravagance, and excessively sumptuous food. They are especially tyrannous toward their menfolk, the enslaved dependent Luke, and those who would normally command them, their husbands and suitors. Later the sins of hypocrisy, ostentation, and impiety are added (IV.iv.110, 113, 116). Clearly, not only social status is at stake. The women offend against a moral and domestic order, too, their actions travestying as much the city's values of thrift, piety, and wifeliness as they do the court's. Holdfast laments that their extravagance "would break an alderman, / And make him give up his cloak," and the point of his description of their vast banquets is not that they challenge a privilege due only to the court, but that they go far beyond that too and outdo *all* example (II.i.16–27). It is the citizens, Sir John and "the cater Holdfast" (II.i.131), who discipline the women, not the courtiers.

All critics accept without qualm the scene in which Luke humiliates the women (IV.iv) as though it expresses unequivocally Massinger's own views. It seems to me much more ambiguous; Luke is, to say the least, not a disinterested party. He does issue a public disclaimer, that he acts "not in revenge / Of your base usage of me" (IV.iv.133–134) but "with judgement" (IV.iv.48; at II.i.92 he expressed admiration for a world where "judgement" had "nought to do"), but alone with Holdfast he admits his tyrannous intentions: "He's cruel to himself, that dares not be / Severe to those that us'd him cruelly" (IV.iv.159–160). We have already *twice* seen the reality behind Luke's pretenses of moral probity. He arrests in IV.iii the very debtors for whom in I.iii he pleaded, announcing that his talk of charity "when I was in poverty . . show'd well; / But I inherit with [Sir John's] state, his mind, / And rougher nature" (IV.iii.37–39); and in IV.ii he arrests the prentices whom he himself encouraged to bad courses ("Will you prove yourself a devil? Tempt us to mischief, / And then discover it?" [IV.ii.82–83]). Massinger puts his condemnation of the women into the mouth of the man whose moral credibility is most thoroughly bankrupt.

Rather than IV.iv representing Massinger's norm, it is a fast after a feast, Lent after carnival (IV.iv.4). Luke, a "rough physician" (IV.iv.150), pretty clearly overdoes his retribution. Although he promises the women their "natural forms and habits" (IV.iv.133), they appear in "*coarse habit*" (IV.iv.23 s.d.) more suited to "Exchange wenches" or "some chandler's daughters / Bleaching linen in Moorfields" (IV.iv.36–37). The true valuation of the city is much higher. Even Luke admits that his sister is a lady and entitled to considerable privileges:

> It being for the city's honour, that
> There should be distinction between
> The wife of a patrician, and plebeian.
>
> (IV.iv.79–81)

This is not just another distinction between court and city,[43] but a discrimination within the city itself. In 1640, Alderman Soames refused to assist the court in a forced loan, saying "his reputation as an honest man, won while a commoner, was as dear to him now that he was an Alderman,"[44] and it is this distinction the women are conceded. As Soames's language indicates, it is a considerable claim. It places the women firmly among the governing classes, and when the suitors complain of the women's scorn, Sir John insists that

> Though they are mine, I must tell you, the perverseness
> Of their manners (which they did not take from me,

43. As Gibson has it, in his note on IV.iv.81.
44. Pearl, *London and . . . Revolution*, p. 192.

But from their mother) qualified, they deserve
Your equals.

                                                            (II.iii.33–36)

This indeed they do get, for Massinger does *not*, in fact, maintain a
distance between city and court, but concludes with intermarriage
between them, the two cooperating under conditions of mutual respect
and benefit, and this state of harmony and reciprocity between the estates
in a well-ordered society is what I believe he intends the point of his moral
to be. It is a more attractive interpretation than the usual one for it
emphasizes the range of his tolerance equally with his intolerance, and
widens the scope of his moral beyond mere respect for rank to imply a
broader ideal of dignified, responsible, and rational social and moral
behavior conducive to the interests of all. In the courteous relationships
that exist between Lord Lacy and Sir John (II.iii.46–51) and between Lacy
and Old Goldwire and Tradewell (V.ii.1–8), Massinger illustrates the
mutual deference at the level of manners which is the exterior manifesta-
tion of a society cooperating healthily and harmoniously at a more fundamental substratum. The play is not opposed to social advancement as
such, but is committed to ensuring that modifications in the shape of
society occur smoothly and without undermining the survival and good
order of the whole.

                                        IV

   Luke Frugal obviously typifies behavior that obstructs such smooth
adjustments, but he must be considered in his own right as the second
prong of Massinger's attack, on *avaricia*. He has been taken to symbolize
the "financial ambitions of the trading classes";[45] however, his crime is
personal and moral, not social. Earlier citizen cheaters, such as
Middleton's Hoard and Quomodo, exhibited an overwhelming desire to
eject the gentry and translate themselves into their place. Luke has nothing of this. He completely lacks social ambition, but preys like a "wolf"
(V.iii.116) on all humanity without distinction, undoing the small tradesman, whore, and gamester as readily as the lord and gentleman. He is

45. Gross, "Social Change and Philip Massinger," p. 335.

motivated by a numbing devotion to his own selfish benefit, made more horrific by a malicious delight in "the fatal curses / Of widows, undone orphans" (V.iii.33). His ambition is to sit

> Alone, and surfeit in my store, while others
> With envy pine at it—my genius pamper'd
> With the thought of what I am, and what they suffer
> I have mark'd out to misery.
>
> (V.i.146–149)

It is a form of self-worship; he agrees with the first Indian that "Temples rais'd to ourselves in the increase / Of wealth, and reputation, speak a wise man" (III.iii.109). He threatens not just the stability of rank, but the survival of human society itself.

Hence it is not the acquisition of wealth that makes Luke what he is; wealth only facilitates his inhumanity. He sees human relationships as power relations; the greatest good is to dominate others, and there is only approbation for success and scorn for failure. This he holds *before* he comes into wealth. In the important soliloquy opening III.ii he discloses he has no pity, only self-contempt, for his own poverty:

> I deserve much more
> Than their scorn can load me with, and 'tis but justice
> That I should live the family's drudge, design'd
> To all the sordid offices their pride
> Imposes on me; since if now I sat
> A judge in mine own cause, I should conclude
> I am not worth their pity.
>
> (III.ii.3–9)

In fact, he *admires* Lady Frugal's tyranny over him for its spirit (II.i.33), and he despises conventional Christian pieties as self-deceiving consolations for weak men. Of Holdfast's "honest care," he says, "With the fortunes / Of a slave, he has a mind like one" (II.i.32–33), an idea of virtue he repeats to the Indians:

> LORD LACY
> Continue
> As in your poverty you were, a pious
> And honest man.   *Exit.*

> LUKE
> That is, interpreted,
> A slave and beggar.
>
> (III.iii.102–104)

The women, having used him as their "slave" (I.i.102), are amazed to find "he that was your slave, by fate appointed / To be your governor" (III.ii.93–94), and the play culminates with the parade of those he has enthralled:

> 'Tis my glory
> That they are wretched, and by me made so;
> It sets my happiness off. I could not triumph
> If these were not my captives.
>
> (V.iii.67–70).

The climax of Luke's career is not his entry into wealth, but the display of the power it has enabled him to gain over others.

It seems to me unlikely that Massinger would have expected any citizen element in his audience to have been offended by Luke. Like the women's pride, Luke's cruelty is as abhorent from a civic as from a courtly perspective. Indeed, since Luke "can brook / No rival in this happiness" (V.iii.14–15), he especially wishes to overreach other London merchants, hoping his "private house in cramm'd abundance / [May] prove the chamber of the City poor" (IV.ii.126–127), and he scorns Sir John's citizenly quality of "thriving industry," boasting that his own riches have come by "dissimulation" (V.iii.22). Massinger carefully establishes that he misuses his fortune; he is wealth without conscience:

> Religion, conscience, charity, farewell!
> To me you are words only, and no more;
> All human happiness consists in store.
>
> (IV.ii.131–133)

The deliberateness of this rejection of conscience is driven home by its repetition to the apprentices (II.i.44; cf. l. 76), their fathers (V.ii.37), and the Indians:

> I fear you will make
> Some scruple in your conscience to grant [our requests].

LUKE

Conscience! No, no; so it may be done with safety,
And without danger of the law.

(V.i. 17–20)

So in clear contrast with Sir John's humane usury, Luke is the malignant,
pitiless usurer. He denies "mercy" to his apprentices (IV.ii. 104) and
debtors (whose pleas move even the sergeants to pity [IV.iii.70]), and
repudiates it conclusively in the final scene:

> Ha, ha, ha!
> This move me to compassion, or raise
> One sign of seeming pity in my face?
> You are deceiv'd. It rather renders me
> More flinty, and obdurate. A south wind
> Shall sooner soften marble . . .
>   than knees, or tears, or groans
> Shall wrest compunction from me.

(V.iii.59–67)

Only Sir John's return restores "Mercy" (V.iii. 125), but Luke is excluded
from the general reconciliation. The man who has abjured pity gets no pity
wasted on him in return (cf. V.iii.58).

In Luke, then, Massinger attacks not the acquisition of wealth but its
abuse, condemning his neglect of humanity, honesty, and pity, values that
are respected by the citizen of conscience, Sir John Frugal, who is returned
to wealth at the end. The full extent of Massinger's respect for the values of
the godly citizen, though, can only be properly appreciated in relation to
the fake Indians who belong entirely to Luke's part of the play.

V

New World visitors were first brought to England by Elizabethan
explorers, but excited greatest comment in the early seventeenth century,
culminating in 1616 with the arrival of a dozen or so including
Pocahontas, the Indian wife of an Englishman, who was presented at
court. Indians appeared in Shakespeare's *Tempest* and in two masques of
1613. In 1635 the governor of the Saybrook colony was still being urged
"to send over some of your Indian Creatures alive," and as late as 1645

Hollar drew a Virginian from life in London.[46] T. S. Eliot ridiculed
Massinger's Indians as "extravagant hocus-pocus,"[47] but they are quite at
home in Sir John's mercantile household and their function must be taken
seriously. They are connected with another of Frugal's charitable activities,
a pious project to convert to Christianity some unfortunate heathen
(III.iii.71–86), and they bring to bear on the Luke plot a consciousness of
the godly citizen ideals underlying the North American trade as a framework within which Luke's actions may be judged.

The travel literature that included descriptions of Indian life was
suffused with religious feeling. Samuel Purchas's monumental compilation
Purchas his Pilgrims (4 vols., London, 1625) opens with Solomon's
"Ophirian *Nauigation*" (I, 2) interpreted as a type of man's pursuit of
Grace; the companion volume, *Purchas his Pilgrimage*, describes all the
religions of the world, beginning at Creation. Purchas saw exploration as
part of the laborious process of overcoming the Fall; God gave man naviga-
tion that he might carry the Gospel to all nations, and regain in return
that dominion over the earth lost by Adam. Colonization would recover
"the right to which the true Children of the Church haue in Christ and by
him in all things" (I, 16). North America, in particular, had been set aside
by Providence as another Eden awaiting English exploitation, and would
bring wealth to the country, new subjects to the king, and further the
political and religious struggle with Spain. If the English sought "the
Kingdome of God" in Virginia, they would have "an earthly Kingdome in
recompence, as the earnest, and the heauenly Kingdome for our full
paiement" (IV, 1816). The Virginia Company attracted investment and
leadership from political and religious puritans, and its propaganda was
written and coordinated by clergymen (Like Purchas); their religious zeal
was inseparable from their zeal for empire.[48]

---

46. J. O. Halliwell (ed.), *The Works of William Shakespeare* (London, 1853), I, 325; F.
Mossiker, *Pocahontas: The Life and the Legend* (London, 1977), pp. 220–221; P. L. Barbour,
Pocahontas and Her World (London, 1971), plate facing p. 140; G. Chalmers, *An Apology for
the Believers in the Shakespeare Papers* (London, 1797), pp. 93–95.

47. *Elizabethan Dramatists* (London, 1963), p. 151.

48. See L. B. Wright, *Religion and Empire*, 2d ed. (New York, 1965), p. 100 and *passim*;
and P. Miller, "Religion and Society in the Early Literature of Virginia," in *Errand Into the
Wilderness* (Cambridge, Mass., 1956), pp. 99–140.

So Purchas encouraged colonists to "plant Christianity, to produce and multiply Christians, by our words and works to further the knowledge of God in his Word and Workes" (IV, 1813), and the Virginia Company declared in 1610 that the first of its *"Principal* and *Maine Endes"* was to "preach and baptize into the *Christian Religion* and by propagation of the *Gospell*, to recover out of the armes of the Divell, a number of poore and miserable soules, wrapt up unto death, in almost *invincible ignorance."*[49] Pocahontas was welcomed as the first Indian convert in England; the Bishop of London entertained her, and her husband defended their marriage as advancing God's glory, "the converting [of] an irregenerate to a regeneration."[50] The idea underlies Chapman's *Memorable Mask* (London, [1613?]) in which Virginian masquers renounce "superstitious worship" in favor of the "heauens true light" of "our *Britan Phoebus"* (Sig. D4ᵛ). The Indians, though, were not meek spiritual innocents, for all authorities agreed that they had already been seduced by the devil. Captain John Smith, who greatly emphasized the "yelling and howling" of Indian religious rites, said, "their chiefe God they worship is the Devill. Him they call *Okee*, and serue him more of feare then loue."[51] Purchas believed the Virginians were enslaved "to Satans tyranny in foolish pieties, mad impieties, wicked idlenesse, busie and bloudy wickednesse; hence haue we fit obiects of zeale and pietie, to *deliver from the power of darknesse"* (IV, 1814), but he was frustrated by his own inability to convert Pocahontas's servant, "a blasphemer of what he knew not, and preferring his God to ours" (IV, 1774), and concluded, "Let vs obserue these things with pitty and compassion, and endeuor to bring these silly soules out of the snare of the Deuill, by our prayers, our purses, and all our best endeuors."[52] Comparable statements can be multiplied almost indefinitely.[53]

49. K. Glenn, "Captain John Smith and the Indians," *The Virginia Magazine of History and Biography*, LII (1944), 229.

50. P. L. Barbour, *The Three Worlds of Captain John Smith* (London, 1964), p. 329.

51. J. Smith, *The General History of Virginia* (London, 1624), p. 35; Massinger echoes this idea at V.i.3–4.

52. *Purchas his Pilgrimage*, 4th ed. (London, 1626), pp. 843–844.

53. E.g., *Purchas his Pilgrims*, IV. 1662, 1774, 1867; W. Wood, *New England's Prospect*, ed. A. T. Vaughan (Amherst, Mass., 1977), p. 101; H. Spelman, "Relation of Virginia," in J. Smith, *Works*, ed. E. Arber (Birmingham, 1884), cv; Wright, *Religion and Empire*, p. 103. Cf. the description of Caliban as a "devil" in *The Tempest*, II.ii.

Moreover, the Indians believed themselves to be in direct contact with
the devil, who "appeareth to them out of the Aire . . . in form of a
personable Virginian, with a long blacke locke on the left side," and
would make their children "hardy and acceptable to the Deuill, that in
time he may appeare vnto them."[54] On these occasions, they take counsel
from him, but also (as do Massinger's Indians, V.i.26–41) receive instruc-
tions for human sacrifice. Henry Spelman said that their "coniurers who
are ther preests, can make [him] apeare unto them at ther pleasuer," and
that annually the tribes go into the woods

> wher ther preests make a great cirkell of fier in ye which after many obseruances
> in ther coniurations they make offer of 2 or 3 children to be giuen to ther god if
> he will apeare unto them and shew his mind whome he will desier. Vppon which
> offringe they heare a noyse out of ye Cirkell Nominatinge such as he will haue,
> whome presently they take bindinge them hand and footte and cast them into y^e
> circle of the fier, for be it the Kinges sonne he must be giuen if [once] named by
> ther god . . .[55]

Purchas's American chapters have many allusions to human sacrifice, but
the best-known instance was probably John Smith's account of the
Huskanaw, a Virginian rite of passage which he mistook for an annual
sacrifice of children. Smith described this as a violent ritual which some of
the boys survived, but the others "the *Okee* or *Divell* did sucke the bloud
from their left breast, who chanced to be his by lot, till they were dead."
Smith himself was captured by Indians in 1607 and expected to be sacri-
ficed "to the *Quiyoughquosicke*, which is a superior power they worship, a
more uglier thing cannot be described." Few theatergoers could have been
ignorant of his celebrated description of the "strange and fearefull Coniura-
tions" practised over him, and of Pocahontas's intervention to prevent his
execution.[56]

Luke's dealings with the devil, *via* the "Indians," and his plans for
human sacrifice, would thus have been entirely serious for Massinger's

54. *Purchas his Pilgrimage*, p. 843; *Purchas his Pilgrims*, IV, 1868.

55. "Relation of Virginia," pp. cv-cvi. Wood, *New England's Prospect*, p. 101, said the
devil, to keep the Indians in fear, "was wont to carry away their wives and children."

56. Smith, *The General History*, pp. 36, 48; *A True Relation of Such Occurrences* (London,
1608), sig. C3^r.

audience. In Virginia, the colonists were actively waging Christ's struggle with Antichrist; "the very prosperity and pregnant hopes of that Plantation made the Deuil and his lims to enuy, feare, and hate it."[57] The great massacre of colonists by Indians was only a decade past, and renewed Indian troubles were coming to be seen as God's war.[58] The arrival of the Indians in *The City Madam*, therefore, is not gratuitous melodrama, for they, devotees of the devil fighting against the true Word, are the negative to Sir John's positive, and introduce this holy war into the design of the play. Against Sir John's pious project, Luke's assertion to the Indians that "You are learn'd Europeans, and we worse / Than ignorant Americans" (III.iii.127–128) would have seemed a horrific and blasphemous inversion. Once again, Massinger evaluates the action with a citizenly eye.

VI

From Sir John's compassionate usury to the women's final "sacrifice of sighs" (V.iii.84), *The City Madam* is pervasively shaped to suggest a religious scheme. The problem of usury is first raised as a choice between angelic and diabolic uses of money:

SIR JOHN
When I lent my moneys I appear'd an angel;
But now I would call in mine own, a devil.
HOIST
Were you the devil's dam, you must stay till I have it.
(I.iii.2–4)

Luke's oration specifically exhorts Sir John to "moral honesty" and "religion," an argument which will "damn him / If he be not converted" (I.iii.95, 80), and his mercy makes his debtors, like Luke, his "beadsmen" (I.iii.101; III.ii.1). Lacy admires Luke as a man "of a clear soul, / Religious, good, and honest" and concludes that "our divines / Cannot speak more effectually" (I.iii.151, 96), whereas he suspects Sir John "an atheist"

57. *Purchas his Pilgrims*, IV, 1819.
58. R. H. Pearce, *Savagism and Civilization*, 2d ed. (Baltimore, 1967), p. 24; cf. J. Underhill, *News from America* (London, 1638), pp. 22, 29–30, 33–35, 40. Some tribes were said to be "cruell bloodie Caniballs"; see P. Vincent, *A True Relation of the Late Battle* (London, 1637), and Wood, *New England's Prospect*, p. 76.

toward his brother (I.iii.123). Later, he presses Luke to use his new wealth
with equal piety:

> . . . use it with due reverence. I once heard you
> Speak most divinely in the opposition
> Of a revengeful humour. To these show it
> And such who then depended on the mercy
> Of your brother, now wholly at your devotion.
>
> (III.ii.100–104)

Watching Luke accept his fortune as "A curse I cannot thank you for," he
exclaims, unctuously, "Honest soul, / With what feeling he receives it"
(III.ii.115, 121).

This angel, however, proves a devil (again, *Othello* comes to mind).
Luke's celebrated soliloquy (III.iii), spoken as if awakening into a higher
reality, a mystery which "weak credulity could have no faith in" (l. 34),
travesties a religious vision. The countinghouse is "Heaven's abstract, or
epitome" (l. 31), and the gold, a god whose body may be touched with
reverence, parodies the Incarnation:

> It did endure the touch;
> I saw and felt it. Yet what I beheld
> And handl'd oft, did so transcend belief
> (My wonder and astonishment pass'd o'er)
> I faintly could give credit to my senses.
>
> (III.iii.4–7)

The arrival of the Indians to initiate Luke into the "sacred principles" that
there is "no religion, nor virtue, / But in abundance, and no vice but
want" (III.iii.106, 126) renders his conversion to false pieties apparent
after the manner of a morality play. Their presence is a visual sign of his
membership of the devil's party; he is to be "confident your better angel is
/ Enter'd your house" (III.iii.115–116).[59]

Usury was of course traditionally associated with the devil,[60] but the
inclusion of the Indians raises this association to the status of a system of

59. Tradewell, at II.i.131, was "converted" to riots by Luke.

60. See, e.g., Middleton's Dampit (*A Trick to Catch the Old One*, 1605) and Brome's
Vermin (*The Damoiselle*, 1638).

belief rivaling Sir John's Christian profession. Luke's pursuit of riches for their own sake leads him naturally into devil worship, for if "you / Desire to wallow in wealth and worldly honours, / You must make haste to be familiar with him" (V.i.26–28). Allusions to his devilishness accumulate overwhelmingly in Acts IV and V. His actions in IV.ii "prove [him] a devil" (l. 82); in IV.iii the "tongues of angels" will not alter him, and he is left to "the devil thy tutor" (ll. 46, 65). His plan for disposing of a "distress'd widow, or poor maids" to the devil is a hideous parody of Sir John's charitable works (V.i.47). Lacy now regrets having thought "This devil a saint" and, describing him as "Such a devil" commends him "To thy damnation"; one is forgiven, he believes, for speaking "unchristianly" of Luke (V.ii.5, 54, 83, 85). In the final scene, Luke glories in his impiety:

> this felicity, not gain'd
> By vows to saints above, and much less purchas'd
> By thriving industry; nor fall'n upon me
> As a reward to piety, and religion,
> Or service for my country.
>
> (V.iii.20–24)

His entertainers, he believes, are the devil's spirits, and the masque—Orpheus descending to hell—powerfully restates his own situation. Luke is indeed *becoming* a devil, for it proves his fiendish nature that music does not soften him (V.iii.44–47), and he delights to watch his victims suffer in the personal hell he has created. Moments later Sir John, condemning him as a "Revengeful, avaricious atheist," consigns him to Virginia where the other devil-worshipers live (V.iii.134, 144).

This pattern of rival pieties is anticipated earlier in the presentation of the Frugal women, themselves left "in hell" by their suitors for a pride "saints and angels" cannot cure (II.ii.110, II.iii.37). The presence of Stargaze makes this more explicit. Keith Thomas has shown that in the Jacobean-Caroline period, astrology came under Puritan attack as the devil's device to draw men from God's worship.[61] For example, the Calvinist bishop George Carleton argued that astrologers predicted "not

61. *Religion and the Decline of Magic*, 2d ed. (London, 1973), pp. 435–439.

by that faith by which God taught his Church: therefore by that faith by
which the Divell teacheth." They operate "by plain compact, or else by a
secret illusion of Satan" whose spirits "make shew of obedience, to catch
the soule of man in these snares; requiring strong Credulity and excessive
desire of the Soule: and so drawing the service of the Soule to themselves,
from God and from godliness."[62] Such devilish irreligion has seduced the
Frugal women. Lady Frugal calls Stargaze's prophecies "oracle" and "The
angels' language" (II.ii.72, 64), and in an act of great blasphemy she and
her daughters kneel to the astrologer. Luke, too, having agreed that
"sacrifice to an imagin'd power" shows man only "A superstitious fool"
(III.iii.108), praises the divinity of his stars:

> Brightness to the star
> That govern'd at my birth! Shoot down thy influence
> And with a perpetuity of being
> Continue this felicity . . .
>
> (V.iii.17–20)

He is defeated by the lawful "sacrifice" and "magic art" of Sir John Frugal
(V.iii.106, 99).

Massinger, then, is closely dependent on a godly, citizen perspective to
articulate his criticism of Luke, for he has deeply embedded the Virginian
struggle between earthly saint and monstrous devil into the structure of
the Luke plot. It accounts for the special intensity of Luke's presentation
and condemnation. He is no ordinary sinner who has fallen into error and
may be recovered to virtue by penitence. Rather, he is frightening because
his malice is entirely deliberate and the depravity of his behavior gratifying
to him. He has consciously and wholeheartedly turned away from piety
and devoted himself to its opposite, a religion of mercilessness that puts
him beyond mercy and makes him more anti-Christian than un-Christian.
Luke is doomed to his damnation, both by his predestined nature and his
own conscious choice, and Sir John's gesture toward reconciliation
(V.iii.150) is empty after Luke's conclusion that "what's" done, with
words / Cannot be undone" (V.iii.146–147).[63] *The City Madam*, in the

---

62. *Astrologamania*, 2d ed. (London, 1651), pp. 16, 38, 132 (first published in 1624).
Compare T. Cooper, *The Mystery of Witchcraft* (London, 1617), p. 142, and James I,
Daemonologie, ed. G. B. Harrison (London, 1924), pp. 10, 14.

63. Compare *Othello*, V.ii.303; *Macbeth*, III.ii.12, V.i.68 (Riverside ed.).

absolute, unpassable divide it makes between the just and the unjust man, is a powerfully puritanical, Calvinist play. The unregenerate being, utterly lost to Grace and actively fighting against it, ends the play more a devil than a man.

Another religious frame of reference also underlies the defeat of Luke. In relation to the other characters, Luke is essentially a bringer of retribution. He imposes a vengefully strict justice on them, vowing that "what I felt [when poor], you all shall feel, and with rigour" (IV.iii.42) and using all the forces of authority from the lord chief justice (IV.ii.74–75) to marshal, sheriff, and sergeants. He flings his victims' own words back into their teeth, ironically condemning or overreaching them out of their own mouths (IV.ii.84–89, 94–96; IV.iii.51–59). Like other usurers he is a "Jew" (IV.iii.60, V.iii.32), and these actions mirror the unredeemed strictness of the rule of the Law, under which all men stand condemned. Sir John's return, though, makes the day "sacred" to mercy (V.iii.126) bringing hope of a new order of forgiveness and freedom to transform the rigors of Law. This moment has the quality of an epiphany: the women's repentance is answered by a miracle—Sir John's metamorphosis from red man to white, and the magical infusion of life into the statues—which overcomes Luke at a stroke. Beneath the concluding reconciliations are suggestions of a wider, sacramental pattern; the supercession of the Jewish rule of loveless Law by the Christian rule of loving Grace.

VII

The City Madam, then, while attacking the excessive or immoral behavior of citizens, adopts a basically sympathetic and enlightened attitude toward the great citizenry, endorsing entirely the values of Sir John Frugal, the godly citizen. It is not, though, an isolated instance of the positive presentation of mercantilism on the early Stuart stage. In 1623, a tragedy of *"The Plantation of Virginia,"* presumably alluding to the Indian massacre of 1622, was produced at the Curtain; in 1625 the officials of the East India Company (some of whom this paper has discussed) tried to stage a play on the massacre of their agents at Amboyna by the Dutch, but were prevented by the Privy Council.[64] Eight years later, the governor, deputy-

64. Bentley, *Jacobean and Caroline Stage*, V, 1395–1396; M. C. Heinemann, *Puritanism and Theatre* (Cambridge, Eng., 1980), pp. 209–210.

governor, and "committees" of the EIC were actually animated on stage in *The Launching of the Mary*, a propaganda play by a minor EIC official. This alternates the story of the puritanical wife of a seaman who, in her husband's absence, heroically defends her chastity from lascivious courtiers and suchlike, with a long vindication of English trade in the East, including several references to England's potential greatness at sea and the Amboyna massacre (expunged by the censor). The EIC spokesmen argue that their trade brings profits to Christendom that would otherwise go to the Infidel Turk, and publicize the Company's charitable works ("Th'East India gates stand open, open wide / to entertayne the needie & the poore, / with good accommodation") which the listening admiral enthusiastically admires ("Heauns blesse theyr store for relligious deeds / such pious actes of Boundles Charitie").[65] England's commercial opponents were again ridiculed in Henry Glapthorne's *The Hollander* (Phoenix, 1635) and Davenant's *News from Plymouth* (Globe, 1635), the latter a popular comedy set among seamen windbound in harbor.[66]

Moreover, whereas earlier criticism has taken Sir John's retirement to Louvain to indicate Massinger's Roman Catholic sympathies, I have suggested that the play's religious coloring is of a much more thoroughly puritan type. The private theaters are normally conceived to have been violently and traditionally aggressive toward citizens and puritans, but Massinger's attack on vanity and unchristian selfishness clearly draws profoundly on their spiritual and moral convictions. In the perspective of our modern historical understanding of puritanism as a powerful social and political movement, there is a level of deep significant contact between the two plots. In just such colonial projects as the Luke plot alludes to, yoking commercial investment and spiritual intention, were foundations laid on which the success of the parliamentary-puritan front of the 1640s was built. In the 1620s and 1630s, many leading "puritan" noblemen, including Massinger's patron Pembroke, engaged in overseas enterprises that established and consolidated their connections with the godly trading class; from these and similar associations would emerge the broad "opposi-

65. W. Mountfort, *The Launching of the Mary*, ed. J. H. Walter (Oxford, 1933), ll. 377, 1713; cf. Heinemann, *Puritanism and Theatre*, pp. 210–213.

66. These two, though, have courtly overtones. *News from Plymouth*, for example, is about privateering rather than commerce.

tion" synthesis of a wide spectrum of moderate puritan feeling which agitated effectively for a return to parliamentary government.[67] Massinger concludes with the establishment—on the understanding that the citizens know their place—of an alliance between aristocracy and citizen, a social development mirroring the evolving political alignments of the 1630s. Insofar as one wishes to extract a crudely political moral from the play, and given that Massinger would never have formulated it this way himself, *The City Madam*, contrary to the usual assumptions about the courtly elitism of the Caroline stage and the traditionalism of city comedy in general, is on the side of progress, rather than of conservatism.

Massinger is here responding to, and helping to shape, the attitudes of an audience which, though not "popular," was still no "Cavalier" coterie. The play is most notable for its distinctively *bourgeois* qualities—its strenuousness and moral severity. There is no temptation toward sentiment or flippancy; rather, the play achieves perfectly that balance between tragedy and comedy which the Caroline drama is most often criticized for lacking. For example, in the tragicomedies of a more courtly dramatist, such as Fletcher, the characters are placed in a dilemma of warring opposites which the playwright does not take seriously and which is resolved when one of the obstacles simply collapses. *The City Madam*, by contrast, is tragicomic in a chaste, non-Fletcherean manner. That is to say, the play is successful as a comedy directly in proportion to the extent to which the conception of Luke is allowed to approach a truly tragic status. Luke is not reintegrated at the end but remains outside, a threatening and, above all, a wholly convincing figure (the echoes of Shakespearean tragedy which I have noted in passing are not gratuitous but contribute to this total effect). Massinger takes the tragic aspect of his plot entirely seriously; being quite in earnest about his conflict of values, he is willing to push it to its limits, and the play's peculiar imaginative vigor is a product and a measure of this seriousness. *The City Madam* exhibits a consistent, coherent, and comprehensive attitude toward life. It cannot be interpreted as evidence of the narrowing of the drama into subservience to the private interests of a single, declining class; it is rooted in a world that is altogether wider, more public, and more complete.

67. See J. H. Hexter, *The Reign of King Pym* (Cambridge, Mass., 1941), pp. 77–88; C. Hill, *Intellectual Origins of the English Revolution* (Oxford, 1965), pp. 161–164; Heinemann, *Puritanism and Theatre*, p. 269.

Arcadia Lost: Politics and
Revision in the Restoration Tempest

KATHARINE EISAMAN MAUS

I

T HE MOST POPULAR PLAY on the Restoration stage was *The Tempest*, as
    revised by John Dryden and William D'Avenant in 1667. Pepys
thought it was "good, above ordinary plays" when he saw it on its opening
night; he was to attend eight performances in the next two years. "After
dinner, to the Duke of York's house to see the play, *The Tempest*, which we
have often seen; but yet I am pleased again, and shall be again to see it."[1]
In 1674 the revised *Tempest* was staged for the first time as an "opera,"
with elaborate scenery and several new songs. According to John Downes,
"All things were perform'd in it so exceedingly well, that not any succeed-
ing Opera got more money."[2] The play was more often revived than any
other between 1660 and 1700; innumerable contemporary allusions indicate that virtually everyone was familiar with it. It continued to be

1. *The Diary of Samuel Pepys*, ed. R. Latham and W. Matthews (London, 1970), IX, 48
(3 February 1668).

2. John Downes, *Roscius Anglicanus* (London, 1708), p. 34. A Restoration "opera" was
not entirely sung; it was usually a lavishly staged production involving vocal and instru-
mental music, and spoken dialogue as well. In its proportion of speech to song it was more
like a modern musical than like a modern opera.

received favorably through the eighteenth century, and into the nineteenth.

Modern critics, however, have not shared the enthusiasm of the Restoration audience. "To appraise this wretched stuff in the light of critical
rules would be absurd," Hazelton Spencer fumes, calling the play "the
worst, as it was the most successful, of the Restoration adaptations prior to
1700."[3] Allardyce Nicoll complains that it panders to "the immoral,
degenerate qualities of the age."[4] The Dryden-D'Avenant *Tempest* has
received more sympathetic, or at least more tactful, attention from a few
critics who see the revision as an attempt to render Shakespeare's dense
language more immediately comprehensible in performance, to reshape
the play according to neoclassic norms, to make Shakespeare's improbable
fictions more acceptable to a scientifically minded audience, or to exploit
the new scenic resources of the Restoration stage.[5] I will argue, however,
that the revised *Tempest* is best understood in terms of sociopolitical issues
which were of primary practical importance in the latter half of the seventeenth century. The new play redefines the limits and uses of sovereignty.

II

It certainly seems plausible enough to assume that the collaborators
undertook the revision with more-or-less coherent goals in mind. Dryden
and D'Avenant alter *The Tempest* far more than *Troilus and Cressida* or

3. *Shakespeare Improved* (Cambridge, Mass., 1927), pp. 201, 203.
4. *Dryden as an Adapter of Shakespeare* (London, 1922), p. 17.
5. The best discussion is in the introduction to the 1667 *Tempest* in Maximilian Novak
and George Guffey, eds., *The Works of John Dryden* (Berkeley, Calif., 1970), X, 319–343.
All line references to the D'Avenant-Dryden *Tempest* are to this edition. Montague
Summers, in *Shakespeare Adaptations* (London, 1922), p. cvii, describes the way the revised
Tempest makes use of the Restoration stage. While helpful, some of the claims these critics
make raise new questions. If D'Avenant and Dryden are writing neoclassic comedy, why do
they observe the unities of time and action so much more loosely than Shakespeare does in
his very tightly constructed play? If their audience is too sophisticated to accept
Shakespeare's implausibilities, why does it applaud the far greater offense to reason represented by Ariel's magical cure of a mortally wounded boy, or the devils impersonating
Fraud, Pride, Rapine, and Murther who dance before the guilty courtiers? If the collaborators wish to take advantage of the new scenic resources of the Restoration stage, why do
they omit Shakespeare's masque of Ceres, a fine opportunity for the display of theatrical
magnificence?

Macbeth—they take only about a third of their material from the original play, displacing and rearranging the Shakespearean material to serve the demands of a substantially new plot.[6] A brief summary will suggest the extent of the alteration.

Like Shakespeare, Dryden and D'Avenant begin their play with a storm and a shipwreck. Shortly thereafter, however, the adaptation diverges from the original. As the revised *Tempest* begins, Prospero has managed to raise his two daughters, Miranda and Dorinda, to adolescence in ignorance of his foster-child Hippolito, whom he also brought as an infant to the island. Hippolito is the rightful Duke of Mantua, disinherited in the same coup that overthrew Prospero himself. Hippolito is doomed, according to his horoscope, if he ever beholds a woman; Prospero therefore keeps the young people apart by threats. The girls, however, finally disobey their father's injunctions. Dorinda begins a conversation with Hippolito; infatuation ensues. When Prospero chides his daughters for their insubordination he quickly discovers Dorinda's passion, and wonders why Hippolito remains unharmed.

Meanwhile, Prospero sends Ariel to bring Ferdinand to Miranda. They fall in love but, as in the Shakespearean version, Prospero refuses to allow an unimpeded courtship. He sends Ferdinand to a cave in which he has sequestered Hippolito. From Ferdinand, Hippolito learns that there is more than one woman in the world, and inductively reasons that if one is good, more are better. The four young people assiduously pursue their courtships—but inevitably, given the inexperience and guileless volubility of the participants, misunderstandings arise on all sides. Eventually a jealous Ferdinand challenges Hippolito to a duel. Hippolito, ignorant of the martial arts, is badly wounded and falls unconscious. Furious, Prospero dismisses Ariel to find Gonzalo, Alonzo, and Antonio, whom he has been tormenting with ingenious apparitions. When the shipwrecked

6. Roughly, the Shakespearean material is disposed as follows: the second half of Shakespeare's I.ii becomes II.ii and III.v in the Dryden-D'Avenant version; Shakespearean material from II.ii and V.i is incorporated with considerable variation into II.iii, III.i, and V.ii of the adapted play. Four scenes (I.i, I.ii, II.i, and II.ii) begin in the same way as their Shakespearean counterparts, but diverge from the earlier play as they proceed. Acts II and IV of the Shakespearean *Tempest* have no equivalent in the Dryden-D'Avenant version. II.iv, II.v, III.iii, III.iv, III.vi, V.i, most of V.ii, and all of Act IV in the revision have no equivalent in Shakespeare.

courtiers arrive, Prospero declares his intention to execute Ferdinand at daybreak for Hippolito's murder.

The next day, Prospero rejects Miranda's last-minute efforts to save her lover's life. Ariel, however, announces that he has revived Hippolito by a combination of medicine and magic. The still-groggy Hippolito claims that he is no longer promiscuously inclined—but more misunderstandings among the lovers nearly lead to another fight at the bedside. All difficulties, though, soon resolve themselves. Alonzo, Antonio, and Prospero are already reconciled by the happy circumstances of Hippolito's recovery and Ferdinand's pardon. The couples prepare to be wed, though Hippolito, Miranda, and Dorinda are still ignorant of their marital responsibilities.

In the revised *Tempest* the low characters—Stephano, Mustacho, Ventoso, and Trincalo—are all sailors, and like their Shakespearean counterparts they quickly find each other once ashore. Stephano proclaims himself duke, Mustacho and Ventoso viceroys. Trincalo rejects their pretensions, and attempts to gain a title himself by marrying Caliban's sister Sycorax. Stephano arrives on an ambassadorial mission, ostensibly to make peace with Trincalo, but actually to seduce Sycorax. The scene ends in uproar. The low characters do not reappear until the end of the final scene, when they and the rest of the company watch Ariel and his lover Milcha perform a saraband.

The script of the operatic *Tempest* differs little from the Dryden-D'Avenant play. Scenes are sometimes rearranged and speeches cut to allow room for new songs and special stage effects; the text includes elaborate descriptions of scenery and other mechanical devices. The initial storm scene features witches who fly about on wires, as does Ariel, throughout the play, at every opportunity. Tables vanish, and holes open onstage to give the guilty courtiers a view of the hell that awaits them. The fifth act includes a nuptial masque, and ends with a choral version of "Where the bee sucks, there suck I." Although D'Avenant had died in 1668, and Dryden did not help with the operatic version, the Restoration *Tempest* was understandably still considered their play. The text of the 1674 opera continued to be ascribed to them on the title pages of subsequent editions.

III

What are we to make of all this? The plot alterations inaugurated by Dryden and D'Avenant react in very significant ways upon the character of Prospero. Shakespeare's Prospero is, by his own account at least, an educator, a dealer in revelatory illusion, who would prefer not to acknowledge the coercive implications of his power. In Milan he puts "the manage of his state," the sordid business of day-to-day politics, in the hands of his practical, opportunistic brother; though he fiercely resents his overthrow, his forced isolation on the island really only completes his retirement, and gives him an opportunity to construct his own Arcadia.[7] In the masque he has performed for Miranda and Ferdinand at the end of Act IV, his imagination need not be constrained by the imperfections of reality. He is free to recreate the golden world:

> Earth's increase, foison plenty,
> Barns and garners never empty.

7. The importance of pastoral to *The Tempest* has received considerable attention. The major treatments are: Frank Kermode, Introduction to *The Tempest*, Arden Shakespeare (London, 1964), xiv-lxiii. This introduction was first published in 1954. Stephen Orgel, "New Uses of Adversity: Tragic Experience in *The Tempest*," *In Defense of Reading*, ed. R. Poirier and R. Brower (New York, 1962), pp. 110–132. Northrop Frye, *A Natural Perspective* (New York, 1965), pp. 149–159. Frye also expounds his views on pastoral in *The Tempest* in his introduction to the play in *The Pelican Shakespeare*, ed. Alfred Harbage (London, 1969), pp. 1369–1372. Harry Berger, "Miraculous Harp: A Reading of Shakespeare's *Tempest*," *ShStud*, V (1969), 253–283. David Young, *The Heart's Forest: A Study of Shakespeare's Pastoral Plays* (New Haven, Conn., 1972), pp. 148–191. Thomas McFarland, *Shakespeare's Pastoral Comedy* (Chapel Hill, N.C., 1972), pp. 146–175. Kermode, Frye, and McFarland emphasize the positive aspects of the pastoral vision and are extremely sympathetic to Prospero. Berger, who stresses the neurotic element in Prospero's constitution, makes a good case for a "darker" reading of *The Tempest*, but I think he misreads the final act. Orgel perceptively distinguishes between Prospero's experience and the experience of the other characters in *The Tempest*, and shows how Prospero's perspective differs from the perspective of the audience. Young is more interested in the theatrical self-consciousness of *The Tempest* than in the issues that directly concern me here, but he agrees that the play moves toward a recognition that "apparently unalterable opposites . . . are mutually complementary, aspects of the same thing" (p. 170).

> Vines with clust'ring branches growing,
> Plants with goodly burden bowing;
> Spring come to you at the farthest
> In the very end of harvest.

                                                    (ll. 110–116)[8]

Gonzalo, Prospero's good-hearted, foolish old supporter, is intuitively sensitive to his lord's version of the marvelous island—he is the only one to notice the miraculous freshness of his salt-drenched clothes—and in his plans for the island he effectively articulates Prospero's ideal:

> All things in common nature should produce
> Without sweat or endeavor. Treason, felony,
> Sword, pike, knife, gun, or need of any engine
> Would I not have; but nature should bring forth,
> Of its own kind, all foison, all abundance
> To feed my innocent people.

                                                    (II.i.155–160)

Gonzalo would "with such perfection govern, sir / T'excel the golden age." His fellows ridicule his guileless refusal to recognize the necessity of labor or the demands of sexuality. "The latter end of his commonwealth forgets the beginning," exclaims the worldly wise Antonio, who understands the contradiction implicit in the idea of a governing power which never asserts itself against the subject's will.

Not surprisingly, the pastoral ambitions of Shakespeare's Prospero render him profoundly suspicious of anything unteachable or unassimilable—anything which, by demanding to be repressed, sets limits upon his power or calls his benevolence into question. He must resort to force or threats of force with Caliban, who rejects his tutelage; with Ariel, who forgets his debt of gratitude; with Alonso and Antonio before they repent of their usurpation; with Trinculo and Stephano when they attempt to overthrow him. Prospero never really need fear that these intransigent elements will successfully displace him from his position of power on the island. He resents them so violently because they force him to realize that

---

8. All line references to the Shakespeare play are to *The Pelican Shakespeare*, ed. Alfred Harbage (London, 1969).

his pastoral vision is anomalously managerial and competitive, that it can be enacted only at the expense of Caliban's or Ariel's version of Arcadia.

Miranda, the apt student, presents no problem until the arrival of Ferdinand divides her loyalties; when she protests against Prospero's treatment of her beloved, she elicits a violent outburst of rage. "What, my foot my tutor? . . . One word more shall make me chide thee, if not hate thee" (I.ii.467–476). Shakespeare's Prospero is anxious about sexuality, particularly female sexuality. The only mother on the island has been a witch whose pregnancy changed her sentence from death to exile, rendered her indestructible. For Prospero the mother is necessary but also stubbornly unassimilable, a potential competitor, and so he fears that Sycorax might be typical. When Miranda asks innocently, "Are you not my father?," he answers with peculiar insistence upon his wife's chastity.

Early in Shakespeare's play, Prospero reacts to all these "things of darkness" by repressing them—enslaving Caliban, subduing Ferdinand, threatening to peg a sullen Ariel in the entrails of an oak. In the Shakespearean version, though, Prospero's repressive impulses are eventually modified and overcome; thus many critics see him as a white magician, or even as a version of the author himself. For Prospero's power is essentially transformational; he aims to alter reality rather than fix it in some eternal shape. He must therefore be acutely conscious of time, of the need to seize the appropriate day. "I find my zenith doth attend upon / A most auspicious star" (I.ii.181–182). He accepts the limits set upon him by fate and by his contract with Ariel, and begins to interpret his own activity in terms of timely revelation, of fruition, rather than as the maintenance of a static order. He supervises the courtship of Miranda and Ferdinand by both encouraging and restraining it, forbidding premature indulgence in the interests of a decorous and fertile consummation. Eventually Prospero's acceptance of the relation between change and creativity modifies his vision of a timeless Arcadia, and leads him to a reconciliation with the un-Arcadian elements he initially finds most threatening. He forgives the courtiers, blesses the daughter he has lost, and acknowledges Caliban as his own.

The Dryden-D'Avenant Prospero begins with the same obsessions and anxieties; the second scene of the play, in which Prospero talks to Miranda, Ariel, and Caliban, is reproduced almost word for word. But Prospero's repressive tendencies are here exaggerated. He is kin to the neurotic and domineering father of a farce. While Shakespeare's Prospero selectively represses the intransigent elements of his world, the Dryden-D'Avenant Prospero makes no such discrimination. Hippolito, Dorinda, and Miranda, who "murmur not . . . but wonder" are kept in caves like Caliban, their freedom of movement severely restricted. Furthermore, the sexual aspects of Prospero's anxiety are developed at much greater length. Instead of dealing frankly with Hippolito or his daughters, he misrepresents vital information; the extreme sexual naïveté of the young people in the revised *Tempest* is the source of much of its comic humor as well as its near-tragedy. Knowing that the children will take metaphor for literal fact, this Prospero employs satiric tropes which betray his own state of mind. He tells his daughters that men are "all that you can imagine ill," more dreadful than "the curled Lion or the rugged Bear."

> DORINDA
> Do they run wild about the Woods?
> PROSPERO
> No, they are wild within Doors, in Chambers
> And in Closets.
>
> (II. iv. 106–108)

To Hippolito, the new Prospero describes women as "the dangerous enemies of man":

> Their voices charm beyond the Nightingales;
> They are all enchantment, those who once behold 'em
> Are made their slaves forever.
>
> (II. iv. 47–49)

The magic of sexual attraction competes with Prospero's art, and (like his own "enchantment") it seems to his mind a negative process, enslavement rather than liberation.

Dorinda, Miranda, and Hippolito discover their sexuality despite Prospero's injunctions: "I find it in my Nature," says Dorinda, "because my father has forbidden me" (II. iv. 132–133). The new Prospero deals not in revelation, but in concealment; the progress of the plot toward marriage and forgiveness represents a violation rather than an expression of his will.

D'Avenant and Dryden part company more and more drastically with the Shakespearean text, as they delimit a fundamentally static and beseiged character, without the means to cope with or reconcile himself to the manifold threats he perceives in his world. Their Prospero can never acknowledge his relationship to Caliban; at the end of the new play he merely orders the savage back into the cave.

In the fifth act of the original *Tempest*, Shakespeare's Prospero struggles to overcome his resentment against his brother and his brother's accomplices.

> Though with their high wrongs I am struck to th' quick,
> Yet with my nobler reason 'gainst my fury
> Do I take part. The rarer action is
> In virtue than in vengeance. They being penitent,
> The sole drift of my purpose doth extend
> Not a frown further.
>
> (V.i.25–30)

Conversion, not persecution, is now his aim. In the revised *Tempest*, on the other hand, the D'Avenant-Dryden Prospero struggles not to outgrow his anxieties and obsessions, but rather to reify them—to impose them on the people he controls. This Prospero torments people who are conscious of their sin from the outset. "Alas, I suffer justly for my crimes," Alonzo exclaims in the first scene, when he believes the ship will sink. Antonio ascribes the shipwreck to divine justice:

> Indeed we first broke truce with Heav'n;
> You to the waves an Infant Prince expos'd,
> And on the waves have lost an only Son;
> I did usurp my Brother's fertile lands, and now
> Am cast upon this desert Isle.
>
> (II.i.21–25)

The new Prospero's persecution of the sinners—much more relentless than in the Shakespearean *Tempest*—thus has no particular moral or educational purpose. His power is essentially sinister, as he admits when he calls upon his spirits in a crisis. "I thought no more to use their aids; (I'm curs'd because I us'd it)" (IV.iii.159–160). He is not inclined to forgiveness even

as the play begins to close; after Ferdinand has wounded Hippolito he tells
Alonzo:

> Blood calls for blood; your Ferdinand shall dye,
> And I in bitterness have sent for you,
> To have the sudden joy of seeing him alive,
> And then the greater grief to see him die.
>
> (IV.iii.150–153)

Not Prospero's will, but the "blessed day," the miraculous and unantici-
pated circumstance of Hippolito's recovery, transforms the Restoration
Tempest from revenge tragedy to comic romance.

It is possible to imagine a play in which the new Prospero's primitive
and unself-conscious moral nature would become the occasion for satire,
but this does not seem to be the point of the Dryden-D'Avenant *Tempest*.
In Shakespeare's version Prospero's Arcadian ideal is not idiosyncratic;
Ariel, Gonzalo, Caliban, Miranda, and Ferdinand all articulate some version of it. In the D'Avenant-Dryden adaptation, though, the pastoral no
longer constitutes a shared ideal—indeed, it does not seem available as an
ideal at all. Gonzalo's speeches are cut, Ariel's songs deleted or shortened.
Caliban is no longer mysteriously susceptible to beauty, but prefers his
sister Sycorax because she is bigger than Prospero's daughters. Lacking the
Arcadian vision, which calls into question the competitive, coercive, and
manipulative aspects of power, the ruler has no impulse to reconcile his
activity with factors that limit and define it.

In the Shakespearean *Tempest* the courtiers are returning from the marriage of Alonso's daughter, Claribel, and the king of Tunis. Gonzalo,
spokesman for Arcadia, identifies Tunis with ancient Carthage, and compares Claribel with "the widow Dido." The Virgilian reference is important, because Aeneas's conquest in Italy depends upon his rejection of the
distraction Dido represents. He must repress the demands of his sexuality
in order to found his city—a city which, in later years, will come into its
own as it once again resists the Punic threat. Against such a background,
the marriage of Claribel represents a new sort of foreign relations—a
political strategy no longer repressive or competitive. Tunis-Carthage is
now accepted rather than resisted; it is the solution of romantic comedy
rather than of tragedy or epic. It is not surprising that the shallow cynics
Antonio and Sebastian, who mock Gonzalo's naïve pastoral vision, reject

also his identification of Tunis with Carthage, and all the consequences implicit in that identification. And it is not surprising that in the D'Avenant-Dryden *Tempest*, the goal of the sea voyage has changed. These courtiers, "in defense of Christianity," have been fighting to drive the Moors out of Portugal—not to wed but to war with Africans upon the competitive Virgilian principle.

In other words, the revised *Tempest* contains no model for the Shakespearean Prospero's ultimate gesture of acceptance and reconcilation. There is no process by which love might be related to death, or poetry to passion; all change is thus of necessity revolutionary or destructive. The Shakespearean Ariel sings "Full fathom five thy father lies" to Ferdinand as he leads him to Miranda, so that the prince decides that she must be "the goddess / On whom these airs attend." In the revised version the funeral song no longer leads to Miranda, and the new Ferdinand unlike the earlier one finds the song simply "mournful." The link between death and sexuality is severed, and Ferdinand cannot now find the rich and strange metamorphoses of his father's drowned body either wonderful or reassuring.

It is, therefore, highly significant that Dryden and D'Avenant omit in their revision the masque of Ceres with which Shakespeare's Prospero celebrates his daughter's betrothal. In the original *Tempest*, Prospero attempts to supply a heretofore missing maternal principle, which in the first act he had been prone to regard as competitive with his own creative and procreative power. The heroine of the masque is the fertile grain goddess, the original patroness of the unproblematic golden world over which Prospero wishes he could preside. Ceres' productivity, though, is dependent upon her daughter, Persephone, and limited by her daughter's affiliation with the king of the underworld, the principle of death. Early in the masque, Juno and Ceres banish Venus and Cupid, the rival mother and child, who represent the darker, uncontrolled aspects of sexuality; and Ceres excludes winter and death from the blessing she gives Miranda and Ferdinand: "Spring come to you at the farthest / In the very end of harvest" (IV.i.115–116). Ceres does not mention her absence. But the proximity of love and death, creation and destruction, is reasserted in the harvest dance which follows.

The nymphs who were cold and chaste at the beginning of the masque are made "fresh" by their encounter with the phallic sicklemen, whose death-dealing "grim reaper" aspect is inseparable from their virile and life-giving sexuality. The sweaty reapers represent all the "things of darkness" which threaten Prospero's Arcadian vision—the necessity of labor, the necessity of death, the necessity of passion—and also the ultimate inseparability of the things of darkness from the things of light. In this scene the proximity of nymphs and reapers reminds Prospero of Caliban's proximity, and of the plot to usurp his kingly power. The same proximity of idealism and necessity, creativity and destructiveness, will also lead Prospero, finally, to acknowledge Caliban as his own.

The Shakespearean Prospero thus uses pastoral to transcend pastoral—or at least to achieve a more mature and comprehensive vision than Gonzalo's naïve utopianism will permit. But while the original Prospero dreams of a world in which repression is unnecessary, the Restoration Prospero, entirely devoid of the Arcadian impulse, dreams instead of a world in which repression is merely unproblematic. In the 1674 operatic *Tempest* he, too, stages a masque—the festivities upon which the play ends.[9] Not surprisingly, its symbolism differs markedy from Shakespeare's. The new masque begins as Amphitrite asks her husband Neptune for calm seas. Good weather is described entirely in negative terms: "Tethys no furrows now shall wear, / Oceanus no wrinkles on his brow." Neptune's control over the elements clearly depends upon sheer power—"You I'll obey," sings Aeolus, "Who at one stroke can make / With your dread trident, the whole earth to shake." Authority here takes the same form as Prospero's did in the first act. All the obstreperous winds are "boistrous prisoners" safe in their "dark caverns," just as Miranda, Dorinda, Hippolito, and Caliban were once sequestered. "To your prisons below / Down, down you must go," Aeolus commands; "We / Will soon obey you cheerfully," reply the tritons and nereids, acquiescing with a thoroughness that Dorinda, Hippolito, Miranda, Caliban, and even Ariel have been unable to match. The Dryden-D'Avenant Prospero learns nothing in the course of the play; in the operatic version, the masque at the end of the fifth act only emphasizes his intransigence.

9. The masque of Amphitrite and Neptune is printed in all seventeenth-century editions of the revised *Tempest* after 1674. It is most easily available to the modern scholar in *The Complete Works of Thomas Shadwell*, ed. Montague Summers (London, 1927), II, 265–267. Shadwell was probably responsible for the additions to the D'Avenant-Dryden script made for the operatic production.

IV

The Restoration audience could not have preferred the revised version of *The Tempest* because it was more poetic, complex, or imaginative than the original. It is tempting to think, in light of the foregoing analysis, that they did find it more plausible. The D'Avenant-Dryden adaptation is much more explicitly and exclusively political than the Shakespeare play. The puns on "art" in I.ii. are cut, and so are the two speeches in Shakespeare's *Tempest* most obviously concerned with artistry—the address to Ferdinand after the masque ("we are such things as dreams are made on"), and Prospero's renunciation speech, his promise to break his rod and drown his book. In the Restoration adaptation, however, Prospero's expanded political role compensates somewhat for his lack of artistic self-consciousness. As he tells Alonzo when he resolves to execute Ferdinand:

> Here I am plac'd by Heav'n, here I am Prince,
> Though you have dispossessed me of my *Millain*.
> (IV.iii.148–149)

He has seven subjects to the Shakespearean Prospero's three—seven subjects whose interaction constantly threatens to overwhelm his authority. In the Restoration *Tempest*, though a political role is no longer synonymous with an artistic or priestly role, politics alone is enough to keep one busy.

Since the revised play is so determinedly a play about government, current political theory might help illuminate reasons for the differences between the two Prospero's, and for the appeal of the later conception to Restoration audiences. In 1612, when Shakespeare's *Tempest* was first performed, James I's earliest theoretical tracts on kingship were little more than a decade old. In *Basilikon Doron* and *The Trew Law of Free Monarchy*, both published at the end of the sixteenth century, James had maintained that he held his royal position by divine right. He used as a supplementary argument a patriarchal theory of kingship which derived the state from the family, and conceived of kingly authority as an extension of fatherly power. Patriarchalists take a limited view of the subject's freedom, maintaining that he has no more right to choose his ruler than children have to choose their fathers. This restriction need not be irksome, however, since the king's fatherly care is originally and ideally loving, and only incidentally coercive. Thus Shakespeare's Prospero, with his vision of an unoppressive golden age, resents Caliban's refusal to accept the role of adoptive child.

The idea that the origin of states is familial was in fact a very old one. [10] But in this particular form it became an important polemical weapon in the seventeenth century, when the Stuarts and their supporters found patriarchalism an attractive basis for their absolutist claims. The theory retained adherents until the end of the century, when the Whiggish John Locke dealt it a death blow, [11] but it had met with fierce opposition even before the Civil War. Populists like Winstanley, and even some absolutists like Hobbes and Digges, wanted to replace the patriarchalist doctrine with a theory of a conventional state—a government based upon a contract among free individuals, rather than one based upon naturally occurring hierarchical relationships. [12] The notion of the father-king came increasingly under attack in the war years and after, and patriarchal theorists became increasingly defensive in their pronouncements. As the century wore on, patriarchalism seemed increasingly nostalgic—an attempt to recover the lost monarchical privilege enjoyed by the early Stuarts.

Clearly, when a theory like this one is current and controversial, a political reading of The Tempest would make Prospero a version of the patriarchalist father-king. But in the 1660s, when Dryden and D'Avenant are collaborating on their revision of The Tempest, the figure of the father-king—at least in its more extravagant or extreme forms—is already becoming anachronistic. It is not surprising that the D'Avenant-Dryden Prospero seems so threatened by change, so willing to employ repressive tactics in order to maintain his shaky authority.

10. See, for example, Aristotle, who begins his Politics with a discussion of the household, arguing that the "elementary relationships" of husband and wife, parent and child, master and servant precede both logically and temporally the more complicated relations among the citizens of the polis. But Aristotle considers patriarchal kingship only one of several kinds (see III.xiv.14). For an account of the fortunes of patriarchalism during the Civil War, Commonwealth, and Restoration, see Gordon Schochet, Patriarchalism in Political Thought (New York, 1975), pp. 159–224.

11. John Locke, The First Treatise of Government (London, 1690).

12. Thomas Hobbes, Leviathan, or the Matter, Form, and Power of a Commonwealth, ecclesiastical and civil (London, 1651), pts. I and II. Dudley Digges, The Unlawfulnesse of subjects taking up armes against their soveraigne . . . (Oxford, 1643).

Shakespeare's Prospero learns to allow for and accept unassimilable and potentially competitive elements—the maternal principle, for example, omitted by patriarchal theorists like James Maxwell, who render the fifth commandment as "Honora patrem etc." [13] But he can afford to be generous. Trinculo and Stephano, or villains like Sebastian, think in terms of usurpation; they implicitly accept a monarchical system of government even while they attempt to subvert the individual in charge. Kingship as an institution is taken for granted.

The low characters in the Dryden-D'Avenant *Tempest* are not even aware of Prospero's existence until the end of the fifth act. Instead, they make their own arrangements among thesmelves:

MUSTACHO

Our ship is sunk, and we can never get home agen: We must e'en turn Salvages, and the next that catches his Fellow may eat him.

VENTOSO

No, no, let us have a Government.

(II.iii.48–51)

Stephano appoints himself duke, and makes Mustacho and Ventoso his viceroys. "Agreed, agreed!" they shout together. Although their pre-governmental state of nature is a sham, since their relations on the island are based on prior relations aboard ship, the low characters obviously believe they are constituting a state on contractual grounds. [14] They immediately and hilariously encounter the difficulties contractual theorists always take pains to treat: the problem of who could "speak for the people" in the absence of any constituted authority or procedures, and the problem of a person who refuses to accept the contract. "I'll have no laws," Trincalo declares, and goes off to form his own government with Caliban as his subject and Caliban's sister as his queen. Main plot and subplot in the Restoration *Tempest* seem curiously exclusive, at least when compared with

13. *Sacro Sancta Regem Majestas, or, the Sacred and Royal Prerogative of Christian Kings* (Oxford, 1644), p. 161.

14. For more information on Dryden and Hobbes, see Louis Teeter, "The Dramatic Use of Hobbes' Political Ideas," pp. 341–373, and John A. Winterbottom, "The Place of Hobbesian Ideas in Dryden's Tragedies," pp. 374–396, in *Essential Articles for the Study of John Dryden*, ed. H. T. Swedenberg (Hamden, Conn., 1966).

the tightly constructed Shakespearean model. In fact, though, the very detachment of the low characters constitutes a threat more subtle, but also more dangerous, than the threat of usurpation in the Shakespeare play. The Dryden-D'Avenant Prospero is besieged, not in his person, as is the Shakespearean Prospero, but in his role. The ideological basis of his authority is subverted by the possibility that the patriarchal conception of monarchy is bankrupt.

The utter failure of the sailors' attempts at self-government is important, though, because it helps define sources for the conservatism of postwar monarchists like Dryden and D'Avenant. The revised *Tempest* is not in the least subversive of the monarchical principle; it merely refuses to grant to the king and father special prerogatives in other kinds of endeavor. Prospero with all his faults is a just and orderly ruler, and the postwar royalists consider justice and order the primary virtues of the good sovereign. The conception of a Prospero who is limited but nonetheless efficient is typical of Dryden's pessimistic conservatism. [15] In *Absalom and Achitophel* and *The Hind and the Panther* he argues for traditional forms not because he has illusions about their transcendent goodness, but because he

---

15. I will concentrate on Dryden in the following few pages, partly because his work is more familiar to the general reader, and also because, according to his introduction to the revised *Tempest*, D'Avenant was concerned less with adapting the main plot than with devising scenes for the low characters. The prologue on Shakespeare is entirely Dryden's work. However, the ideas that I attribute to Dryden here are commonplace enough in the later seventeenth century; they are shared not only by D'Avenant but by many Restoration conservatives—including, most likely, the majority of playgoers in the 1660s and '70s. For D'Avenant's simultaneous loyalty to, and disenchantment with, Charles II, see Alfred Harbage, *Sir William D'Avenant: Poet Venturer 1606–1668* (Philadelphia, 1935), pp. 135–141. David Ogg, in *England in the Reign of Charles II* (Oxford, 1934), gives a thorough and entertaining account of the way political and theoretical issues intersect during the later part of the seventeenth century. See particularly I.139–141, and II.450–523. The importance of Dryden's politics for his literary practice has received a great deal of attention. See, e.g., Bernard Schilling, *Dryden and the Conservative Myth: A Reading of Absalom and Achitophel* (New Haven, Conn., 1961), pp. 1–95; Alan Roper, *Dryden's Poetic Kingdom* (London, 1965), pp. 50–103; Ann T. Barbeau, *The Intellectual Design of John Dryden's Heroic Plays* (New Haven, Conn., 1970), pp. 3–54; Stephen N. Zwicker, *Dryden's Political Poetry* (Providence, R.I., 1972); Isabel Rivers, *The Poetry of Conservatism 1600–1745* (Cambridge, Eng., 1973), pp. 127–174; Sanford Budick, *The Poetry of Civilization* (New Haven, Conn., 1974), pp. 81–110.

believes that radical change necessarily brings about worse evils. Any tradition, any constituted authority, is better than none. Like his Prospero, he has a lively suspicion of lurking chaos; the source of satiric vigor in poems like *MacFlecknoe* and *The Medall* lies largely in the tension between immoral disorder and a justly repressive authority.

Dryden sides with the forces of order, but he defines that order carefully; Charles II is no omnipotent Shakespearean Prospero, but "a king, who is just and moderate in his nature, and who rules according to the laws, whom God has made happy by joining the temper of his soul to the Constitution of his government." [16] Charles's virtue, for Dryden, lies not in his extravagant assertions of power, but in his willingness to limit that assertion. Shakespeare throughout his long career is fascinated by the managerial personality, whether good or evil; in Dryden's plays absolutist aspirations are inevitably and unmistakably foul both in their sources and their effects.

This is not to say that Dryden is insensitive to a conception of authority which is both more ambitious and less coercive. His prologue begins with a recognition, somewhat like the Shakespearean Prospero's, that creative and destructive potentials are inseparable.

> As when a Tree's cut down, the secret root
> Lives under ground, and thence new branches shoot,
> So, from old *Shakespeare's* honoured dust, this day
> Springs up and buds a new reviving Play.
>
> (ll. 1–4)

Shakespeare, not Prospero, is the ultimate patriarchalist authority figure, embodying the monarch, the father, the artist, and the magician all at once:

> *Shakespeare*, who (taught by none) did first impart
> To Fletcher wit, to labouring Jonson art,
> He, Monarch-like, gave those his subjects law,
> And is the nature which they paint and draw.

16. Dedication to *All For Love*, a play not yet available in the California Dryden. It is reproduced in *Dryden: The Dramatic Works*, ed. Montague Summers (London, 1932), IV, 177.

> But *Shakespeare's* Magick could not copy'd be,
> Within that Circle none durst walk but he.
>
> (ll. 6–9, 19–20)

This kind of omnipotence, however, is both unique—an attribute of the creatively heroic ancestor—and archaic, inimitable in a self-conscious modern world.

> I must confess t'was bold nor would you now
> That liberty to vulgar wits allow
> Which works by Magick supernatural things:
> But *Shakespeare's* pow'r is sacred as a Kings.
> Those legends from old Priesthood were received,
> And he then writ, as people then believed.
>
> (ll. 21–26)

Modern artist and audience lack the confident vision conferred by the old unquestioning belief—they can recapture it, if at all, only in a prologue's moment of sentimental nostalgia. Perhaps a sense of loss always accompanies the evocation of traditional simplicity, but here that loss seems so absolute and irrevocable that the naïve golden world of fifty years ago lacks any contemporary urgency at all. However regretfully, the adapters find that they must shoulder aside Shakespeare's central concerns, or at best grant them a marginal status. The fundamental problems are different now, and demand a new, if in some ways inferior, treatment.

In fact, though, when D'Avenant and Dryden separate Prospero's kingly authority from any special innovative genius, they do not so much repudiate the possibility of political creativity as relocate it. The real hero of the Dryden-D'Avenant *Tempest* is Ariel, who believes that Prospero's power over him is unjust. "Why should a mortal by Enchantments hold / In chains a spirit of aetherial mold?" (IV.iii.274–275). Nevertheless, he obeys Prospero in very trying circumstances. Finally, when Prospero assumes that Hippolito is dead, and resolves to execute Ferdinand, Ariel on his own initiative succeeds in resurrecting the wounded boy. Ariel, not Prospero, is responsible for the happy denouement; Ariel, not Prospero, learns to exploit repressive circumstances in productive ways. The potential for a creative political order resides not with the benevolent monarch, but with the loyal, resourceful subject.

Like the treatment of Prospero, the new emphasis on Ariel in the revised *Tempest* has parallels in Dryden's other work. In the Shakespearean *Tempest*, Prospero's sense of his imaginative resources is bound up with his sense of control over other people. Dryden, however, characteristically makes a sharp distinction between political power and creative potency, and locates the latter not with the monarch but with the subject. In *Astraea Redux, Annus Mirabilis, Absalom and Achitophel*, and *Britannia Redivivia*, poetic vocation finds its best and fullest employment in the celebration of the sovereign. The panegyric in *Annus Mirabilis* becomes an alternative to "serving King and Country" in the wars; [17] it is the literary version of a service required of all loyal and capable subjects. Poets are not kings, nor kings poets; Flecknoe's pretenses to sovereignty only emphasize his creative bankruptcy, and in the preface to *All For Love* Dionysius and Nero (bad kings both) render themselves ridiculous by aspiring to poetic laurels. [18] Ariel, whose creative initiative preserves the comic ending to the revised *Tempest*, is a type of the imaginatively loyal subject so crucial to Dryden's sense of himself as a citizen and, eventually, as laureate.

The revised *Tempest*, in other words, is the product of a staunch but distinctively Restoration brand of conservatism. Politicized by the traumatic events of the mid-seventeenth century, D'Avenant and Dryden believe that between Shakespeare and themselves, 1612 and 1667, there is a great gulf set. They find themselves forced to reconceive Prospero and his subjects, in order to bring them into line with their version of a well-run state. This kind of preoccupation cannot have seemed anomalous or unintelligible to contemporaries. Certainly the published script of the operatic version indicates that the set designer, at least, was fully aware of the play's political implications. The published text of the opera lovingly describes the new scenery:

the Curtain rises, and discovers a new Frontispiece, join'd to the great Pilasters, on each side of the Stage. This frontispiece is a noble Arch, supported by large wreathed Columns of the Corinthian order; the wreathings of the Columns are beautifi'd with Roses wound round them, and several Cupids flying about them. On the Cornice, just over the Capitals, sits a Figure with a Trumpet in one hand,

17. *The Works of John Dryden*, I, 50.
18. Preface to *All for Love, Dryden: The Dramatic Works*, IV, 185.

and a Palm in the other, representing *Fame*. A little further on the same Cornice, on each side of the Compass-pediment, lie a Lion and a Unicorn, the supporters of the Royal Arms of *England*. In the middle of the arch are several Angels, holding the King's Arms, as if they were placing them in the midst of that Compass-pediment. Behind this is the Scene, which represents a thick Cloudy Sky, a very Rocky Coast, and a Tempestuous Sea in perpetual Agitation.[19]

This explicit reference to England's real king must be intended as a sort of defense, as a way of pointing out the differences where art and life might otherwise seem uncomfortably close. Charles II is *not* Prospero, the frontispiece claims. Its tranquil, symmetrical design flatly contradicts the scene behind it, which depicts nature confused, dangerous, "in perpetual Agitation." The frontispiece makes traditional claims for the king's stable, central position in the natural and divine order of things. Its iconology recalls precisely those myths of royal omnipotence central to the prewar court masque—the myths so conscientiously purged from the revised *Tempest*.

As the description indicates, this frontispiece acts as a sort of visual frame for the dramatic action. It is, on one hand, a way of containing and limiting the significance of the play—a warning to the audience not to confuse the impotent, repressive Restoration Prospero with the real powers that be. Mediating between the play and the audience, it emphasizes the unreality of the dramatic spectacle, and thus keeps the potentially frightening implications of the fiction within reassuring bounds. However, the frontispiece is also (like the prologue celebrating Shakespeare) a marginal, nostalgic element, subverted by the action at center stage. The frame can seem not more true or reliable than the dramatic fiction, but less—a sort of *de post facto* window dressing which unfortunately stresses just those analogies it was apparently designed to defeat.

One suspects, in fact, that the ambivalence of this new scenery, which denied and at the same time emphasized the contemporary relevance of the Restoration *Tempest*, constituted part of its appeal. In an era when the Stuart mythology seemed increasingly inappropriate, as well as indispensable, the average Restoration playgoer must have been keenly—even painfully—sensitive to the various claims of competing ideologies. A play

19. *The Complete Works of Thomas Shadwell*, ed. Montague Summers, II, 199.

which acknowledged such difficulties, but which also transmuted them into gorgeous and apparently escapist spectacle, must have been extraordinarily compelling. If the Restoration audience greeted the revised *Tempest* with unparalleled enthusiasm, it is probably because Dryden and D'Avenant, and the operatic producers after them, managed to address the hopes and fears of large numbers of their contemporaries.

Notes on Contributors

CATHERINE BELSEY lectures in English at University College, Cardiff, Wales. She has published articles on medieval and Renaissance drama and *Critical Practice* (1980).

PETER BEREK, Professor of English at Williams College, has published essays recently on *Antony and Cleopatra, Locrine* and *Selimus*, and Lyly, Nashe, and *Love's Labor's Lost*. He is now working on a study of realism and control in English drama between *Tamburlaine* and *1 Henry IV*.

MARTIN BUTLER is a Research Fellow of Trinity Hall, Cambridge. He is currently at work on a study of Massinger and on a book on English drama and politics, 1632–1642.

KATHARINE E. MAUS is an Assistant Professor of English at Princeton University. She has published articles in the *Journal of English Literary History* and *Studies in the Novel* and is presently writing a book on Ben Jonson's use of the classics.

CATHERINE MINSHULL, formerly a lecturer in English at the University of Hull, is presently teaching at the City Literary Institute in London and working on a study of sixteenth-century attitudes toward rhetoric.

THOMAS PETTITT is a Lecturer at the English Institute, Odense University, Denmark, where he teaches early English literature and folklore. His current research focuses primarily on early popular culture, particularly folk drama and ballads, and on their interaction with literary traditions. He has published studies on these topics in *Comparative Drama, Journal of American Folklore, Lore and Language*, and *Folklore*.

WILLIAM SHULLENBERGER is Assistant Professor of Literature at Sarah Lawrence College. Sections of his dissertation, a study of Milton's

211

poetics of faith, have appeared recently in *Milton Studies, Notre Dame English Journal*, and *English Language Notes*.

DON E. WAYNE, Assistant Professor of English Literature at the University of California, San Diego, has published essays on Jonson and on contemporary criticism and theory. He has recently completed a book, *Penshurst: The Semiotics of Place and the Poetics of History*.